# The 371 Chorales of Johann Sebastian Bach

# The
# 371 Chorales
## of JOHANN SEBASTIAN BACH

*⟨With English Texts and Twenty-three Instrumental Obbligatos⟩*

## Frank D. Mainous      Robert W. Ottman

NORTH TEXAS STATE UNIVERSITY

HOLT, RINEHART AND WINSTON, INC.

New York     Chicago

San Francisco

# Acknowledgments

The editors wish to express their gratitude to the following for their aid in locating English translations of the German hymns: Robert Douglass of the faculty of Southwestern Baptist Theological Seminary, Fort Worth, Texas; Angelina Jacobson, librarian of Luther College, Decorah, Iowa; Edgar Krentz, librarian of Concordia Lutheran Seminary, St. Louis, Missouri; Sara Thompson, librarian of Southwestern Baptist Theological Seminary; Mrs. Jerry Warmath, librarian of Southern Baptist Theological Seminary, Louisville, Kentucky; Henry Williams, librarian of Moravian College, Bethlehem, Pennsylvania; and John Young, librarian of Union Theological Seminary, New York City.

For their cooperation in offering the facilities of the North Texas State University Libraries, recognition is due to members of the library staff and in particular to Lois S. Cook, secretary; Vinita Bond Davis, librarian; Anna Harriett Heyer, music librarian; Elizabeth Teasley, assistant music librarian; and David A. Webb, director of libraries.

Special acknowledgment is due to members of the North Texas State University faculty for providing translations of German hymns: Samuel Adler (193, 232), Stephen T. Farish (207, 208), William H. Gardner (238, 242, 264), Thomas S. Harllee (202, 203, 206) and Jack L. Roberts (173).

*Copyright © 1966 by Holt, Rinehart and Winston, Inc.*

*All Rights Reserved*

*Library of Congress Catalog Card Number: 65–14877*

ISBN: 0-03-051245-X

*Printed in the United States of America*

56789  005  987

# Contents

# Introduction

## The Chorale of Bach's Time

The four-voice chorales of Johann Sebastian Bach (1685–1750) are his harmonizations of hymn-tunes in use during his time. They were not, however, intended for inclusion in hymn books. Most of the chorales were written as parts of larger choral works such as the cantatas, the *St. Matthew Passion*, the *St. John Passion*, and the *Christmas Oratorio*. It is improbable that such chorales were intended for congregational use. The variety and complexity of the harmonies, the contrapuntal intricacies and the vocal range of the individual parts seem to indicate that performance by the choir was their intended purpose. The fact that Bach used the popular hymn-tunes of his day, not only in the chorales but also in many extended contrapuntal sections of the choral works, gave the congregation a sense of participation in the production. It is not unlikely that the congregation joined the choir in singing the melody of the chorale, especially in the cantatas where a chorale is usually the final number of the work.

## Early Chorale Collections

The circumstances under which the chorales were first collected are unknown. Many of the chorales were taken from cantatas and other choral works which to this day have not been found, indicating that the chorales had been copied before the disappearance of the original manuscripts, possibly during Bach's lifetime.

The first collection of chorales was published in 1765 in an edition of one hundred chorales edited by Bach's son, Carl Philipp Emanuel Bach (1714–1788). This was followed in 1769 by a second group of one hundred chorales edited by J. F. Agricola. Dissatisfied with Agricola's editorial practices, C. P. E. Bach undertook a more ambitious compilation of the chorales, resulting in a collection of four volumes: 1784, chorales 1–96; 1785, chorales 97–194; 1786, chorales 195–283; and 1787, chorales 283–370. The error in assigning the number 283 to two successive chorales was corrected in an edition of 1831 so that the entire collection numbered 371. C.P.E. Bach did not arrange the chorales alphabetically, chronologically or in any particular order, but merely assigned numbers to each. Except for a few changes in numerical order in editions soon after those of C. P. E. Bach, the chorales have enjoyed widespread circulation using his basic numbering. In books on music theory and literature it is common to find reference to the chorales by these numbers. The present edition uses the traditional numbering.

None of the early editions of the chorales contained words.

## The Hymns

The hymn texts used by J. S. Bach in the extant choral works are readily available. But in the case of lost works, it is difficult to know for what hymn and for what stanza the chorale was intended since the original and anonymous copyists preserved only the music. Each of the chorales in the editions of C. P. E. Bach is given a title, but this is not always an indication of his father's intentions; even C. P. E.'s title for a chorale from an extant work is sometimes different from the hymn actually used.

Ludwig Erk, in his collection of the chorales (1850 and 1865), was the first to add German hymn texts to the music. For chorales from lost works, he supplied hymns appropriate to the tradition of the tunes.

## Translations

In the present edition, each chorale is furnished with the English translation of the first stanza of its hymn and at least one other. All stanzas known to have been used by J. S. Bach are included with the chorale. It is not the intention of the editors to present translations in conformity with present-day theology. Rather, the translations cover a long chronological period, ranging from John Cosin, who died thirteen years before the birth of Bach, to translators of the present day. Thus the translations display a wide variety of literary styles and interpretations of the original German hymns.

## Duplicate Chorales

The four-volume edition of C. P. E. Bach contained

twenty-three chorales which were duplicates of other chorales in the collection. Some were exact duplicates, others exact except for transposition to another key, and others which displayed only a few minor differences. These twenty-three chorales are not reproduced here, but their numbers and titles are placed in normal position in the sequence of chorales, each with a cross reference to the printed version of the chorale.

### Scoring of the Chorales; The Obbligato Chorales

With few exceptions, the chorales from Bach's extant works are scored with instruments. The original instrumentation is listed in the appendix. Usually the instrumental parts are merely doublings of the vocal parts. In these chorales, if an instrumental part varies momentarily from the vocal part it is shown in small notes with an identifying name or abbreviation.

A number of the chorales contain obbligatos. The following are included: Chorales 11, 46, 51, 82, 93, 116, 255, 256, 270, 292, 298, 313, 323, 327, 329, 330, 331, 333, 337, 344, 347, 348, and 362. To facilitate study and performance, all parts are reproduced in concert key in G and F clefs and assigned to instruments most resembling those of the baroque period. If necessary for performance, substitute instru-ments should be used. For example, a clarinet or a oboe would be an acceptable substitute for a trump

### The Continuo

An essential part of the chorale instrumentation wa the baroque continuo. This part was ordinarily playe by the organ and at least one other instrument suc as a violoncello, violone, or bassoon. For present-da performance the continuo may be played by th violoncello, double (string) bass, or bassoon, an optionally by the organ depending on the size of th ensemble and the discretion of the conductor. In th chorales the continuo part and the vocal bass usuall coincide. Exceptions are shown in the present editio by small bass notes which indicate the continuo par

For students of harmony it is significant that th double bass or organ playing sixteen foot stops pro duces a sound one octave lower than written. Thi nullifies a number of apparent second inversion ($^6_4$ chords.

Arabic numerals supplied with the organ continu constitute a figured bass—a system of musical short hand which enabled the player to fill in the harmonie above the bass part.

# A Note to the Reader

## Titles

The English title is the first line of the translation of the German hymn. The first German title is the first line of the hymn as well as the name of the German hymn (poem). The second German title is the name of the hymn-tune (melody). If only one German title is given, the names of the hymn and the hymn-tune are identical. The Hymn-Tune Index provides information concerning other stanzas, hymns and translations used with a given hymn-tune.

## Cross Reference

The heading *see also* refers to other chorales in the collection that display different harmonizations of the same melody.

The symbol (D) indicates a duplicate chorale and that no music will be found under that number.

## Source

This is the name of the larger choral work or other source from which the chorale is taken. When not specified the original source is unknown.

## Hymn; Melody

These headings list the author of the hymn and the composer of the melody of the chorale, together with the dates of composition or earliest appearance in a hymn book.

## Translators

TR. means *translated by*. The abbreviation *alt.* indicates that the original translation has been altered in some respect. Such alteration has been kept to a minimum and usually occurs only when the meters of the German hymn and the English translation do not coincide.

## The Chorale

Small bass notes in parentheses are alternate notes used for convenience in singing when the regular notes are in an uncomfortable singing range for the average voice. Small bass notes not in parentheses indicate the continuo when it differs from the bass line. Other small notes are identified by name or abbreviation as instrumental notes and are used to indicate an instrumental part that varies momentarily from the doubling of a vocal part.

The fermata ($\curvearrowright$) is commonly used in many editions of the chorales to mark the end of each line in the stanza. In this context the sign does not mean to hold. Therefore, the fermata is not used in this edition.

The asterisk (*) denotes the stanza used by Bach in the work from which the chorale is taken.

A symbol such as (3/5) at the end of a stanza indicates the stanza of the original hymn and the total number of stanzas in the original hymn. (3/5) means the third stanza from a hymn of five stanzas. The first stanza in the present edition is always the first stanza of the original hymn, unless otherwise indicated.

## Text Setting

In much of the music of the chorales, a word or syllable is sung in all four voices simultaneously as in the usual church hymn. Rather frequently, however, a syllable, a word, or several successive words are to be sung at different times. Where necessary, these offset words are placed above or below the appropriate voice lines. When a single syllable or word, placed correctly for one voice, is no further away than one beat from its correct place in another voice, the offset word is usually not repeated in its other location.

Two or more notes connected either by a beam or by a slur are always sung with a single syllable or one-syllable word. When an offset word is not actually written in, observing this function of beams and slurs will make clear the placement of the offset syllable or word in a particular voice line.

## Footnotes

In the present edition, chorales from the extant works are found in their original keys and with their original titles. Different keys and titles often found in other editions are indicated in the footnotes. Many of these titles and transposed keys have been traditionally reprinted from the editions of C. P. E. Bach.

# The 371 Chorales of Johann Sebastian Bach

# 1. My Inmost Heart Now Raises

AUS MEINES HERZENS GRUNDE

HYMN: Johannes Mathesius(?), 1592
MELODY: Anonymous, 1598

TR.: Catherine Winkworth, 1863, *alt.*

My in - most heart now rais - es, In this fair
A song of thank - ful prais - es To Thine al -

morn - ing hour, O God upon Thy throne. To
might - y power,

hon - or and a - dore Thee, I bring my

praise be - fore Thee, Through Christ Thy on - ly Son.

[ 2 ]
For Thou from me hast warded
All perils of the night;
From every harm hast guarded
My soul till morning's light;

To Thee I humbly cry,
Do Thou my sins forgive me
That in my life offend Thee;
Have mercy, Lord most High!    (2/7)

1

## 2. We Thank Thee, Lord, for Sending

*see also:* 272, 341
HYMN: Johann Kolross, c.1535
MELODY: Anonymous, 1544

*ICH DANK DIR, LIEBER HERRE*

TR.: Henry S. Drinker, 1944

We__ thank Thee, Lord, for send - ing A - gain the__ morn - ing light,
That__ Thou hast safe a - vert - ed The dan - gers of _____ the night;
With dark - ness deep a - round _____ us, We lay__ in dead - ly fear, But__
foes could not con - found ___ us, For Thou, our God _____ wert__ near.

[2]

Confer Thou faith upon me
In Jesus Christ Thy Son,
And grant me now the pardon,
That He for me has won.

Thou wilt not now deny me
That which Thou didst agree;
From sin to purify me,
And lift its load from me.  *(4/9)*

## 3. How Many They, How Many Rail

*see also:* 253, 262
SOURCE: Cantata No. 153, 1727
HYMN: David Denicke(?), 1646
MELODY: Anonymous, 1524

*SCHAU, LIEBER GOTT, WIE MEINE FEIND*
ACH GOTT VOM HIMMEL, SIEH DAREIN

TR.: Charles Sanford Terry, 1929. By permission of Oxford University Press, London.

*How man - y they, how man - y__ rail, The foes who press up - on _____ me!
Sore griev - ous - ly do__ they as - sail, My spir - it__ faints with - in _____ me.

Lord, with Thy grace my soul re-fresh! So shall the Dev-il,

World, and Flesh No more pre-vail a - gainst me.

[2]
O grant Thy Holy Spirit's grace
To govern and direct me;
Toward heaven guide and set my face,
Let nought from Thee distract me!

Bring swift to ruin all my foes,
And set me on the path that goes
To where Thou reign'st in glory. (7/8)

## 4. Our Whole Salvation Doth Depend

⧊ *ES IST DAS HEIL UNS KOMMEN HER*

see also: 248, 290, 329, 335, 354(D)
SOURCE: Cantata No. 86, c.1725
HYMN: Paul Speratus, 1524
MELODY: Anonymous, fifteenth century

TR.: John Christian Jacobi, 1725, *alt.*

Our whole sal-va-tion doth de-pend On God's free grace and
All our good works can ne'er pre-tend To boast of an-y

spir - it,
mer - it;
'Tis faith re-ceives its right-eous-ness From

Christian and His a - ton-ing Grace, He is our me - di - a - tor.

[2]*
The living hope with patience waits
God's promised consolation;
Takes all the ways of life and fate
With Christian resignation;

God knows the time for our relief
To rest us from our pain and grief,
In Him we have reliance.  (*11/14*)

## 5. A Lamb Goes Forth: The Sins He Bears

*EIN LÄMMLEIN GEHT UND TRÄGT DIE SCHULD*

AN WASSERFLÜSSEN BABYLON

*see also:* 309(D)
HYMN: Paul Gerhardt, 1647
MELODY: Wolfgang Dachstein(?), 1525

TR.: Arthur Tozer Russell, 1851

A Lamb goes forth: the sins He bears Of ev - ery gen - er - a - tion:
Him - self with pa - tience He pre-pares To die for ev - ery na - tion.

All faint and weak, be - hold! He goes, His life re - sign - ing

to His foes: No thought His grief can meas - ure. He

yields to__ scorn, re - proach, dis - dain, Wounds, an - guish, cross and__

"It is __ my pleas - ure."

dy - ing pain, And__ saith, "It__ is __ my__ pleas - ure."

"It is__ my pleas - ure."

[ 2 ]
This Lamb the greatest friend I own,
He is my soul's redemption:
Sin to destroy is His alone,
And give from wrath exemption.
In sighs His spirit melts away,
His blood, my life in heav'nly day,

In purple streams is flowing.
O Lamb, belov'd, how shall I Thee
Requite for all, thus unto me
Such wondrous goodness showing. *(2/10)*

## 6. For Me to Live Is Jesus

*see also:* 316
HYMN: Anonymous, 1609
MELODY: Melchior Vulpius, 1609

⚜ *CHRISTUS, DER IST MEIN LEBEN*

TR.: Anonymous (*Evangelical Lutheran Hymn Book,* 1894)

For me to live is Je - sus, To die is __ gain for me; To

Him__ I __ glad - ly__ yield__ me, And die__ most cheer - ful - ly.

[ 2 ]
From hence I go with gladness
To Christ, my Brother's side,
That I may soon be with Him,
And e'er with Him abide. *(2/7)*

5

## 7. My Soul Now Praise Thy Maker

*see also:* 116, 268, 296
SOURCE: Cantata No. 17, 1735(?)
HYMN: Johann Graumann, 1540, (Psalm 103)
MELODY: Johann Kugelmann(?), 1540

NUN LOB, MEIN SEEL, DEN HERREN

TR.: Catherine Winkworth, 1863

My soul now praise Thy Mak - er! Let all__ with - in__ me bless His name,
Who mak-eth thee par-tak - er Of__ mer - cies more than thou dar'st claim.

For - get__ Him not__ whose meek - ness Still bears with all thy__ sin, Who

heal - eth all__ thy weak - ness, Re - news__ thy__ life___ with - in, Whose

grace and care are end - less And sav'd thee through the past; Who

leaves no . suf - f'rer friend - less, But rights the wrong'd___ at__ last!

[2]*

For as a tender father
Hath pity on his children here,
He in His arms will gather
All who are His in childlike fear;
He knows how frail our powers,
Who but from dust are made,
We flourish as the flowers,
And even so we fade,

A stormwind o'er them passes,
And all their bloom is o'er,
We wither like the grasses,
Our place knows us no more.    (3/4)

6

# 8. O Rejoice, Ye Christians, Loudly

SOURCE: Cantata No. 40, 1723
HYMN: Christian Keimann, 1646
MELODY: Andreas Hammerschmidt, 1646

FREUET EUCH, IHR CHRISTEN ALLE

TR.: Catherine Winkworth, 1863

O re-joice, ye Chris-tians, loud-ly, For your joy is now_ be-gun;

Won-drous things our_ God hath done. Tell a-broad His_ good-ness proud-ly,

Who_ our_ race hath_ hon-ored thus That He deigns to dwell with_ us.

Joy,_ O_ joy_ be-yond all glad-ness! Christ hath done a-way_ with sad-ness!

Hence, all_ sor-row and re-pin-ing, For_ the_ Sun of_ grace is shin-ing.

[ 2 ]*
Jesus, guard and guide Thy members,
Fill Thy brethren with Thy grace,
Hear their pray'rs in ev'ry place,
Quicken now life's faintest embers;
Grant all Christians, far and near,
Holy peace, a glad New Year!

Joy, O joy beyond all gladness!
Christ hath done away with sadness!
Hence, all sorrow and repining,
For the Sun of grace is shining. (4/4)

## 9. Bestir Thyself, My Feeble Soul

*see also:* 102, 343, 361(D)
SOURCE: Christmas Oratorio, 1734
HYMN: Johann Rist, 1641
MELODY: Johann Schop, 1641

*ERMUNTRE DICH, MEIN SCHWACHER GEIST*

TR.: Henry S. Drinker, 1944, (stanza 1); John Trout-beck, 1832–1899, (stanza 2), by permission of G. Schirmer, Inc., New York.

Be - stir thy - self, my feeble soul, And come with ju - bi - la - tion
To greet the lit - tle Je - sus child With joy and a - dor - a - tion.

This is the night on which He came, And took a hu - man form and frame, The

Fa - ther's Son with - in it, To woo the world and win it.

[2]*
Break forth, O beauteous heav'nly light,
And usher in the morning;
Ye shepherds, shrink not with affright,
But hear the angels' warning.

This Child now weak in infancy,
Our confidence and joy shall be,
The pow'r of Satan breaking,
Our peace eternal making.  *(9/12)*

# 10. Out of the Depths I Cry to Thee

SOURCE: Cantata No. 38, c.1740
HYMN: Martin Luther, 1524
MELODY: Martin Luther(?), 1524

*AUS TIEFER NOT SCHREI ICH ZU DIR*

TR.: Catherine Winkworth, 1863

Out of the depths I __ cry __ to Thee, Lord, hear me, I __ im - plore __ Thee!
Bend down Thy gra - cious ear __ to me, My prayer let come be - fore __ Thee!

If Thou re - mem - b'rest each mis - deed, If each should have its

Thy pres - ence?

right - ful meed, Who may a - bide Thy pres - ence?

[2]*
Though great my sins and sore my woes,
His grace much more aboundeth;
His helping love no limit knows,
Our utmost need it soundeth;

Our kind and faithful Shepherd He,
Who shall at last set Israel free
From all their sin and sorrow. (5/5)

9

## 11. Now Join We All to Praise Thee

JESU, NUN SEI GEPREISET

see also: 252, 327
SOURCE: Cantata No. 41, 1736; Cantata No. 171, c.1730    TR.: Henry S. Drinker, 1944
   (in the key of D major)
HYMN: Johann Hermann(?), 1591
MELODY: Anonymous, 1591

bless - ings That drive our cares a - way.
lad - en, And last - ing peace sub - lime;

That free and_ un - de - feat - ed, The old_ year we_ com - plet - ed. To

Thee_ in deep_ de - vo - tion, Would we be ev - er

near._____ Pre - serve_ us, soul_ and bod - y, Through-

out_ the com - ing year,_____ In_ safe - ty_ watch and

guard_ us,_ Through all the_ com - ing year.

[ 2 ]*
To Thee alone be glory,
To Thee alone be praise;
In trouble teach us patience,
And govern all our ways,
Until at last in heaven,
From care and trouble free,
In peace and joy and gladness,
We may be one with Thee.

Our needs and ventures measure,
According to Thy pleasure,
And so Thy people, bringing,
To Thee their faith sincere,
With trusting hearts are singing:
Bless Thou this coming year;
With trusting hearts are singing:
Bless Thou this coming year.  (3/3)

## 12. A Child Is Born in Bethlehem†

SOURCE: Cantata No. 65, 1724
HYMN: Anonymous, fourteenth century
MELODY: Anonymous, 1553

*EIN KIND GEBORN ZU BETHLEHEM*

TR.: H. M. MacGill, 1876, *alt.*

† Sometimes published under the title *Puer Natus in Bethlehem.*

A child is born in Beth - le - hem, Beth - le - hem. Ex - ult for joy,_ Je - ru - sa - lem. Al - le - lu - ia!_ Al - le - lu - ia.

[ 2 ]*
And three kingly pilgrims long foretold, long foretold.
Bring from the East, myrrh, incense and gold.
Alleluia! Alleluia. (*4/10*)

## 13. Lord Jesus Christ, in Thee Alone

*see also:* 359
SOURCE: Cantata No. 33, *c.*1740
HYMN: Johannes Schneesing, *c.*1540
MELODY: Anonymous, 1541(?)

*ALLEIN ZU DIR, HERR JESU CHRIST*

TR.: Catherine Winkworth, 1863, *alt.*

Lord Je - sus Christ, in_ Thee _____ a - lone My hope in earth _____
For oth - er_ com - fort - er _____ is none, Help in_ Thy grace _____
re - sid - ing.
a - bid - ing. There is_ no_ man nor_ crea - ture here, No

13

an - gel_ in_ the heav'n - ly sphere, Who at_ my_ need can suc - cor me, I
I_
cry, Lord_ to Thee, For Thou canst end_ my_ mis - er - y.
_ cry,_ Lord to Thee,

[ 2 ]*
Glory to God in highest heav'n,
The Father God Almighty;
To His dear Son for sinners giv'n,
Who cares for us most dearly;

To God the Holy Ghost on high;
O ever be His comfort nigh,
And teach us, free from sin and fear,
To so please Him here,
And serve Him in the sinless sphere.   (4/4)

## 14. O God, Our Lord, Thy Holy Word

HYMN: Anark von Wildenfels(?), 1527
MELODY: Anonymous, 1527

*O HERRE GOTT, DEIN GÖTTLICHS WORT*

TR.: Anonymous (*Lutheran Hymnal,* 1942). Reprinted by permission of Concordia Publishing House from *The Handbook of the Lutheran Hymnal* by W. G. Polack (1942).

O God, our Lord, Thy ho - ly Word Was long a_ hid - den treas - ure.
Till to its place it was by grace Re - stored in_ full - est meas - ure.

For this to - day our thanks_ we say And_ glad - ly glo - ri - fy_ Thee. Thy

mer-cy_ show and grace be-stow On_ all who still _____ de - ny_ Thee.

[ 2 ]

My Lord art Thou, and for me now
Death holds for me no terrors;
Thy precious blood, my highest good,
Hath blotted out my errors.

My thanks to Thee! Thou wilt to me
Fulfill Thy promise ever
And mercy give while here I live,
And heav'nly bliss forever. (7/8)

## 15. Christ in the Bonds of Death Was Laid

*CHRIST LAG IN TODESBANDEN*

HYMN: Martin Luther, 1524
MELODY: Adaptation, 1524, of *Christ ist erstanden*

TR.: Arthur Tozer Russell, 1851, *alt.*

*see also:* 184, 261, 371

Christ in_ the bonds of_ death was laid, For our_ trans-gres-sions giv - en:
He_ rose: the_ way He_ o - pen made To life, the_ life of_ heav - en.

There-fore we_ will now re - joice, And praise our God_ with thank - ful voice, So

sing_ we_ now_ Hal - le - lu - jah. Hal - le - lu - jah.

[ 2 ]

By none of all the sons of men
Could death's dark realm be shaken.
Sin made our strength all weak and vain;
All have of guilt partaken.

Thus came death upon us all,
And bound the fallen world in thrall,
In his dominion buried all.
Hallelujah. (2/7)

15

## 16. May God unto Us Gracious Be

*see also:* 333, 352
HYMN: Martin Luther, 1524
MELODY: Anonymous, 1524

ES WOLLT UNS GOTT GENÄDIG SEIN

TR.: Arthur Tozer Russell, 1851, *alt.*

May God un-to us gra - cious be, And
Lord, show Thy face to us through Thee E-

grant to us His bless - ing;
ter - nal life pos - sess - ing:

That all Thy work and will, O God, To us may be re-

veal - èd, And Christ's sal - va - tion spread a-broad To hea-then lands un-

con - vert them.
seal - èd, And un-to God con - vert them.
con - vert them.

[2]
Thine over all shall be the praise
And thanks of every nation,
And all the world with joy shall raise
The voice of exultation.

For Thou dost wield Thy scepter, Lord,
Sin to Thyself subjecting;
Thy people's pasture is Thy word,
Thy fence their feet protecting;
In righteous ways O keep them. *(2/3)*

16

## 17. The Day Hath Dawned, the Day of Days†

SOURCE: Cantata No. 145, *c.*1729
HYMN: Nikolaus Herman, 1560
MELODY: Nikolaus Herman, 1560

❧ *ERSCHIENEN IST DER HERRLICH TAG*

TR.: Arthur Tozer Russell, 1851

† Sometimes published with a key signature of one sharp
and transposed one whole step lower.

The day hath dawned, the day of days Tran-scend-ing all our
joy and praise: This day our Lord tri-um-phant rose; This
day He cap-tive led our foes. Hal-le-lu-jah.

[ 2 ]*
Then as is meet, we now will sing
Glad hallelujahs to our King:
To Thee, Lord, doth our praise pertain,
Who for our joy art ris'n again.
Hallelujah!  (*14/14*)

## 18. Once He Came in Blessing

HYMN: Johann Roh, 1544
MELODY: Anonymous, 1531

❧ *GOTTES SOHN IST KOMMEN*

TR.: Catherine Winkworth, 1863

Once He came in bless - ing, All our ills re - dress - ing,

Came in like-ness low-ly, Son of God most ho - ly;

Bore the cross to save us, Hope and free-dom gave us.

[2]
Still He comes within us,
Still His voice would win us
From the sins that hurt us;
Would to truth convert us
From our foolish errors,
Ere He comes in terrors.  (2/9)

## 19. My Cause Is God's, and I Am Still

ICH HAB MEIN SACH GOTT HEIMGESTELLT

HYMN: Johannes Leon, 1589
MELODY: Anonymous, 1589

TR.: Catherine Winkworth, 1863

My cause is God's, and I am still, Let Him do with me

as He will; Wheth-er for me the race is won, Or

[ 2 ]
My sins are more than I can bear,
Yet not for this will I despair;
I know to death and to the grave
The Father gave His dearest Son that He might save.
 (11/18)

## 20. A Mighty Fortress Is Our God

*see also:* 250, 273
HYMN: Martin Luther, 1529
MELODY: Martin Luther, 1529

*EIN FESTE BURG IST UNSER GOTT*

TR.: Frederick Henry Hedge, 1805–1890, *alt.*

[ 2 ]
Did we in our own strength confide,
Our striving would be losing,
Were not the right man on our side,
The man of God's own choosing.

Dost ask who that be?
Jesus, it is He,
Christ Jesus His name,
From age to age the same,
And He must win the battle.  (2/4)

## 21. Entrust Thy Ways unto Him

*see also:* 74, 80, 89, 98, 270, 286, 345, 367
SOURCE: Cantata No. 153, 1727
HYMN: Paul Gerhardt, 1653
MELODY: Hans Leo Hassler, 1601

TR.: Henry S. Drinker, 1944

*BEFIEHL DU DEINE WEG*
HERZLICH TUT MICH VERLANGE

En - trust thy ways un - to Him, And all thy spir-it craves,
The ev - er faith-ful Guard - ian Who guides the wind and waves,

Who rules the clouds of heav - en And bids the breez-es blow; He

best can choose the path - way On which our steps shall go.

[ 2 ]*
Though all the fiends are striving,
O'er heaven to prevail,
All vain their fell contriving,
Their hellish plot will fail.
What God has well provided no mortal can amend,
And what He has decided will happen in the end.
(5/12)

## 22. Deck Thyself, My Soul, with Gladness

SOURCE: Cantata No. 180, c.1740
HYMN: Johann Franck, 1649
MELODY: Johann Crüger, 1649

TR.: Catherine Winkworth, 1863

*SCHMÜCKE DICH, O LIEBE SEEL*

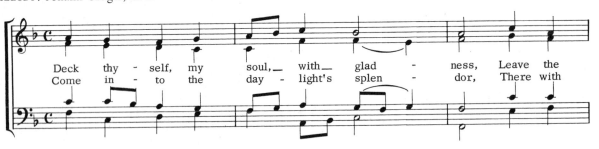

Deck thy - self, my soul, with glad - ness, Leave the
Come in - to the day - light's splen - dor, There with

gloom-y haunts of sad - ness,
joy thy prais-es ren - der

Un - to Him whose grace un-bound-
ed Hath this won-drous ban-quet found - ed,
High o'er all the heav'ns He reign-eth,
Yet to dwell with thee He deign - eth.

[ 2 ]*
Jesus, Bread of Life, I pray Thee,
Let me gladly here obey Thee,
Never to my hurt invited,
Be Thy love with love requited;

From this banquet let me measure,
Lord, how vast and deep its treasure;
Through the gifts Thou here dost give me
As Thy guest in heav'n receive me.   (9/9)

## 23. Ye Christians in This Nation†

*see also:* 88(D), 99, 123
SOURCE: Cantata No. 28, *c.*1736
HYMN: Paul Eber, *c.*1580
MELODY: Anonymous, 1569

🎵 *HELFT MIR GOTTS GÜTE PREISEN*

TR.: John Christian Jacobi, 1722

† Sometimes published under the title *Zeuch ein zu deinen Toren.*

Ye Chris-tians in this na - tion! Come all, and praise with me,
Our Mak-er's pres-er - va - tion, In joy-ful har-mo - ny,

E'en at_ this pre - sent time, When we new date_ our_ sea - son, And have the_ great-est_ rea - son To love_ our_ Lord di - vine.

[2]*
These mercies we're adoring,
O Lord, who dwelt above:
Which Thou hast been restoring
Through Christ the Son of Love;

In whom thou wilt be pleased
To grant this year ensuing,
Grace, constant in welldoing,
'Till we're from sin released.  (6/6)

## 24. Farewell I Gladly Bid Thee

VALET WILL ICH DIR GEBEN

see also: 108
HYMN: Valerius Herberger, 1613
MELODY: Melchior Teschner, 1613

TR.: Catherine Winkworth, 1863

Fare - well I_ glad - ly_ bid___ thee, False e - vil_ world, fare - well!
Thy_ life is_ dark and_ sin - ful, With thee I_ would not dwell:

In_ heav'n are joys un - trou - bled, I_ long for that bright sphere Where

God__ re - wards them dou - bled, Who serv'd Him__ tru - ly__ here.

[ 2 ]
Do with me as it pleases
Thy heart, O Son of God;
When anguish on me seizes,
Help me to bear my load;

Nor then my sorrows lengthen,
But take me hence on high;
My fearful heart, oh strengthen,
And let me calmly die.    (2/5)

## 25. O Whither Shall I Flee†

*see also:* 281, 304, 331
SOURCE: Cantata No. 148, *c.*1725
HYMN: Johann Heermann, 1630
MELODY: Anonymous, 1609

⚜ *WO SOLL ICH FLIEHEN HIN*
    AUF MEINEN LIEBEN GOTT

TR.: Anonymous (*Moravian Hymn Book*, 1789)

† Sometimes published in the transposed key of F minor.

O__ whith-er shall I flee, De - pressed with mis - er - y? Who

is__ it__ that can__ ease__ me, And from my__ sins re - lease____ me? Man's

help I__ vain have prov - ĕd, Sin's load re - mains un - mov - ĕd.

[ 2 ]*
Lord, strengthen Thou my heart;
Such grace to me impart,
That nought which may await me
From Thee may separate me;
Let me with Thee, my Saviour,
United be forever.    (11/11)

23

## 26. Eternity! Tremendous Word

*see also:* 274
SOURCE: Cantata No. 20, *c.*1725
HYMN: Johann Rist, 1642
MELODY: Johann Schop, 1642

O EWIGKEIT, DU DONNERWORT

TR.: John Christian Jacobi, 1722

Lyrics under first staff:
E - ter - ni - ty!__ Tre - men - dous word. Home strik - ing__ point, heart
E - ter - ni - ty!__ With - out__ a shore, Where ev - er - fi - ery

Lyrics under second staff:
pierc - ing__ sword, Be - gin - ning__ with - out__ end - ing!
bil - lows__ roar, What is__ Thy__ sight__ por - tend - ing?

Lyrics under third staff:
One glimpse of Thine un - fath - omed deep Would rouse a __ wretch from sin - ful sleep.

[ 2 ]*
As long as God eternal reigns
And His Almighty sway retains,
Hell's torment will be lasting;
They shall be plagued with cold and heat,
Thirst, hunger, fire shall be their meat,
Their worm is never wasting;
Then this eternal misery
Will end when God shall cease to be.  (*11/16*)

[ 3 ]*
Eternity! Tremendous word.
Home striking point, heart piercing sword,
Beginning without ending!
Eternity! Without a shore!
Where ever fiery billows roar,
What is Thy sight portending?
Lord Jesu! When it pleases Thee,
Bring me to blest eternity.  (*16/16*)

## 27. Vain Foolish Men Absurdly Boast

HYMN: Martin Luther, 1524, (Psalm 14)
MELODY: Martin Luther(?), 1524

ES SPRICHT DER UNWEISEN MUND WOHL

TR.: Anonymous (*Moravian Hymn Book*, 1754)

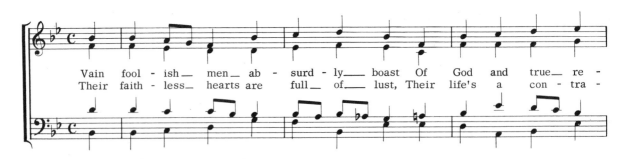

Lyrics under staff:
Vain fool - ish__ men ab - surd - ly__ boast Of God and true__ re -
Their faith - less__ hearts are full__ of__ lust, Their life's a con - tra -

li - gion;
dic - tion: Cor - rupt - ed is _ their _ ver - y _ frame, God's

ho - li - ness _ ab - hors the same, There's none doth good, but e - vil.
good, _____ but e - vil.

good, but e - vil.

[2]
O that the joyful day would come
To change our mournful station,
When God will bring His children home
And finish our salvation!

Then shall the tribes of Jacob sing,
And Judah praise their Lord and King
With lasting hallelujahs.   (6/6)


## 28. Come Redeemer of Our Race

*see also:* 170
SOURCE: Cantata No. 36, *c.*1730
HYMN: Martin Luther, 1524
MELODY: Anonymous, 1524

*NUN KOMM, DER HEIDEN HEILAND*

TR.: B. M. Craster (stanza 1), by permission of Novello
& Co., Ltd., London; Richard Massie, 1800–1887,
(stanza 2).

Come re - deem - er _ of _ our race Vir - gin _ born by _ Ho - ly _ grace,

Hail'd by _ all _ the _ won - d'ring earth: God of _ old _ or - dained His birth.

[2]*
Praise be to the Father done,
Praise be to the only Son,
Praises to the Spirit be,
Now and to eternity.   (8/8)

## 29. Hence My Heart, and [■■■■] Thinking

*WEG, MEIN HERZ, MIT DEM GEDANKEN*
FREU DICH SEHR, O MEINE SEELE

*see also:* 64(D), 67, 76, 254, 256, 282(D), [■■■]
SOURCE: Cantata No. 32, c.1740
HYMN: Paul Gerhardt, 1647
MELODY: Louis Bourgeois, 1551

TR.: Catherine Winkworth, 1863, *alt.*

Hence my heart, and cease such think-ing As that thou art cast a-way!
For God's word is nev-er fail-ing, Heed not then what oth-ers say.

Art thou e-vil and un-just? God is good, be He thy trust.

Art thou cursed by death and sin - ning? Faint not, God is all for-giv - ing.

[ 2 ]*
Open wide Thy gates before me
Whence such tender mercies flow,
Longs my heart to stand before Thee
Let me all Thy sweetness know,

Everywhere and every hour
Own Thy love's constraining power;
And this one thing I implore Thee,
Nevermore that I should grieve Thee.   *(12/12)*

## 30. Christ, Who Freed Our Souls from Danger

*JESUS CHRISTUS, UNSER HEILAND, DER VON UNS*

HYMN: Martin Luther, 1524
MELODY: Anonymous, 1524

TR.: Richard Massie, 1800–1887, *alt.*

Christ, who freed _____ our_ souls from dan - ger, And hath turned a-

way__ God's an ___ ger, Suf - fered pains no__ tongue__ can__

tell, To__ save us__ all__ from pains __ of __ Hell:
pains __ of __ Hell:

pains __ of __ Hell.

[2]
That we never might forget it,
"Take my flesh," He said, "and eat it,
Hidden in this piece of bread,
My blood drink in this wine," He said.  *(2/10)*

## 31. Ye Christians Take Your Courage Up

*ACH, LIEBEN CHRISTEN, SEID GETROST*
WO GOTT DER HERR NICHT BEI UNS HÄLT

see also: 285, 301, 336
HYMN: Johann Gigas, 1561
MELODY: Anonymous, 1535

TR.: John Christian Jacobi, 1725

Ye__ Chris - tians__ take__ your cour - age__ up, Shake off your__ soul's op -
Will you re - ject__ the gen - erous cup Of God's own__ vis - it -

pres - sion! Let us__ con - fess His judg - ment's just, And Ad - am's__ sons but
a ___ tion?

mor - tal — dust, From death none — is — ex - emp - ted.

[2]
Lord, we resign unto Thy hands
Our body, soul and spirit,
We come and go at Thy commands,
Death only our real merit:

While dwelling in this mortal clay,
Pain will attend us every way,
But wait for joy thereafter. *(2/6)*

## 32. Now Thank We All Our God

*NUN DANKET ALLE GOTT*

*see also:* 330
HYMN: Martin Rinkart, 1636
MELODY: Johann Crüger, 1648

TR.: Catherine Winkworth, 1863

Now thank we — all — our God, With heart, and hands and — voi - ces,
Who won - drous things hath done, In whom His world re - joi - ces.

Who from our moth - er's arms Hath blessed us — on — our way With

count - less — gifts — of — love, And still is — ours to - day.

[2]
O may this bounteous God
Through all our life be near us,
With ever joyful hearts
And blessèd peace to cheer us;

And keep us in His grace,
And guide us when perplex'd,
And free us from all ills
In this world and the next. *(2/3)*

## 33. Lord, to Thee I Make Confession

*see also:* 287

HYMN: Johann Franck, 1649

MELODY: Johann Crüger, 1649

⚜ *HERR, ICH HABE MISSGEHANDELT*

TR.: Catherine Winkworth, 1863

Lord, to Thee I make confession, I have sinned and gone astray,
I have multiplied transgression, Chosen for myself my way:

Forced at last to see my errors,
Forced at last to see my errors, Lord, I tremble at Thy terrors.

Forced at last to see my errors,

[2]
But from Thee how can I hide me;
Thou, O God, art everywhere.
Refuge from Thee is denied me,
Or by land, or sea, or air.
Nor death's darkness can enfold me
So that Thou shoulds't not behold me. *(2/8)*

## 34. Show Pity Lord! O Lord Forgive!

HYMN: Erhart Hegenwalt, 1524

MELODY: Johann Walther(?), 1524

⚜ *ERBARM DICH MEIN, O HERRE GOTT*

TR.: John Christian Jacobi, 1722

Show pity Lord! O Lord forgive! Are not Thy mercies
Let a repenting rebel live Whose guilt is great, yet

large and free? My lips with shame my sins confess, Lord
trusts in Thee;

should Thy judg-ment grow se-vere, And mark what's done a-gainst Thy Grace, I am con-demn'd, but Thou art clear.

[2]
Cleanse me, O Lord, and clear my soul,
By means of Thy forgiving love;
O make my broken spirit whole,
And bid my guilty pains remove.

Let not Thy spirit quite depart,
Nor drive me from Thy Holy Face,
Create anew my vicious heart,
And fill it with Thy saving grace.   (3/5)

## 35. All Ye Stars and Winds of Heaven

*IHR GESTIRN, IHR HOHEN LÜFTE*
GOTT DES HIMMELS UND DER ERDEN

SOURCE: Christmas Oratorio, 1734
HYMN: Johann Franck, 1655          TR.: Henry S. Drinker, 1944
MELODY: Heinrich Albert, 1642

All ye stars and winds of heav-en, Thou the spa-cious fir-ma-ment,
Deep ra-vines and loft-y moun-tains, Hills and vales with ech-oes rent,

Shout and sing in ex-ul-ta-tion, Cleave the clouds with ju-bi-la-tion.

[2]*
In my heart of hearts the chamber
Was a gloomy dreary place,
All unlike a royal palace;
Thou didst fill it with Thy grace,
Royally its walls adorning,
Like the sunshine in the morning.   (9/9)

## 36. Now Do We Pray God, the Holy Ghost

see also: 84, 97
HYMN†: Anonymous (stanza 1); Martin Luther, 1524, (stanza 2).
MELODY: Anonymous

*NUN BITTEN WIR DEN HEILIGEN GEIST*

TR.: Anonymous (*Selah Song Book*, 1936)

† Kyrie eleis from Kyrie eleison (Gk.), "Lord, have mercy."

Now do we pray God, the Holy Ghost, For the true faith which we need the most, And that He defend us When life is ending, And from exile home we shall be wending. Kyrie e-leis!

God, the Holy Ghost,

[2]
Shine in our hearts, O most precious Light,
That we Jesus Christ may know aright,
Clinging to our Savior,

Whose blood has bought us;
Who again to our true home has brought us.
Kyrie eleis!   (2/4)

## 37. Jesu, Who in Sorrow Dying

see also: 269, 297, 369
HYMN: Johann Rist, 1641
MELODY: Anonymous, 1642

*JESU, DER DU MEINE SEELE*

TR.: Arthur Tozer Russell, 1851

Jesu, who in sorrow dying, Didst deliv'rance bring to me,
Whilst my sins for vengeance crying, Nail'd Thee to the shameful tree;

[2]
Born in sin—my life transgression,
O how have I gone astray!
But I make Thee full confession:
Nought but sin hath marked my way.

Grant me graciously remission,
Who am wounded with contrition.
Be no more my trespass sought
Which on me Thy wrath hath brought.  (3/12)

## 38. Rise, My Soul, to Watch and Pray†

SOURCE: Cantata No. 115, c.1740
HYMN: Johann Burchard Freystein, 1697
MELODY: Anonymous, 1694

*MACHE DICH, MEIN GEIST, BEREIT*
STRAF MICH NICHT IN DEINEM ZORN

TR.: Catherine Winkworth, 1863

† Sometimes published in the transposed key of E♭ major.

Oft_ his_ har-vest reap — est While the_ Chris-tian sleep — est.

[ 2 ]*

Courage then, for He will give
All that we are needing,
Through the Son, in whom we live
Who for us is pleading.

Day by day
Watch and pray,
While the tempest lower,
Till He comes with power. (10/10)

## 39. What Shall I, a Sinner, Do, Lord

HYMN: Johann Flittner, 1661
MELODY: Anonymous, 1661

*ACH! WAS SOLL ICH SÜNDER MACHEN*

TR.: Catherine Winkworth, 1863, *alt.*

What shall I, a _ sin-ner, do, Lord? With-er_ shall I_ turn for_aid?

Sins that make me_ sore a-fraid Con-science wak-ing brings to view, Lord.

This my_ con-fi-dence shall be, Je-sus,_ I will cleave to _ Thee.

[ 2 ]

True I have transgressed Thy will, Lord,
Oft have grieved Thee by my sins.
Yet I know Thou lov'st me still,

For I hear Thy voice within, Lord;
Then, though sin accuses me,
Jesus, I will cleave to Thee. (2/7)

33

## 40. Alas! My God!

**ACH GOTT UND HERR**

*see also:* 279
HYMN: Johann Major(?) and Martin Rutilius(?), 1613   TR.: Catherine Winkworth, 1863
MELODY: Anonymous, 1625

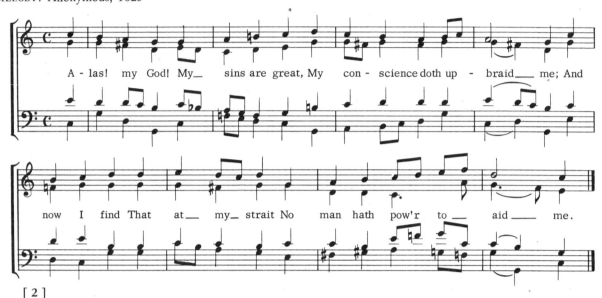

A - las! my God! My sins are great, My con - science doth up - braid me; And
now I find That at my strait No man hath pow'r to aid me.

[ 2 ]
If fled I hence,
In my despair,
In some lone spot to hide me,
My griefs would still
Be with me there,
Thy hand still hold and guide me.   (2/6)

## 41. I into God's Own Heart and Mind

**ICH HAB IN GOTTES HERZ UND SINN**
WAS MEIN GOTT WILL, DAS G'SCHEH ALLZEIT

*see also:* 115, 120, 265, 349(D)       TR.: John Kelly, 1867
SOURCE: Cantata No. 65, 1724
HYMN: Paul Gerhardt, 1647
MELODY: Anonymous, c.1529

I in - to God's own heart and mind My heart and mind de -
What e - vil seems, a gain I find, E'en death is life for -

liv - er,
ev - er.

I am His son, Who spread the

throne Of heav-en_ high_ a - bove_ me. Though I bend

low Be-neath His blow, Yet still His_ heart_ doth love me.

His_ heart doth love_ me.

[ 2 ]*
My God! My God! Into Thy hand
I joyfully now yield me,
Keep me, a stranger in the land,
E'en to the end, Lord! Shield me.

Deal with me now
As well dost know,
That I may profit by it;
Then more and more
Thy glorious pow'r,
Lord! Show and magnify it.   (10/12)

## 42. Lord Jesus Christ, the Prince of Peace

                *DU FRIEDEFÜRST, HERR JESU CHRIST*

SOURCE: Cantata No. 67, *c.*1725
HYMN: Jakob Ebert, 1601          TR.: Catherine Winkworth, 1863
MELODY: Bartholomäus Gesius(?), 1601

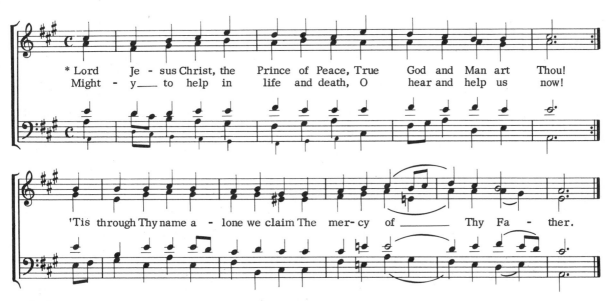

* Lord   Je - sus Christ, the   Prince of Peace, True   God and Man art   Thou!
Might - y_ to help in   life and death, O   hear and help us   now!

'Tis through Thy name a - lone we claim The mer-cy of _____ Thy Fa - ther.

[ 2 ]
We have deserved, and patiently
Would bear what-e'er Thou wilt,
But grace is mightier for Thee
Than all our sin and guilt;
Forgive us then, dear Lord again,
Thy love is ever faithful.  (4/7)

35

## 43. Gracious God, When Wilt Thou Call Me

*LIEBSTER GOTT, WANN WERD ICH STERBEN*

SOURCE: Cantata No. 8, *c.*1725
HYMN: Caspar Neumann, *c.*1700
MELODY: Daniel Vetter, 1713

gels,    I will praise Thy_ won -    'drous love;

an - gels,    I will praise Thy    won - 'drous love;

an - gels,    I will praise Thy    won - 'drous love;

an - gels,    I    will praise Thy    won - 'drous love;

7    6 —— 5        6    5    4
2

7
4
2

5
4

'Tis the fate    of    man    to    know,    Pain and sor - row

'Tis the fate    of_    man_    to_    know,    Pain and sor - row

'Tis the    fate    of man to    know,    Pain and sor - row

'Tis the    fate of man to    know, Pain and    sor -    row_

6    5    6        5    6        6        6 —— 5    4    6
3    4    3        2

[ 2 ]*

Lord of life, and King all glorious,
Be Thou still my guide and friend,
Over death and sin victorious,
On Thy promise I depend!

Grant that I an honored grave
With the saints of earth may have,
There to wait th' eternal morrow,
Nevermore to suffer sorrow.   (5/5)

## 44. Deal with Me, God, in Mercy Now

*see also:* 310
HYMN: Johann Hermann Schein, 1629
MELODY: Johann Hermann Schein, 1629

*MACHS MIT MIR, GOTT, NACH DEINER GÜT*

TR.: Catherine Winkworth, 1863, *alt.*

Deal with me, God, in mercy now, Give help to me when dying,
Thine ear to me in pity bow, When hence my soul is flying,
Receive me as my God and friend, For all is right if right the end.

[2]
Now, O my Lord, I follow Thee,
Safe where Thy steps are tracing;
Ah, now Thou art not far from me,
Though death I now am facing,
And I must leave the friends most dear
Who loved me well and truly here. (2/5)

## 45. O Father! Send the Spirit Down

*see also:* 370
SOURCE: Cantata No. 108, 1735
HYMN: Paul Gerhardt, 1653
MELODY: Anonymous, 1530

*GOTT VATER, SENDE DEINEN GEIST*
KOMMT HER ZU MIR, SPRICHT GOTTES SOHN

TR.: John Kelly, 1867

O Father! Send the spirit down, Whom we are bidden
by Thy Son To seek, from Thy high heav-

[2]*
No mortal man upon the earth
Is of this gift so noble worth,
No merit we've to gain it;

Here only grace availeth aught,
That Jesus Christ for us hath bought,
His tears and death obtain it.  (2/12)

## 46. From Heav'n Above to Earth I Come

see also: 344
SOURCE: Christmas Oratorio, 1734
HYMN: Martin Luther, 1535
MELODY: Martin Luther(?), 1539

✠ VOM HIMMEL HOCH DA KOMM ICH HER

TR.: Catherine Winkworth, 1863

Trumpet I, II

Trumpet III

Timpani

Soprano, Flute I, II in 8va, Oboe I, II, Violin I
Alto, Violin II

Tenor, Viola
Bass

Bassoon, Organ and Continuo

joy I bring,        Where-of I

will now say and sing.

[ 2 ]*
Ah, dearest Jesus, Holy Child,
Make Thee a bed, soft, undefiled,
Within my heart, that it may be
A quiet chamber kept for Thee.   (13/15)

# 47. Our Father, Thou in Heav'n Above

see also: 110, 267, 292
HYMN: Martin Luther, 1539, (Lord's Prayer)
MELODY: Anonymous, 1539

⁓ *VATER UNSER IM HIMMELREICH*

TR.: Catherine Winkworth, 1863

Our Fa-ther, Thou in heav'n a-bove, Who bid-dest us to dwell in love, As breth-ren of one fam-i-ly, And cry for all we need to Thee; Teach us to mean the words we say, And from the in-most heart to pray.

[2]*
Thy will be done on earth, O Lord,
As where in heav'n Thou art ador'd!
Patience in time of grief bestow,

Obedience true through weal and woe;
Strength, tempting wishes to control
That thwart Thy will within the soul.  (4/9)

# 48. O How Cheating, O How Fleeting

SOURCE: Cantata No. 26, *c.*1740
HYMN: Michael Franck, 1652
MELODY: Michael Franck, 1652

⁓ *ACH WIE FLÜCHTIG, ACH WIE NICHTIG*

TR.: Sir John Bowring, 1825

O how cheat-ing, O how fleet-ing, Is our earth-ly be-ing!

'Tis__ a__ mist in__ win-try__ weath-er, Gath-ered in__ an__ hour to-geth-er, And as__ soon dis-persed in__ e ther.

[ 2 ]*
O how cheating, O how fleeting,
Is all earthly beauty!
Everything is fading, flying,
Man is mortal, earth is dying,
Christian, live on heav'n relying.   *(13/13)*

## 49. In Peace and Joy I Now Depart

*see also:* 325
HYMN: Martin Luther, 1524
MELODY: Martin Luther(?), 1524

*MIT FRIED UND FREUD ICH FAHR DAHIN*

TR.: Catherine Winkworth, 1869, *alt.*

In__ peace and joy I__ now__ de-part, O-bey-ing God's__ will; For full of__ com-fort is__ my heart, Peace-ful and__ still. So doth

44

naught but sleep - ing.

God His prom-ise— keep, And death is naught but sleep - ing.

[2]
'Tis Christ has wrought this work for me;
Thy only dear Son,
Whom Thou hast suffered me to see,

And made Him known
As our help when woes are rife,
And e'en in death is living.  (2/4)

## 50. O World, Thy Life Doth Languish†

see also: 63, 103, 117, 275, 289, 355, 363, 366
SOURCE: St. Matthew Passion, 1729
HYMN: Paul Gerhardt, 1647
MELODY: Anonymous, 1539

⤙ *O WELT, SIEH HIER DEIN LEBEN*
O WELT, ICH MUSS DICH LASSEN

TR.: Anna Hoppe, 1922. By permission of Erie Printing
Co., Erie, Pennsylvania.

† Sometimes published under the title *In allen meinen
Taten.*

O world, thy— life— doth lan - guish, Up-on— the cross in — an - guish, Thy

dy - ing Sav - iour— see! The Prince of Glo - ry of - fers His—

life— for— thee, and— suf - fers Scorn, stripes and— mal - ice— will - ing - ly.

[2]*
O Saviour mine, who dareth
To smite Thee thus? Who beareth
The guilt of Thy deep pain?

All we must make confession
Of sin, but no transgression
Hath ever left on Thee a stain.  (3/16)

## 51. All Praise to Jesus' Hallowed Name

see also: 160, 288
SOURCE: Cantata No. 91, *c.*1740
HYMN†: Martin Luther, 1524
MELODY: Anonymous, 1524

⚜ *GELOBET SEIST DU, JESUS CHRIST*

TR.: Richard Massie, 1854

† Kyrieleis from Kyrie eleison (Gk.), "Lord, have mercy."

Horn I, II

Timpani

Soprano, Oboe I, II, III, Violin I
Alto, Violin II

Tenor, Viola
Bass, Continuo

All __ praise to __ Je - sus' __ hal - lowed name,

Who of Vir - gin __ pure be - came True man for __ us! The an - gels sing, As __

[2]*
All this He did, that He might prove
To us sinners His great love;
For this let Christendom adore
And praise His name forevermore.
Kyrieleis.  (7/7)

## 52. When My Last Hour Is Close at Hand

*WENN MEIN STÜNDLEIN VORHANDEN IST*

*see also:* 322, 351
HYMN: Nikolaus Herman, 1574
MELODY: Nikolaus Herman, 1569

TR.: Catherine Winkworth, 1869

[2]
My sins may sting my mem'ry sore,
And guilt my heart encumber;
But though as sands upon the shore
My sins may be in number,

I will not quail, but think of Thee,
Thy death, Thy sorrows, borne for me,
And sink in peace to slumber.   (2/5)

## 53. The Holy Son, the New-born Child

*see also:* 178(D)
SOURCE: Cantata No. 122, c.1742
HYMN: Cyriakus Schneegass, 1595
MELODY: Melchior Vulpius, 1609

◄ *DAS NEUGEBORNE KINDELEIN*

TR.: Arthur Tozer Russell, 1851

er year of grace, To us, His lov'd,—— His cho-sen race.

year— of grace, To us, His lov'd,— His cho-sen race.

er year of grace,

[ 2 ]*
Behold! He brings a year of praise;
O waste no more in grief your days;
Awake, your time in songs employ;
Lo! Jesus turns your grief to joy!  (4/4)

## 54. Praise God the Lord, Ye Sons of Men

see also: 276, 342
SOURCE: Cantata No. 151, c.1735–1740
HYMN: Nikolaus Herman, 1560
MELODY: Nikolaus Herman, 1554

*LOBT GOTT, IHR CHRISTEN ALLZUGLEICH*

TR.: August Crull, 1845–1923

Praise God the Lord, ye sons of_men, Be - fore His high-est throne; To - day He o - pens heav'n a - gain And gives us_ His_ own Son,—— And gives us_ His own Son.

[ 2 ]*
He opens unto us the door
Of Paradise today;
The angel guards the gate no more;
To God our thanks we pay,
To God our thanks we pay.  (8/8)

## 55. We Christians May Rejoice Today

WIR CHRISTENLEUT

*see also:* 321, 360
SOURCE: Cantata No. 110, after 1734
HYMN: Caspar Fuger, 1592
MELODY: Caspar Fuger, the younger(?), 1593

TR.: Catherine Winkworth, 1863, *alt.*

We_ Chris-tians may, We_ Chris-tians may Re - joice to-day, When Christ was born to_ com-fort and to save_ us; Who thus be-lieves No_ long-er_ grieves, For none are_ lost who_ grasp the_ hope He_ gave_ us.

[2]
Alleluia, Alleluia,
Sing thanks to God,
Sing hallelujahs to the skies above us;
The bliss bestowed
Today by God,
To ceaseless thankfulness and joy should move us.
(5/5)

# 56. Now Must We Jesus Laud and Sing

SOURCE: Cantata No. 121, c.1740
HYMN: Martin Luther, 1524
MELODY: Anonymous

*CHRISTUM WIR SOLLEN LOBEN SCHON*

TR.: George Macdonald, 1876

[ 2 ]*
Praise, honor, thanks to Thee be said,
Christ Jesus, born of holy maid!
With Father and with Holy Ghost,
Now and forever, ending not. *(8/8)*

51

## 57. O Darkest Woe! Ye Tears that Flow!

O TRAURIGKEIT! O HERZELEID!

HYMN: Johann Rist, 1641
MELODY: Anonymous, 1628

TR.: Catherine Winkworth, 1863

O dark-est woe! Ye tears that flow! Has earth so sad a wonder,
That the Father's only Son Now lies buried yonder.

[ 2 ]
Behold thy Lord,
The Lamb of God,
Bloodsprinkled lies before thee,
Pouring out His life that He
May to life restore thee. (4/8)

## 58. Lord, All My Heart Is Fixed on Thee

HERZLICH LIEB HAB ICH DICH, O HERR

see also: 107, 277
SOURCE: Cantata No. 174, 1729
HYMN: Martin Schalling, 1571
MELODY: Anonymous, 1577

TR.: Catherine Winkworth, 1863

*Lord, all my heart is fixed on Thee, I pray Thee, be not
The whole wide world delights me not, Of heav'n or earth, Lord,

far from me, With tender grace uphold me.
ask I not, If but Thy love enfold me.

Yes, though my heart be— like to break, Thou art my trust that— nought can shake, My por - tion and my— hid - den joy, Whose Cross could all my— bonds de - stroy. Lord Je - su Christ, Lord Je - su Christ, my God and Lord, For - sake me not who trust Thy word!

[2]
Rich are Thy gifts! 'Twas God that gave
Body and soul and all I have
In this poor life of labor.
O grant that I may through Thy grace
Use all my powers to show Thy praise,
And serve and help my neighbor.

From all false doctrine keep me, Lord;
All lies and malice from me ward,
In every cross uphold Thou me,
That I may bear it patiently.
Lord Jesu Christ, Lord Jesu Christ, my God and Lord,
In death Thy comfort still afford!  (2/3)

## 59. Alas, Dear Lord, What Law Then Hast Thou Broken

see also: 78, 105, 111

HERZLIEBSTER JESU, WAS HAST DU VERBROCHEN

SOURCE: St. John Passion, 1723
HYMN: Johann Heermann, 1630
MELODY: Johann Crüger, 1640

TR.: Catherine Winkworth, 1863

A - las,— dear Lord, what law— then hast Thou bro - ken, That such sharp sen - tence should on— Thee be— spo - ken? Of— what great crime hast

Thou to__ make con - fes - sion--What dark trans-gres - sion?

**[ 2 ]***

O wondrous love! Whose depths no heart hath
  sounded,
That brought Thee here by foes and thieves
  surrounded;
All worldly pleasures, heedless was I trying,
While Thou wert dying! *(7/15)*

## 60. O Lord, We Welcome Thee

SOURCE: Cantata No. 133, *c*.1735
HYMN: Caspar Ziegler, 1697
MELODY: Anonymous, 1738

*ICH FREUE MICH IN DIR*

TR.: Composite (*Lutheran Hymnal*, 1942). Reprinted
by permission of Concordia Publishing House from
*The Handbook of the Lutheran Hymnal* by W. G.
Polack (1942).

O__ Lord, we wel - come Thee, Our hearts for Thee are__ leap - ing,
Thou, Je - sus dear - est__ Child, Thy pre-cious prom -ise__ keep - ing.

Art__ come from heav'n to earth To be__ our Broth - er dear; Thou

gra - cious Son__ of __ God, Wilt ban - ish all__ our fear.

**[ 2 ]***

To Thee alone we cling,
For Thee all else forsaking;
On Thee alone we build
Though heav'n and earth be quaking.

To Thee alone we live,
In Thee alone we die;
O Jesus, dearest Lord,
With Thee we reign on high. *(4/8)*

54

## 61. Jesu's Suffering, Pain and Death

*see also:* 83, 106
SOURCE: Cantata No. 159, 1729
HYMN: Paul Stockmann, 1633
MELODY: Melchior Vulpius, 1609

*JESU LEIDEN, PEIN UND TOD*

TR.: Anonymous (*Moravian Hymn Book*, 1754), alt.

Je - su's_ suf - f'ring, pain and_ death, Je - su's love so_ lav - ish,

We poor folk, while we_ have breath, Whole-some-ly_ do_ rav - ish.
We poor folk,_____ while we have breath,

O ye_ men, all sin re - nounce, Since we_ now are Chris - tians;

From that pit,_ we_ mount at_ once Through our_ Lamb's as - sist - ance.

[ 2 ]*
Jesu, Thy sore Passion is
To me perfect sweetness:
There's between Thy miseries
And my heart, a fitness;
When thereof I meditate,
My soul walks on roses.
Grant to me a place in heav'n
As Thy hand disposes.   (*33/34*)

## 62. If Thou but Suffer God to Guide Thee

see also: 104, 112, 146, 204, 339
SOURCE: Cantata No. 197, 1737
HYMN: Georg Neumark, 1657
MELODY: Georg Neumark, 1657

*WER NUR DEN LIEBEN GOTT LÄSST WALTEN*

TR.: Catherine Winkworth, 1863

If thou but suf-fer God to guide thee And hope in Him thro' all thy ways, He'll give thee strength, what-e'er be-tide thee, And bear thee thro' the e-vil days; Who trusts in God's un-chang-ing love Builds on the Rock that naught can move.

[ 2 ]*
Sing, pray, and keep His ways unswerving,
So do thine own part faithfully,
And trust His Word, tho' undeserving,

Thou yet shalt find it true for thee.
God never will forsake in need
The soul that trusted Him indeed.   (7/7)

## 63. See World, Thy Lord in Anguish†

see also: 50, 103, 117, 275, 289, 355, 363, 366
SOURCE: St. John Passion, 1723
HYMN: Paul Gerhardt, 1647
MELODY: Anonymous, 1539

*O WELT, SIEH HIER DEIN LEBEN*
O WELT, ICH MUSS DICH LASSEN

TR.: John Kelly, 1867, *alt.*

† Sometimes published under the title *Nun ruhen alle Wälder.*

See world, thy__ Lord in an - guish Up - on__ the cross doth__ lan - guish, The
Sav - iour sinks__ in__ death! The might -y Prince from Heav - en Him -
self__ hath free - ly__ giv - en To shame and blows, and cru - el wrath.

[ 2 ]*
Who is it that afflicts Thee?
My Saviour what dejects Thee
And causes all Thy woes?
Sin Thou committed never,
As we and our seed ever
Of deeds and evil nought dost know. (3/16)

[ 3 ]*
I many times transgressing,
In number far surpassing
The sand upon the coast,
I thus the cause have given,
That Thou with grief are riven,
And the afflicted martyr host. (4/16)

### 64. Faithful God, I Lay before Thee

TREUER GOTT, ICH MUSS DIR KLAGEN
FREU DICH SEHR, O MEINE SEELE

Duplicate of Chorale 256. Chorale 64 is sometimes published in the transposed key of G major whereas Chorale 256 appears in B flat major, the original cantata key.

### 65. What-e'er My God Ordains Is Right

WAS GOTT TUT, DAS IST WOHLGETAN

see also: 293, 347
SOURCE: Cantata No. 144, c.1725
HYMN: Samuel Rodigast, 1676
MELODY: Johann Pachelbel(?), 1690

TR.: Catherine Winkworth, 1863, alt.

* What - e'er my God or - dains is right; His_ Ho - ly_ will a - bid - eth;
I _ will be still, what - e'er He doth, And_ fol - low where He_ guid - eth.

He is_ my God; Though dark my road, From fall - ing_ He_ doth_

hold _ me, Where - fore_ I _ trust Him _ sure - ly.

[ 2 ]
What-e'er my God ordains is right;
His loving thought attends me;
No poison'd draught the cup can be
That my Physician sends me,

But comfort due;
For God is true,
And on that truth now building
My heart with hope is filling. (3/6)

## 66. To Jordan When Our Lord Had Gone

*see also:* 119
HYMN: Martin Luther, 1541
MELODY: Johann Walther(?), 1524

*CHRIST UNSER HERR ZUM JORDAN KAM*

TR.: George Macdonald, 1876

To Jor-dan when our Lord had gone, His Fa-ther's pleas-ure will - ing,
He took His bap-tism of Saint John, His work and task ful - fill - ing;

There - in He would ap - point a bath To wash us from de -

file - ment, And al - so drown that cru - el death In

His blood of as - soil - ment: 'Twas no less than a new life.

[ 2 ]
The eye but water doth behold,
As from man's hand it floweth;
But inward faith the power untold
Of Jesus Christ's blood knoweth.

Faith sees therein a red flood roll,
With Christ's blood dyed and blended,
Which hurts of all kinds maketh whole,
From Adam here descended,
Or by ourselves brought on us.　(7/7)

59

## 67. Come and Hear Our Blessed Saviour†

KOMMT, LASST EUCH DEN HERREN LEHREN

FREU DICH SEHR, O MEINE SEELE

see also: 29, 64(D), 76, 254, 256, 282(D), 298
SOURCE: Cantata No. 39, 1732
HYMN: David Denicke, 1648
MELODY: Louis Bourgeois, 1551

TR.: John Christian Jacobi, 1722

† Sometimes published in the transposed key of G major.

Come and hear our bless-ed_ Sav-iour, All that have a mind to_ learn,
What's their life and whole be-hav-ior, Who the Chris-tian ti-tle_ earn;

Who not_ on-ly_ do_ con-fess, But_ with hearts and hands ex-press,

That their whole de-light and la - bor Is_ to serve their God and_ neigh-bor.

[ 2 ]*
Blest are those who with compassion,
Look upon their neighbor's grief,
Pitying poverty's oppression,
Pray to God for its relief;

Who assist the suff'rers need
Not with words alone, but deed,
They shall never be discarded,
But with mercy be rewarded.  (6/11)

## 68. When in the Hour of Utmost Need

WENN WIR IN HÖCHSTEN NOTEN SEIN

see also: 247
HYMN: Paul Eber, c.1560
MELODY: Louis Bourgeois, 1547

TR.: Catherine Winkworth, 1863

When in the_ hour of _ ut - most need We_
hour of ut - most_ need

hour of ut - most need

know not where to look for aid, When days and nights of

anx - ious thought Nor help nor coun - sel yet have brought,

[2]
Then this our comfort is alone:
That we may meet before Thy throne,

And cry, O faithful God, to Thee,
For rescue from our misery. (2/7)

## 69. Come, Holy Spirit, God and Lord†

SOURCE: Motet No. 2, *Der Geist hilft,* 1729
HYMN: Martin Luther, 1524
MELODY: Anonymous, 1524

*KOMM, HEILIGER GEIST, HERRE GOTT*

TR.: Catherine Winkworth, 1863

† Sometimes published in the transposed key of G major.

Come, Ho - ly Spir - it, God and Lord, Be all Thy grac - es

now out-poured On the be - liev - er's mind and spir - it, And

On the be - liev - er's mind and spir - it,

with liv - ing coal.

touch our hearts with liv - ing coal. Thy Light this day shone

[ 2 ]*

Thou Sacred Ardour, Comfort sweet,
Help us to wait with ready feet
And willing heart at Thy dread command,
Nor trial fright us from Thy band.

Lord, make us ready with Thy powers,
Strengthen the flesh in weaker hours,
That as good warriors we may force
Through life and death, unto Thee our course.
Alleluia, Alleluia.   (3/3)

## 70. O Lord, We Praise Thee, Bless Thee, and Adore Thee

GOTT SEI GELOBET UND GEBENEDEIET

HYMN†: Martin Luther, 1524
MELODY: Anonymous, 1524

TR.: Composite (*Lutheran Hymnal*, 1942). Reprinted
by permission of Concordia Publishing House from
*The Handbook of the Lutheran Hymnal* by W. G.
Polack (1942).

† Kyrieleison from Kyrie eleison, (Gk.), "Lord, have
mercy."

[ 2 ]
Thy holy body into death was given,
Life to win for us in heaven.
No greater love than this to Thee could bind us;
May this feast thereof remind us.
Kyrieleison.

Lord, Thy kindness did Thee so constrain
That Thy blood should bless and me sustain,
All our debt Thou hast paid;
Peace with God once more is made:
Kyrieleison. *(2/3)*

63

## 71. I Cry to Thee, My Dearest Lord†

SOURCE: Cantata No. 177, 1732
HYMN: Johannes Agricola, 1529
MELODY: Anonymous, 1529

*ICH RUF ZU DIR, HERR JESU CHRIST*

TR.: John Christian Jacobi, 1722

† Sometimes published in the transposed key of E minor.

[ 2 ]*
I fight, Lord Jesus, and withstand,
Do Thou relieve my weakness,
Support me with Thy mighty hand,
And Thine abundant greatness.

When sin and Satan raise their force,
Let me be never frighted,
But delighted
To run my Christian course
'Till I'm with Thee united.  (5/5)

## 72. Lord, Keep Us Steadfast in Thy Word

SOURCE: Cantata No. 6, 1736
HYMN: Martin Luther, 1542
MELODY: Anonymous, 1543

*ERHALT UNS, HERR, BEI DEINEM WORT*

TR.: Catherine Winkworth, 1863

Lord, keep us steadfast in Thy word; Curb those who fain by craft or sword Would wrest the king-dom from Thy Son, And set at nought all He hath done.

[ 2 ]*
Lord Jesus Christ, Thy pow'r make known,
For Thou art Lord of lords alone;
Defend Thy Christendom, that we
May evermore sing praise to Thee.   (2/3)

## 73. Lord Jesus Christ, My Sovereign Good

*see also:* 92, 266, 294
HYMN: Bartholomäus Ringwaldt, 1588
MELODY: Anonymous, 1593

*HERR JESU CHRIST, DU HÖCHSTES GUT*

TR.: Anonymous (*Moravian Hymn Book*, 1890)

Lord Je-sus Christ, my sov-ereign good, Thou foun-tain of sal-va-tion,
Be-hold me bowed be-neath the load Of guilt and con-dem-na-tion:

My sins_ in-deed are_ num-ber-less; O_ Lord, re-gard my
deep dis-tress, Re-ject not_ my_ pe-ti-tion.
O Lord re-gard_
_ my deep dis-tress,

[2]
In pity look upon my need,
Remove my sore oppression;
Since Thou hast suffered in my stead,
And paid for my transgression;
Let me not yield to dark despair;
A wounded spirit who can bear?
O show me Thy salvation.   (2/8)

## 74. O Sacred Head Now Wounded

*O HAUPT VOLL BLUT UND WUNDEN*
HERZLICH TUT MICH VERLANGEN

*see also:* 21, 80, 89, 98, 270, 286, 345, 367
SOURCE: St. Matthew Passion, 1729
HYMN: Paul Gerhardt, 1656
MELODY: Hans Leo Hassler, 1601

TR.: James W. Alexander, 1804–1859

*O_ sa-cred Head now wound-ed, With grief and shame weighed down,
Now_ scorn-ful-ly_ sur-round-ed With thorns, Thy on-ly_ crown!
How_ pale art_ Thou with an-guish, With sore a-buse and scorn! How

does_ that_ vis-age lan - guish Which once was_ bright_ as_ morn!

[ 2 ]*
O Lord of life and glory,
What bliss till now was Thine!
I read the wondrous story;
I joy to call Thee mine.
Thy grief and bitter Passion
Were all for sinners' gain:
Mine, mine was the transgression,
But Thine the deadly pain.  (2/10)


## 75. As Willed the Three

*DAS WALT MEIN GOTT*

HYMN: Basilius Förtsch(?), 1613
MELODY: Anonymous, 1648

TR.: Henry S. Drinker, 1944

As willed the_ Three, Fa-ther, Son and_ Ho-ly_ Ghost, They

have cre-a-ted me. My_ bod-y they al-lowed_ me, With

soul and_ life_ en-dowed_ me, In_ like-ness, Lord, to_ Thee.

[ 2 ]
My ev'ry step in the name of God I take,
Send Thou Thy help to me.
Come early, Lord, to meet me,
With grace and blessing greet me,
Deny not Thou my plea.  (2/8)

## 76. Comfort, Comfort Ye My People†

*see also:* 29, 64(D), 67, 254, 256, 282(D), 298
SOURCE: Cantata No. 30, 1738
HYMN: Johann Olearius, 1671
MELODY: Louis Bourgeois, 1551

*TRÖSTET, TRÖSTET MEINE LIEBEN*
FREU DICH SEHR, O MEINE SEELE

TR.: Catherine Winkworth, 1863

† Sometimes published in the transposed key of G major.

Com-fort, com-fort_ ye_ My peo - ple, Seek ye_
Com-fort, those_ who_ sit_ in _ dark - ness, Mourn-ing_

peace, thus_ saith our_ God; Speak ye_ to_ Je - ru - sa - lem
'neath their_ sor - row's load;

Of _ the_ peace that_ waits for them, Tell_ her_ that_ her_

sins I cov - er And_ her_ war - fare now is _ o - ver.

[ 2 ]*
For Elijah's voice is crying
In the desert far and near,
Bidding all men to repentance,
Since the kingdom now is here.

O that warning cry obey,
Now prepare for God a way;
Let the valleys rise to meet Him,
And the hills bow down to greet Him. *(3/4)*

## 77. Awake Ye Souls, This Is the Day

*NUN LIEBE SEEL, NUN IST ES ZEIT*
IN DICH HAB ICH GEHOFFET, HERR

*see also:* 118
SOURCE: Christmas Oratorio, 1734
HYMN: Georg Weissel, 1642
MELODY: Sethus Calvisius(?), 1581

TR.: Henry S. Drinker, 1944

[2]*
Thy splendor drives the night away,
And turns the darkness into day.
Shed Thou Thy glory o'er me,
Thy beauteous face and radiant grace,
My light and guide before me.  (6/6)

## 78. Alas, Dear Lord, What Law Then Hast Thou Broken

*see also:* 59, 105, 111
SOURCE: St. Matthew Passion, 1729
HYMN: Johann Heermann, 1630
MELODY: Johann Crüger, 1640

TR.: Catherine Winkworth, 1863

HERZLIEBSTER JESU, WAS HAST DU VERBROCHEN

*A - las,_ dear_ Lord, what law then hast_ Thou bro - ken, That such sharp sen - tence should on Thee be_ spo - ken? Of_ what great crime hast Thou to_ make con - fes - sion--What dark_ trans - gres - sion?

[2]
And when, dear Lord, before Thy throne in heaven
The crown of joy to me at last is given,

Where sweetest hymns Thy saints forever raise Thee,
I too shall praise Thee!  *(15/15)*

## 79. Today the Lord in Triumph Reigns

HEUT TRIUMPHIERET GOTTES SOHN

HYMN: Bartholomäus Gesius(?) and Basilius Förtsch(?), 1601
MELODY: Bartholomäus Gesius(?), 1601

TR.: John Christian Jacobi, 1722

To - day the Lord_ in tri - umph reigns, Breaks death and Hell's in -

fer - nal chains; Al - le - lu - ia! __ Al - le - lu - ia!

Re - takes His __ life _____ and maj - es - ty, Praise Him to all __ e-

ter - ni - ty. Al - le - lu - ia! __ Al - le - lu - ia!

[2]
O sweet Redeemer, Jesus Christ!
Our Sacrifice and great High Priest;
Alleluia! Alleluia!
Lead us by Thine almighty grace,
To end with joy our Christian race.
Alleluia! Alleluia!  (4/6)

## 80. Commit Thou Every Grievance†

*BEFIEHL DU DEINE WEGE*
HERZLICH TUT MICH VERLANGEN

*see also:* 21, 74, 89, 98, 270, 286, 345, 367
SOURCE: St. Matthew Passion, 1729
HYMN: Paul Gerhardt, 1653
MELODY: Hans Leo Hassler, 1601

TR.: Anonymous (*Moravian Hymn Book*, 1890)

† Sometimes published under the title *O Haupt voll Blut und Wunden.*

*Com - mit thou ev - ery __ griev - ance In - to __ His __ faith - ful hands,
To His sure care __ and __ guid - ance, Who heav'n and __ earth com - mands;

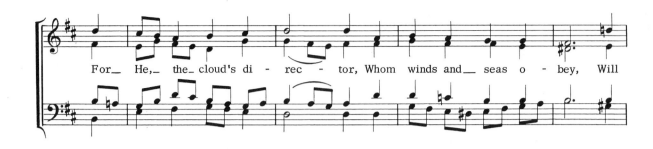

For_ He,_ the_ cloud's di - rec - tor, Whom winds and_ seas o - bey, Will

be_ thy kind_ pro - tec - tor, And_ will_ pre - pare_ thy way.

[ 2 ]

Rely on God thy Saviour,
So shalt thou safe go on;
Build on His grace and favor,
So shall thy work be done:

Thou can'st make no advances,
By self consuming care;
But He His help dispenses
When called upon by prayer.  (2/12)

## 81. See the Lord of Life and Light

see also: 113, 198, 307(D)
SOURCE: St. John Passion, 1723
HYMN: Michael Weisse, 1531
MELODY: Anonymous, 1531

✠ CHRISTUS, DER UNS SELIG MACHT

TR.: John Troutbeck, 1832–1897, (stanza 1), used by
permission of Novello & Co., Ltd.; John Christian
Jacobi, 1725, (stanza 2).

* See the Lord of_ light_ and_ life, Sav - iour meek and_ low - ly,

Tak - en like_ a_ thief_ at night, Bound by hands un - ho - ly.

See the_ sin-less_ Son of_ God Shame-ful mock-ings_ bear- ing,

shar - ing.____

Bit-ter taunts, a_ cru-el rod, Doom of sin-ners shar - ing.

Oboe

shar - ing.____

[2]
Grant, O Jesu, blessed Lord,
By Thy cross and passion,
That Thy love may be adored
By Thy whole creation;

Hating sin, the woeful cause
Of Thy death and suff'ring,
Let our hearts obey Thy laws
As our best thanksgiving.  (8/8)

## 82. O God of Power and Might

SOURCE: Cantata No. 46, c.1725
HYMN: Balthasar Schnurr, 1633
MELODY: Melchior Franck(?), 1632

⧉ *O GROSSER GOTT VON MACHT*

TR.: Charles Sanford Terry, 1929. By permission of
Oxford University Press, London.

Flute I, a due

Flute II, a due

Soprano, Trumpet, Violin I
Alto, Violin II

O God of power and_ might,

Tenor, Viola
Bass, Continuo

And lov-ing mer-cy too, With-

draw Thy_venge-ful hand, Nor with_ just_ wrath pur-

sue. Per-chance there are a-mong us

74

still ... A faith - ful few to do Thy will.

For their sake, Lord, O__ hear__ us,

And on Thy__ mer-cy bear__ us. __

[ 2 ]*
O Lord, Thou God of Truth,
Before Whom none may stand
If Jesus Christ Thy Son
Stay not Thy wrathful hand.

O, to His wounds have Thou regard,
His anguish, pain, and body marred:
For His dear sake, O spare us,
And on Thy mercy bear us!   (9/9)

## 83. Jesus, Thou Who Once Was Dead

JESU LEIDEN, PEIN UND TOD

*see also:* 61, 106
SOURCE: St. John Passion, 1723
HYMN: Paul Stockmann, 1633
MELODY: Melchior Vulpius, 1609

TR.: Anonymous (*Moravian Hymn Book,* 1908)

Je - sus, Thou who once was dead, But now ev - er — liv - est;

Who in ev - 'ry time of need Kind - ly me re - liev - est,

And — dost help to — me af - ford; Faith - ful Lord and Sav - iour,

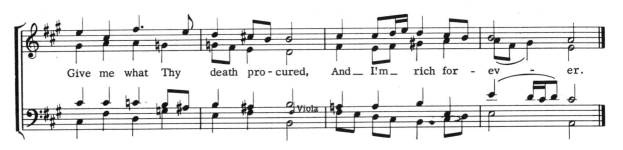

Give me what Thy death pro - cured, And — I'm — rich for - ev - er.

[ 2 ]*
Peter, faithless, thrice denies
That his Lord he knoweth;
When he meets those earnest eyes,
Weeping, forth he goeth.

Jesus, when we will not turn,
Look on us in kindness;
Make our hearts within us burn,
Rouse us from our blindness. (*10/34*)

## 84. Now Do We Pray God, the Holy Ghost

*see also:* 36, 97
SOURCE: Cantata No. 197, 1737
HYMN†: Anonymous (stanza 1); Martin Luther, 1524, (stanza 2).
MELODY: Anonymous

*NUN BITTEN WIR DEN HEILIGEN GEIST*

TR.: Anonymous (*Selah Song Book*, 1936)

† Kyrie eleis from Kyrie eleison (Gk.), "Lord, have mercy."

Now do we pray God, the Holy Ghost, For

the true faith which we need the most, And that

He defend us, when life is ending, And from exile

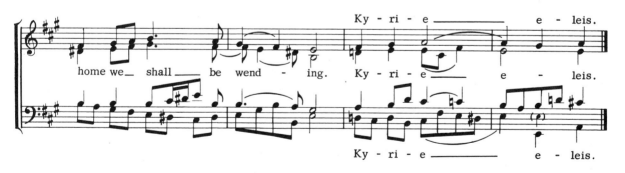

home we shall be wending. Kyrie eleis. Kyrie eleis.

Kyrie eleis.

[2]*
Thou sweetest Love, grace on us bestow;
Set our hearts with heav'nly fire aglow,

That with hearts united we love each other
Of one mind, in peace with ev'ry brother.
Kyrie eleis. (3/4)

## 85. O God, Thou Faithful God

*see also:* 255, 291, 312
SOURCE: Cantata No. 45, *c.*1740
HYMN: Johann Heermann, 1630
MELODY: Anonymous, 1679

*O GOTT, DU FROMMER GOTT*†

TR.: Catherine Winkworth, 1863

† First tune.

O— God, Thou faith-ful— God, Thou Foun-tain ev - er flow - ing, With-

out— whom noth - ing— is, All per-fect gifts— be - stow - ing; A—

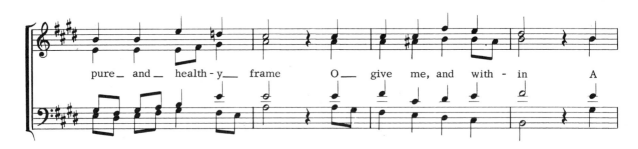

pure— and— health-y— frame O— give me, and with - in A—

con - science free— from blame, A —— soul un - hurt by— sin.

[2]*
And grant me, Lord, to do,
With ready heart and willing,
What-e'er Thou shalt command,
My calling here fulfilling,

And do it where I ought
With all my strength, and bless
The work I thus have wrought,
For Thou must give success. (2/8)

# 86. How Bright Appears the Morning Star

**see also:** 195(D), 278, 305(D), 323
SOURCE: Cantata No. 36, c.1730
HYMN: Philipp Nicolai, 1599
MELODY: Philipp Nicolai(?), 1599

*WIE SCHÖN LEUCHTET DER MORGENSTERN*

TR.: John Christian Jacobi, 1722

How bright ap - pears_ the_ morn - ing star With grace and_ truth_ be -
O Da - vid's Son_ of_ Ja - cob's line, My soul's de - light_ and_

yond _ com - pare, The roy - al root _ of Jes - se.
spouse _ di - vine, Thy love can on - ly bless _____ me.

Pre - cious, gra - cious, Fair and _ glo - rious, e'er vic - to - rious,

Thou my_ treas - ure Art_ be - yond all joy_ and_ meas - ure.

[ 2 ]*
Tune all your strings of lute and harp,
Resolve the notes of flat and sharp
Into celestial concords,
That nothing may disturb my frame
Which is wrapt up in Jesus' name,
The sweetest of all comforts.

Ringing, singing
Be your praises, that the phrases
Of your duty
Please the Lord of bliss and beauty.  (6/7)

## 87. Let Who Will Receive Thy Pleasure

 DU, O SCHÖNES WELTGEBÄUDE

*see also:* 134
SOURCE: Cantata No. 56, *c.*1731
HYMN: Johann Franck, 1653
MELODY: Johann Crüger, 1649

TR.: Catherine Winkworth, 1855, *alt.*

Let who will receive thy pleasure, O thou
Ever anguished sorrow's measure Pierces
fair and wondrous earth! Let thy vain delights be given
through thy seeming mirth; Unto them who love not heaven,
My desire is fixed on Thee, Jesus, dearest far to me!

[ 2 ]*
Come, O Death, thou twin of Sleeping
Lead me hence,—I pray thee come,
Guide my rudder, aimless drifting,
Take my vessel safely home.

At Thy coming some are fearful,
But for me to die is joyful,
Death but leads the way to Thee,
Jesus, dearest Friend to me!   (6/8)

## 88. Ye Christians in This Nation

 HELFT MIR GOTTS GÜTE PREISEN

Duplicate of Chorale 23.

# 89. O Sacred Head Now Wounded†

see also: 21, 74, 80, 98, 270, 286, 345, 367
SOURCE: St. Matthew Passion, 1729
HYMN: Paul Gerhardt, 1656
MELODY: Hans Leo Hassler, 1601

*⚜ O HAUPT VOLL BLUT UND WUNDEN*
HERZLICH TUT MICH VERLANGEN

TR.: James W. Alexander, 1804–1859

† Sometimes published in the transposed key of B minor.

O sa-cred Head now wound-ed, With grief and shame weighed down,
Now scorn-ful-ly sur-round-ed With thorns, Thy on-ly crown!

How pale art Thou with an-guish, With sore a-buse and scorn! How

does that vis-age lan-guish Which once was bright as morn!

[ 2 ]*
Be near me, Lord, when dying;
Show Thou Thyself to me;
And for my succor flying,
Come, Lord, to set me free.

These eyes, new faith receiving,
From Jesus shall not move;
For he who dies believing
Dies safely through Thy love. (9/10)

# 90. Why Hast Thou Hidden Thee, Jesus, and Left Me Neglected

SOURCE: Cantata No. 57, c.1740
HYMN: Ahasuerus Fritsch, 1668
MELODY: Anonymous, 1665

*⚜ HAST DU DENN, JESU, DEIN ANGESICHT
GÄNZLICH VERBORGEN*

TR.: Henry S. Drinker, 1944

Why hast Thou hid-den Thee, Je-sus, and left me ne-
All through the night have my thoughts un-to Thee been di-

glect - ed?
rect - ed.
Why dost Thou still, Sweet - est One,

treat me so ill? Leave me for - lorn and ne - glect - ed?

[ 2 ]*
Know thou, beloved one, naught will I ever deny
    thee;
Friend of thy soul, will I ever and always be nigh
    thee;

Thee do I love,
Come then to heaven above;
There will thy God glorify thee.   (6/12)

## 91. In These Our Days So Perilous

see also: 215, 259(D)
SOURCE: Cantata No. 42, 1731
HYMN: Martin Luther, 1529
MELODY: Anonymous, 1531

VERLEIH UNS FRIEDEN GNÄDIGLICH

TR.: Richard Massie, 1800–1877, alt.

In these our days so per - il - ous, Lord, peace in mer - cy
*[1.] In these our days so per - il-ous, Lord, peace in mer -
In these our days so per - il - ous, Lord, peace in mer - cy

send us;
- cy send us; No God but Thee can fight for us, No
send us;

82

God_ but_ Thee de - fend_____ us; Thou art our_ one_ and_ on - ly God.

[2.] Grant to_ our King and all_ au - thor - i - ties Peace and pro - fi - cient

rule. That we_ may live_ in_ peace And that,_ un - der our rul - ers,_

live_ in_ qui - et hon - or; Liv - ing_ in_ all_ god - li - ness_

And hon - es - ty. A - - - - - men.

## 92. Lord Jesus Christ, My Highest Good

see also: 73, 266, 294
SOURCE: Cantata No. 168, c.1725
HYMN: Bartholomäus Ringwaldt, 1588
MELODY: Anonymous, 1593

HERR JESU CHRIST, DU HÖCHSTES GUT

TR.: Catherine Winkworth, 1869, alt.

Lord Je - sus Christ, my_ high - est good, Who show-ers grace up - on __ me,
Be - hold how heav - y_ is _ my mood, Re - call - ing sins a - gainst __ Thee;

How sore my_ con - science is_ be - set With keen - est_ ar - rows

cease to pierce _____ me.

of _ re - gret That nev - er cease _____ to _ pierce __ me.

[ 2 ]*
Thy joyful Spirit give me strength,
Heal by Thy wounds, my Saviour,
When my last hour must come at length,

Cleanse Thou my soul forever,
And take me when it seems Thee best,
In Thy true faith to heav'nly rest,
My bonds with Thee ne'er sever.  (8/8)

# 93. Awake, My Heart, Rejoicing

*see also:* 257(D)
SOURCE: Cantata No. 194, 1723
HYMN: Paul Gerhardt, 1647
MELODY: Nikolaus Selnecker(?), 1587

*WACH AUF, MEIN HERZ, UND SINGE*
NUN LASST UNS GOTT DEM HERREN

TR.: Alfred Ramsey, 1890

Oboe I, II

Oboe III

Soprano, Violin I
Alto, Violin II

Tenor, Viola
Bass, Continuo

A - wake, my_ heart, re - joic - ing, Thy Mak - er's

prais - es voic - ing, The Giv - er good gifts send -

ing, Their Shield,— His fold_____ de - fend - ing.

[ 2 ]*
Approve my works when shown Thee;
Help Thou good councils only;
Beginning, middle, closing,
Lord, for the best disposing. *(9/10)*

[ 3 ]*
With blessings guard me waking,
My heart Thy dwelling making,
And with Thy Word, Lord, feed me,
While heav'nward Thou dost lead me. *(10/10)*

## 94. Why Art Thou Thus Cast Down, My Heart?†

*WARUM BETRÜBST DU DICH, MEIN HERZ?*

*see also:* 145, 300
SOURCE: Cantata No. 47, 1720
HYMN: Hans Sachs(?), 1565
MELODY: Anonymous, 1565

TR.: Henry S. Drinker, 1944

† Lines one and two of stanza 11 of this hymn, as used by Bach in Cantata No. 47, contain more syllables than lines one and two of other stanzas. For this reason, only stanza 11 is included.

All glo-ries of earth glad-ly I fore-go,

*All glo-ries of earth glad-ly I fore-go, If__ on-ly__ on me

All glo-ries of earth glad-ly I fore-go,

Thou wilt be - stow

Thou wilt be-stow For-ev-er that re-ward, The__ guer-don__ of__ Thy__

Thou wilt be - stow

bit- ter__ woe. This ask__ I Thee,__ My__ God__ and__ Lord.
(11/14)

## 95. Sink Not Yet, My Soul, to Slumber

*see also:* 121, 233, 350, 365
SOURCE: Cantata No. 55, c.1731
HYMN: Johann Rist, 1642
MELODY: Johann Schop, 1642

*WERDE MUNTER, MEIN GEMÜTE*

TR.: Catherine Winkworth, 1861

[2]*
Have I e'er from Thee departed,
Now I seek Thy face again,
And Thy Son, the lovinghearted,
Made our peace through bitter pain.

Yes, far greater than our sin,
Though it still be strong within,
Is the love that fails us never,
Mercy that endures forever. (6/12)

## 96. Blessed Is the Spirit

see also: 138, 263, 283, 324, 356
SOURCE: Cantata No. 87, 1735
HYMN: Heinrich Müller, 1659
MELODY: Johann Crüger, 1653

SELIG IST DIE SEELE
JESU, MEINE FREUDE

TR.: Henry S. Drinker, 1944

Bless-ed_ is_ the_ spir - it, That has ev - er_ near____ it,
Thou wilt warm em - brace____ it, At_ Thy_ side_ will_ place____ it,

Thee_ and_ love for_ Thee.
From af - flic - tion_ free.

Thou our_ light_ and_ jew - el_ bright,

Thou the_ heart's most pre - cious treas - ure, Life and joy_ and_ pleas - ure.

Oboe da caccia

[ 2 ]*
What is there to grieve me?
Jesus will not leave me,
He will love me still.
Through His love I capture
Heaven's joyous rapture,
Conquer every ill.
For my grief he sends relief,
Through His love the deepest sadness
Changes into gladness. (9/9)

## 97. Now Let Us Pray to God and Holy Ghost

*see also:* 36, 84
SOURCE: Cantata No. 169, 1731
HYMN†: Anonymous (stanza 1); Martin Luther, 1524, (stanza 2).
MELODY: Anonymous

*NUN BITTEN WIR DEN HEILIGEN GEIST*

TR.: George Macdonald, 1876, *alt.*

† Kyrie eleison (Gk.), "Lord, have mercy."

Now let us pray to God and Ho - ly Ghost For the true faith, of all things the most, That He help and aid us when we are dy - ing, And are go - ing from this vale of

And are go - ing from this vale of cry - ing Ky - rie e - lei - son!

Ky - rie e - lei - son!

And are go - ing from this vale of cry - ing Ky - rie e - e - lei - son!

[2]*
Thou sweet Love, favor us this day, that so
We of Thy love feel within the glow,

That we from our hearts may be true to others,
And in peace dwell with the minds of brothers.
Kyrie eleison.  (3/4)

89

## 98. Ah Wounded Head That Bearest†

see also: 21, 74, 80, 89, 270, 286, 345, 367
SOURCE: St. Matthew Passion, 1729
HYMN: Paul Gerhardt, 1656
MELODY: Hans Leo Hassler, 1601

⚜ *O HAUPT VOLL BLUT UND WUNDEN*
HERZLICH TUT MICH VERLANGEN

TR.: Catherine Winkworth, 1863, (stanzas 1, 2); John Troutbeck, 1832–1899, (stanza 3), by permission of G. Schirmer, Inc., New York.

† In the *St. Matthew Passion* this harmonization is found twice in the keys of E♭ major and E major. It is also sometimes published in the transposed key of D major.

Ah wound-ed Head that bear-est Such bit-ter shame and scorn,
That now so meek-ly wear-est The mock-ing crown of thorn!

Erst reign-ing in the high-est In light and maj-es-ty, Dis-

hon-ored here Thou di-est, Yet here I wor-ship Thee.

[ 2 ]*
My Guardian, deign to own me,
My Shepherd, I am Thine;
What goodness hast Thou shown me,
O Fount of Love Divine!
How oft Thy lips have fed me
On earth with angels' food!
How oft Thy spirit led me
To stores of heav'nly good. (5/10)

[ 3 ]*
Near Thee would I be staying;
O Lord, disdain me not;
From Thee would ne'er be straying,
How dark soe'er Thy lot.
Till Thou dost yield Thy spirit
To meet the stroke of death,
Thy love I'd seek to merit,
And soothe Thy latest breath. (6/10)

## 99. Ye Christians in This Nation

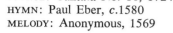

see also: 23, 88(D), 123
SOURCE: Cantata No. 16, 1724
HYMN: Paul Eber, c.1580
MELODY: Anonymous, 1569

*HELFT MIR GOTTS GÜTE PREISEN*

TR.: John Christian Jacobi, 1722

[ 2 ]*
These mercies we're adoring,
O Lord, who dwelt above:
Which Thou hast been restoring,
Through Christ the Son of Love;

In whom thou wilt be pleased
To grant this year ensuing,
Grace, constant in welldoing,
'Till we're from sin released.   (6/6)

## 100. All Mankind Fell in Adam's Fall

see also: 126(D)
SOURCE: Cantata No. 18, 1714
HYMN: Lazarus Spengler, 1524
MELODY: Anonymous, 1535

*DURCH ADAMS FALL IST GANZ VERDERBT*

TR.: Matthias Loy, 1880, (stanza 1), *alt.*; John Christian
   Jacobi, 1722, (stanza 2).

Through all_man's pow'rs cor - rup -tion creeps And_ him in_dread-ful_ sin_ steeps; In

guilt he_draws his in - fant breath And reaps its_ fruits of _ woe, _____ death.

[ 2 ]*
I send my cries unto the Lord,
My heart implores His favor:
To grant me of His living word
A never failing savor;

That sin and shame may lose their claim
Of shaking my salvation;
In Christ, the scope of all my hope,
I 'scape death and damnation.   (8/9)

## 101. O Thou, of God the Father

see also: 303
SOURCE: Cantata No. 164, 1715
HYMN: Elisabethe Cruciger, 1524
MELODY: Anonymous, 1524

*{ HERR CHRIST, DER EIN'GE GOTTS SOHN *

TR.: Catherine Winkworth, 1863, (stanza 1), *alt.*; Henry
S. Drinker, 1944, (stanza 2).

O  Thou, of God_ the  Fa -  ther, The  true  e - ter - nal_ Son,
Of  whom 'tis  sure - ly  writ - ten  That Thou with  Him  art_ One,

Thou_ art_ the_ Star_ of _ Morn - ing Whose  rad - iance  marks the_

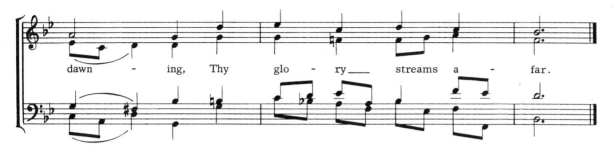

dawn - ing, Thy glo - ry___ streams a - far.

[ 2 ]*
Transform us by Thy kindness,
Awake us through Thy grace,
That we put on the New Man,
The Old Man's power efface.

While here as mortals living
With heartiest thanksgiving,
Our trust in Thee we place.   (5/5)

## 102. Lord Jesus Christ, Thou Prince of Love

*DU LEBENSFÜRST, HERR JESU CHRIST*
ERMUNTRE DICH, MEIN SCHWACHER GEIST

*see also:* 9, 343, 361(D)
SOURCE: Cantata No. 43, *c*.1735                    TR.: Henry S. Drinker, 1944
HYMN: Johann Rist, 1641
MELODY: Johann Schop, 1641

*Lord Je - sus Christ,___ Thou Prince of Love, When past Thy res - ur - rec - tion,
Thou did'st re - turn___ to God a - bove And those of His e - lec - tion.

For Thy most glo - rious vic - to - ry, O - ver a might - y en - e -

my Which Thou hast gained in splen - dor, Our heart - y praise we ren - der.

[ 2 ]*
Draw us to Thee, and draw Thou near;
Give us an eagle's pinions,
That we may soar far, far from here
To heaven's high dominions.

O Lord, when may I come to Thee,
Where I may ever joyful be?
When shall I stand before Thee,
To worship and adore Thee?   (13/14)

## 103. In All That I Am Doing†

*see also:* 50, 63, 117, 275, 289, 355, 363, 366
SOURCE: Cantata No. 13, *c.*1740
HYMN: Paul Flemming, 1642
MELODY: Anonymous, 1539

*IN ALLEN MEINEN TATEN*
O WELT, ICH MUSS DICH LASSEN

TR.: Henry S. Drinker, 1944

† Sometimes published under the title *Nun ruhen alle Wälder.*

In all that I am do - ing, Each en - ter - prise pur - su - ing, I

fol - low God's ad - vice; For he who this is heed - ing Is

ev - er well suc - ceed - ing, His ven - tures ev - er pay him thrice.

[ 2 ]*
Be His, my soul, forever,
That naught from thee can sever,
Him who created thee.
Whatever ill assail thee,
Thy Father will not fail thee,
Thine ev'ry need will He foresee.   (*15/15*)

# 104. If Thou but Suffer God to Guide Thee

WER NUR DEN LIEBEN GOTT LÄSST WALTEN

see also: 62, 112, 146, 204, 339
SOURCE: Cantata No. 88, 1732
HYMN: Georg Neumark, 1657
MELODY: Georg Neumark, 1657

TR.: Catherine Winkworth, 1863

If \_ thou but suf - fer \_ God \_ to \_ guide thee, And \_ hope in \_
He'll give thee strength what \_ e'er \_ be - tide thee, And \_ bear thee \_

Him \_ through all \_ thy ways, Who trusts in \_ God's un -
through the \_ e - vil days;

chang - ing \_ love Builds \_ on the \_ rock \_ that \_ nought can \_ move.

[ 2 ]*
Sing, pray, and keep His ways unswerving,
So do thine own part faithfully,
And trust His word;—though undeserving,
Thou yet shalt find it true for thee;
God never yet forsook in need
The soul that trusted Him indeed.   (7/7)

95

## 105. Alas, Dear Lord, What Law Then Hast Thou Broken

see also: 59, 78, 111
SOURCE: St. Matthew Passion, 1729
HYMN: Johann Heermann, 1630
MELODY: Johann Crüger, 1640

*HERZLIEBSTER JESU, WAS HAST DU VERBROCHEN*

TR.: Catherine Winkworth, 1863

A - las, dear Lord, what law then hast Thou bro - ken, That

such sharp sen - tence should on Thee be spo - ken? Of what great crime hast

Thou to make con - fes - sion--What dark trans - gres - sion?

[ 2 ]*
What strangest punishment is sufferred yonder!
The Shepherd dies for sheep that wayward wander!

The Master pays the debts His servants owe Him,
Who would not know Him. *(4/15)*

## 106. Jesus' Death in Bitter Pain

see also: 61, 83
SOURCE: St. John Passion, 1723
HYMN: Paul Stockmann, 1633
MELODY: Melchior Vulpius, 1609

*JESU LEIDEN, PEIN UND TOD*

TR.: Henry S. Drinker, 1944

Je - sus' death in bit - ter pain, Je - sus' tri - bu - la - tion,

Caused our mor - tal clay to gain Heal - ing and sal - va - tion.

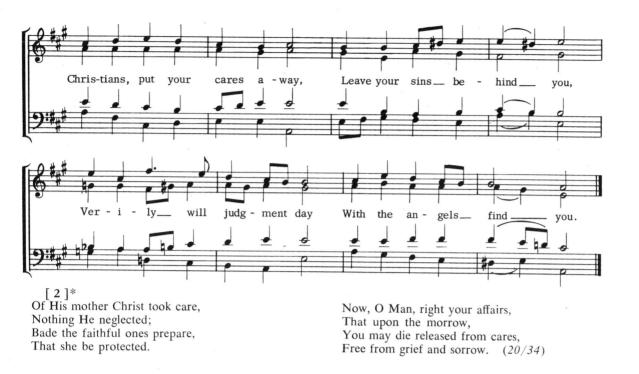

Christ-ians, put your cares a-way, Leave your sins be-hind you,
Ver-i-ly will judg-ment day With the an-gels find you.

**[ 2 ]***

Of His mother Christ took care,
Nothing He neglected;
Bade the faithful ones prepare,
That she be protected.

Now, O Man, right your affairs,
That upon the morrow,
You may die released from cares,
Free from grief and sorrow. (20/34)

### 107. Lord, All My Heart Is Fixed on Thee

see also: 58, 277
SOURCE: St. John Passion, 1723
HYMN: Martin Schalling, 1571
MELODY: Anonymous, 1577

*HERZLICH LIEB HAB ICH DICH, O HERR*

TR.: Catherine Winkworth, 1863

Lord, all my heart is fixed on Thee, I pray Thee, be not
The whole wide world delights me not, Of heaven or earth, Lord,

far from me, With ten-der grace up-hold me.
ask I not, If but Thy love en-fold me.

97

Yea, though my heart be like to break, Thou art my trust that nought can shake, My

por - tion and my hid - den joy, Whose Cross could all my bonds de - stroy. Lord

Je - su Christ, Lord Je - su Christ, my God and Lord, For - sake me not who trust Thy Word!

[2]*
Ah, Lord, let Thy dear angels come
At my last end to bear me home,
That I may die unfearing.
And in its narrow chamber keep
My body safe in painless sleep
Until my Lord's appearing.

And then from death awaken me,
That these mine eyes with joy may see,
O Son of God, Thy glorious face,
My Saviour and my Fount of Grace!
Lord Jesu Christ, Lord Jesu Christ, receive my
    prayer:
Thy love will I for aye declare.  (3/3)

## 108. Farewell I Gladly Bid Thee

*see also:* 24
SOURCE: St. John Passion, 1723
HYMN: Valerius Herberger, 1613
MELODY: Melchior Teschner, 1613

❧ *VALET WILL ICH DIR GEBEN*

TR.: Catherine Winkworth, 1863

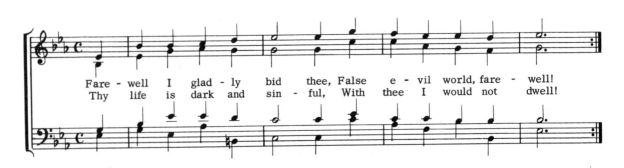

Fare - well I glad - ly bid thee, False e - vil world, fare - well!
Thy life is dark and sin - ful, With thee I would not dwell!

In heav'n are joys untroubled, I long for that bright sphere Where
God rewards them doubled, Who serv'd Him truly here.

[2]*
When all around is darkling,
Thy name and cross still bright,
Deep in my heart are sparkling,
Like stars in blackest night;

Appear Thou in Thy sorrow,
For Thine was woe indeed,
And from Thy cross I borrow
All comfort heart can need. (3/5)

## 109. Now Give Ye Thanks, Both Old and Young

◦┤ SINGEN WIR AUS HERZENSGRUND

SOURCE: Cantata No. 187, 1732
HYMN: Anonymous, c.1560
MELODY: Anonymous, 1544

TR.: John Christian Jacobi, 1725, alt.

Now give ye thanks, both old and young, Praise the
heart and tongue.
mer-ci-
Lord with heart and tongue. For our God most mer-ci-
ful
har-vest
ful Sends a harvest plentiful; As He

feeds ___ the birds ___ and beasts, So ___ we are ___ His

we are blessed.

dai - ly guests, In ___ His ___ boun - ty we ___ are ___ blessed.

In ___ His

[ 2 ]*
God yet adorne this earth below,
Numbers of provisions grow.
Hills and dales, the woods and fields,
Our Creator's blessings yield:
Wine and bread, the best of food,
He bestows on bad and good,
Were His love but understood.  (4/6)

[ 3 ]*
Lord, now enlarge our narrow sense,
Thank Thee for Thy providence,
That our body, soul and mind
Still may rest to Thee resigned,
Keeping up a thankful frame,
As we praise Thy glorious name
At the supper of the Lord.  (6/6)

## 110. As Sure I Live, My Maker Saith

*SO WAHR ICH LEBE, SPRICHT DEIN GOTT*
VATER UNSER IM HIMMELREICH

see also: 47, 267, 292
SOURCE: Cantata No. 102, 1731
HYMN: Johann Heermann, 1630
MELODY: Anonymous, 1539

TR.: John Christian Jacobi, 1725

As sure I live, my_ Mak - er saith, I ne'er de - sire the_ sin - ner's death, But_

rath - er_ that he_ turn be - times From all his for - mer_ ways and crimes, With

[2]*
Today thou liv'st, today repent,
Lest all thy life should be misspent.
Who seems today so fair and red,
May lie tomorrow sick or dead.
Who dies in His impenitence
Will ever curse his negligence.  (6/7)

[3]*
O blessed Jesu! Grant I may
Return to Thee this very day,
And live in constant penitence,
'Till death appears to call me hence,
That I in every time and place
Be well prepared to end my race.  (7/7)

## 111. Ah, Holy Jesus, How Hast Thou Offended

*HERZLIEBSTER JESU, WAS HAST DU VERBROCHEN*

*see also:* 59, 78, 105
SOURCE: St. John Passion, 1723
HYMN: Johann Heermann, 1630
MELODY: Johann Crüger, 1640

TR.: Anonymous, 1899, (stanza 1); T. A. Lacey, 1929, (stanzas 2, 3), Copyright 1929 by Novello & Co., Ltd. Used by permission.

[2]*
O King of Glory, King for time unending,
How can I serve Thee, what for Thee be spending?
No heart may find wherewith due thanks to render
Or service tender.  (8/15)

[3]*
How can I, straining sight and expectation,
Find aught wherewith to measure Thy compassion,
Or how requite Thee, working thus in blindness,
Thy loving kindness.  (9/15)

## 112. Who Knows How Near Will Be My Ending?

WER WEISS, WIE NAHE MIR MEIN ENDE!
WER NUR DEN LIEBEN GOTT LÄSST WALTEN

see also: 62, 104, 146, 204, 339
SOURCE: Cantata No. 84, c.1731
HYMN: Emilie Juliane, Countess of Schwarzburg-Rudol-
stadt, 1695
MELODY: Georg Neumark, 1657

TR.: Catherine Winkworth, 1863, alt.

Who knows how near will be my ending? Time speeds a-way, and Death comes on;
How swift-ly, ah, how swift de-scend-ing, May Death be here and Life be gone!

My God, for Je-sus' sake I pray Thy peace may bless my dy-ing day.

[ 2 ]*
And thus at peace with God I'm living,
And die without a thought of fear,
Content to take my God's decreeing,
For through His Son my faith is clear,
His grace shall be in death my stay,
And peace shall bless my dying day. *(12/12)*

102

# 113. See the Lord of Life and Light

*see also:* 81, 198, 307(D)
SOURCE: St. John Passion, 1723
HYMN: Michael Weisse, 1531
MELODY: Anonymous, 1531

CHRISTUS, DER UNS SELIG MACHT

TR.: John Troutbeck, 1832–1897, (stanza 1), used by permission of Novello & Co., Ltd.; John Christian Jacobi, 1725, (stanza 2).

See the Lord of life and light, Sav-iour meek and low-ly,

Tak-en like a thief at night, Bound by hands un-ho-ly.

See the sin-less Son of God Shame-ful mock-ings bear-ing,

shar-ing.

Bit-ter taunts, a cru-el rod, Doom of sin-ners shar-ing.

shar-ing.

[ 2 ]*
Grant, O Jesu, blessed Lord,
By Thy cross and passion,
That Thy love may be adored
By Thy whole creation;
Hating sin, the woeful cause
Of Thy death and suff'ring,
Let our hearts obey Thy laws
As our best thanksgiving. (8/8)

## 114. From God Shall Nought Divide Me

*VON GOTT WILL ICH NICHT LASSEN*

TR.: Catherine Winkworth, 1863

*see also:* 191, 332, 364
HYMN: Ludwig Helmbold, 1563
MELODY: Anonymous, 1571

From God shall nought di - vide ___ me, For He is ___ true for ___ aye,
And ___ on my ___ path will guide _____ me, Who **else** should of - ten ___ stray. ___

His ___ ev - er boun - teous hand By night and ___ day is ___ heed - ful, And

gives me what ___ is ___ need - ful, Wher - e'er I ___ go ___ or ___ stand.

[2]
O praise Him, for He never
Forgets our daily need;
O blest the hour whenever
To Him our thoughts can speed;

Yea, all the time we spend
Without Him is but wasted,
Till we His joy have tasted,
The joy that hath no end.  (5/9)

# 115. The Will of God Be Alway Done

see also: 41, 120, 265, 349(D)
SOURCE: St. Matthew Passion, 1729
HYMN: Albrecht, Markgraf of Brandenburg-Culmbach,
   c.1554
MELODY: Anonymous, c.1529

WAS MEIN GOTT WILL, DAS G'SCHEH
ALLZEIT

TR.: John Troutbeck, 1832–1899, (stanza 1), by permission of G. Schirmer, Inc., New York; Henry S. Drinker, 1944, (stanza 2).

*The will of God be alway done, His will that wise-ly guid-eth;
His help is nigh to ev-'ry one Whose faith on Him a-bid-eth.
What though His end we fail to see, What though His face He hid-eth? For-
sak-en he shall nev-er be, Whose heart in Him con-fid-eth.

[2]
Once more, O God, I ask of Thee,
Nor will Thou this deny me:
When base temptations trouble me,
With faith and hope supply me.

O God, our Lord, Thy help afford,
Thy name to render glorious;
And send, I pray, that promised day,
When right will be victorious. (4/4)

## 116. My Soul! Exalt the Lord, God

see also: 7, 268, 296
SOURCE: Cantata No. 29, 1731
HYMN: Johann Graumann, 1540, (Psalm 103)
MELODY: Johann Kugelmann(?), 1540

*NUN LOB, MEIN SEEL, DEN HERREN*

TR.: John Christian Jacobi, 1722, *alt.*

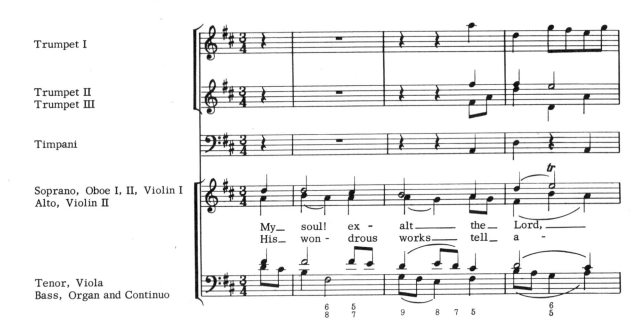

Thy tres - pass - es _____ for - gives _____ He, Thy frail - ties
Thy _____ frail-ties
Thy frail-ties _ He _

6      6   7    4  3  6   5       6          5  6  6  6  6  5
       4   4                      5          6
       2   2

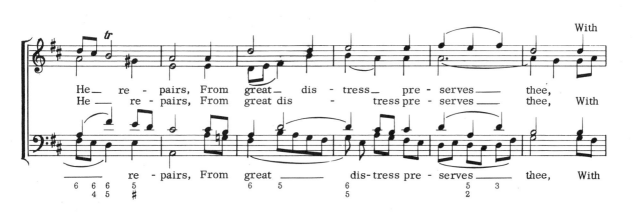

He _ re - pairs, From great _ dis - tress _ pre - serves _____ thee,
He _ re - pairs, From great dis - tress pre - serves _____ thee, With
_ re - pairs, From great _____ dis-tress pre - serves _____ thee, With

6  6  6   5           6    5       6              5   3
4  5   #                                          2

mer - cy crowns thy years. With good He sat - is -
mer - cy _____ crowns thy _ years. With good _____ He _ sat -
mer - cy crowns thy years. With good He sat - is -
mer - cy _____ crowns thy years. With good _____ He _ sat-is-fies

5 _____   7    4  3  6  #                         7   5          7
          ♮        5                              5              5
                                                                ♮

[ 2 ]*

All glory, might, and blessing,
To Father, Son, and Holy Ghost,
Upon His faith relying,
He is the God of whom we boast;
Let our brave zeal be showing
His glorious fame to raise,
For He's the God, whose naming
Deserves our endless praise.

Thus we in humble praying
Conclude our best desires,
With this our glad Amen saying
Our faith shall ne'er expire.   (5/5)

# 117. O World, Thy Life Is Ended†

O WELT, SIEH HIER DEIN LEBEN
O WELT, ICH MUSS DICH LASSEN

see also: 50, 63, 103, 275, 289, 355, 363, 366
SOURCE: St. Matthew Passion, 1729
HYMN: Paul Gerhardt, 1647
MELODY: Anonymous, 1539

TR.: Henry S. Drinker, 1944, (stanza 1); John Trout-beck, 1832–1899, (stanza 2), by permission of G. Schirmer, Inc., New York.

† Sometimes published under the title *Nun ruhen alle Wälder.*

O world, thy life is end-ed, High on the Cross sus-pend-ed, To-day the Sav-iour died. The Lord of all cre-a-tion, in shame and deg-ra-da-tion, Was scourged, re-viled and cru-ci-fied.

[ 2 ]*
The sorrows thou art bearing,
With none their burden sharing,
On me they ought to fall.
The torture Thou art feeling,
Thy patient love revealing,
'Tis I that should endure it all.  (5/16)

## 118. In Thee, Lord, Have I Put My Trust

𝄞 IN DICH HAB ICH GEHOFFET, HERR

see also: 77
SOURCE: St. Matthew Passion, 1729
HYMN: Adam Reissner, 1533, (Psalm 31)
MELODY: Sethus Calvisius(?), 1581

TR.: Catherine Winkworth, 1863, alt.

In Thee, Lord, have I put my trust, Leave me not help-less in the dust, But let my hope be shame - less, And still sus - tain, Through want and pain, My faith that Thou wilt save us.

[ 2 ]*
The world for me hath falsely set
Full many a secret snare and net,
Dark lies and vain delusions;
Lord, hear my pray'rs,
And break these snares,
And save me from confusion.   (5/7)

## 119. Scarce Tongue Can Speak, nor Human Know

𝄞 WAS ALLE WEISHEIT IN DER WELT
CHRIST UNSER HERR ZUM JORDAN KAM

see also: 66
SOURCE: Cantata No. 176, 1735
HYMN: Paul Gerhardt, 1653
MELODY: Johann Walther(?), 1524

TR.: John Kelly, 1867, alt.

Scarce tongue can speak, nor human know The mys - t'ry here un -

foud - ing, That\_ God\_ a - bove from His high throne Makes known to\_ men\_ be -

hold - ing: That\_ He a - lone is\_ King a - bove All\_ oth - er gods\_ what-

ev - er, Great, might - y,\_ faith - ful,\_ full\_ of love, His\_

saints doth aye\_ de - liv - er, One sub - stance but\_ three per - sons!

[ 2 ]*
Grant this, that we Thy people may
All reach the heav'nly portals,
And in Thy kingdom sing for aye,
'Mid all the bless'd immortals:

That Thou above art King alone,
All other gods high over,
The Father, Son, and Spirit, One,
Thy people's Shield and Cover,
One substance but three persons!     (8/8)

## 120. Father of Mercies! God Most High

*see also:* 41, 115, 265, 349(D)
SOURCE: Cantata No. 103, 1735
HYMN: Paul Gerhardt, *c.*1653
MELODY: Anonymous, *c.*1529

*BARMHERZGER VATER, HÖCHSTER GOTT*
WAS MEIN GOTT WILL, DAS G'SCHEH ALLZEIT

TR.: John Kelly, 1867

Fa - ther of Mer - cies! God most high, Deign gra - cious-ly\_ to\_ hear\_\_ me,
Thou say'st "Knock at\_ My\_ door and cry, In time of\_ need draw near\_\_ Me.

As _ ur _ gent - ly _ thou longst, to _ thee I'll _ come to _ help and _ raise _ thee, That
with thy _ mouth, In _ ver - y - truth, Thou joy - ful - ly _ may'st praise _ Me."

[2]*
"A moment I've forsaken thee,
And left thee in temptation;
With mercy great, as thou shalt see,
And boundless consolation,

I'll give the crown and to the throne
Of glory shall I raise thee,
To joy convert,
Thy grief and hurt,
Thou evermore shalt praise Me."    (9/18)


## 121. Sink Not Yet, My Soul, to Slumber

*see also:* 95, 233, 350, 365
SOURCE: St. Matthew Passion, 1729
HYMN: Johann Rist, 1642
MELODY: Johann Schop, 1642

*WERDE MUNTER, MEIN GEMÜTE*

TR.: Catherine Winkworth, 1861

Sink not _ yet, my _ soul, to _ slum - ber, Wake, my _ heart, go _ forth _ and tell
All _ the _ mer - cies _ with - out num - ber That this _ by - gone day _ be - fell;

Tell how God hath kept a-far All things that a-gainst me war,
Hath up-held me and de-fend-ed, And His grace my soul be-friend-ed.

[ 2 ]*
Have I e'er from Thee departed,
Now I seek Thy face again,
And Thy Son, the lovinghearted,
Made our peace through bitter pain.

Yes, far greater than our sin,
Though it still be strong within,
Is the love that fails us never,
Mercy that endures forever.  (6/12)

## 122. With God My Shield and Surety

*IST GOTT MEIN SCHILD UND HELFERSMANN*

SOURCE: Cantata No. 85, 1735
HYMN: Ernst Christoph Homburg, 1659
MELODY: Anonymous, 1694

TR.: Henry S. Drinker, 1944

With God my shield and sur-e-ty, What can there be to in-jure me? I bid my foes de-fi-ance. Ye who with guile my

steps would trace Will gain you noth-ing__ but dis-grace, For__ God is__ my re-li-ance, For__ God__ is__ my re-li-ance.

[ 2 ]*

My Shepherd true, with mighty arm,
Protects me safe from ev'ry harm
And foe who would assail me.
They who would give me grief or pain
Will to their sorrow strive in vain,
For God will never fail me,
For God will never fail me.  (4/7)

## 123. O Enter Lord, Thy Temple

*ZEUCH EIN ZU DEINEN TOREN*
HELFT MIR GOTTS GÜTE PREISEN

*see also:* 23, 88(D), 99
SOURCE: Cantata No. 183, 1735            TR.: Catherine Winkworth, 1863
HYMN: Paul Gerhardt, 1653
MELODY: Anonymous, 1569

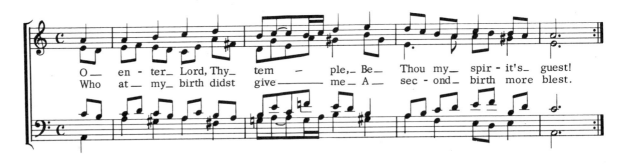

O__ en-ter__ Lord, Thy__ tem — ple,__ Be Thou my__ spir-it's__ guest!
Who at__ my__ birth didst give————— me A__ sec-ond__ birth more blest.

Thou in — the — God - head, Lord, Though here to — dwell Thou deign - est, For-

ev - er e - qual — reign - est, Art — e - qual - ly — a — dored.

[ 2 ]*
'Tis Thou, O spirit, teachest
The soul to pray aright;
Thy songs have sweetest music,
Thy pray'rs have wondrous might;
Unheard they cannot fall,
They pierce the highest heaven,
Till He His help hath given
Who surely helpeth all.  (5/12)

## 124. Awake My Heart

HYMN: Martin Opitz, 1625
MELODY: Johann Staden(?), 1663

🙴 *AUF, AUF, MEIN HERZ*

TR.: Walter E. Buszin, 1952. From *101 Chorales Harmonized by Johann Sebastian Bach,* Copyright 1952 by Hall & McCreary Company. Used by permission of the publishers, Schmitt, Hall & McCreary Company, Minneapolis, Minn.

A - wake, my — heart! Be — roused from sloth, my — mind! Re - ject — all —

lust, leave world-ly__ cares__ be - hind! Fol - low__ the__ Christ, please God in__ life__ and

spir - it, Ac - cept__ His__ grace, and__ bless-ings__ rich in - her - it.

[ 2 ]
If thou wilt not the carnal urge obey,
But heed instead what God the Lord doth say,
Esteem His Word, His promise, and His mercy;
Then will no foe, nor death, nor Satan hurt thee.
    (6/10)

## 125. The Lord My Shepherd Is and True

*DER HERR IST MEIN GETREUER HIRT, DEM*
ALLEIN GOTT IN DER HÖH SEI EHR

*see also:* 249, 313, 326, 353(D)
HYMN: Cornelius Becker, 1598, (Psalm 23)
MELODY: Anonymous, 1539

TR.: Charles Sanford Terry, 1929. By permission of
Oxford University Press, London.

The__ Lord my Shep-herd is__ and true, To Him my__ trust I ren - der.
He__ lead-eth me to__ pas-tures new, To mead - ows green and ten - der.
To _____ Him my trust I __ ren-der.
To _____ mead-ows green and ten - der.

To__ Him my trust I ren - der.
To__ mead-ows green and ten - der.

By wa - ters__ clear He__ guides me__ still, He doth__ my soul with__

glad - ness fill, Through His great love and fa - vor.

**[2]**

My feet in surety He doth guide
And for His Name's sake lead me:
Though troubles sore do here abide
And death stalks on beside me.

No matter what may happen here,
My Shepherd hath me in His care,
His rod and staff shall guide me.    *(2/3)*

## 126. All Mankind Fell in Adam's Fall

*DURCH ADAMS FALL IST GANZ VERDERBT*

Duplicate of Chorale 100. Chorale 126 is sometimes
published in the key of A minor.

## 127. These Are the Holy Ten Commands

*DIES SIND DIE HEILIGEN ZEHN GEBOT*

HYMN: Martin Luther, 1524
MELODY: Anonymous, 1524

TR.: George Macdonald, 1876

These are the ho - ly ten com - mands, Which came to us from
God's own hands By Mo - ses, who o - beyed His will, Stand -
ing up - on Si - nai's hill. Have mer - cy, Lord!
Have mer - cy, Lord!
Have mer - cy, Lord!

**[2]**

May Christ our Lord help us in this,
For He our Mediator is;

Our own work is a hopeless thing,
Judgment alone it can bring.
Have mercy, Lord!    *(12/12)*

## 128. All Things Wait on Our Possessing

HYMN: Anonymous, 1676
MELODY: Johann Löhner, 1691

*ALLES IST AN GOTTES SEGEN*

TR.: Catherine Winkworth, 1863

All things wait_ on our pos-sess-ing God's free love and_ grace_ and bless-ing,

Though all_ earth-ly_ love de-part; He_ who God for_ his_ has tak-en,

'Mid_ the_ chang-ing_ world un-shak-en Keeps a_ free he-ro-ic_ heart.

[ 2 ]
If on earth He bids me linger,
He will guide me with His finger
Through the years that now look dim;
All that earth has fleets and changes
As a river onward ranges,
But I rest in peace on Him.  (6/6)

## 129. His Own God Ne'er Neglecteth

*KEINEN HAT GOTT VERLASSEN*

HYMN: Andreas Kesler(?), 1611(?)
MELODY: Anonymous, 1609

TR.: Charles Sanford Terry, 1929. By permission of
Oxford University Press, London.

His own_ God_ ne'er ne-glect - eth Who_ in _ Him_ put their trust,
He who_ his_ sin_ re-pent - eth He _ rais-eth_ from the dust.

God will pro-tect His chil - dren And one day call them home, On earth let noth-ing harm them, But to their com - fort come.

[2]
Both good and ill He sendeth;
He chooseth which alone.
He foolish is that groaneth
Or troubled makes his moan.
How can God e'er reject me,
My Helper, truest, best?
No, when care rubs most sorely,
He'll give me quiet rest.   (4/8)

## 130. My Soul Doth Magnify the Lord

*MEINE SEELE ERHEBT DEN HERREN*

*see also:* 320, 358
HYMN: St. Luke, 1:46–47
MELODY: *Tonus peregrinus*

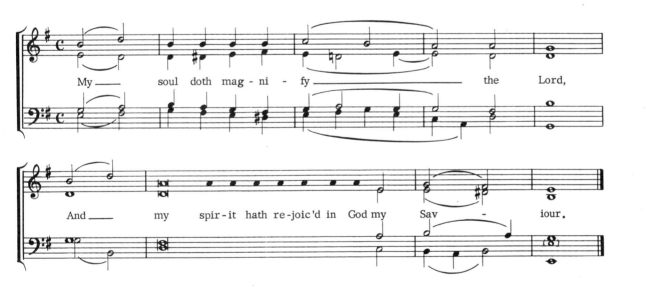

My soul doth mag - ni - fy the Lord, And my spir-it hath re-joic'd in God my Sav - iour.

## 131. Blessed Jesu, at Thy Word

*see also:* 328(D)†
HYMN: Tobias Clausnitzer, 1663
MELODY: Johann Rodolph Ahle, 1664

LIEBSTER JESU, WIR SIND HIER

TR.: Catherine Winkworth, 1863

† Chorale 328 is a duplicate except for minor differences.

Measure 7, soprano:   Measure 9, alto:

Measure 9, bass:

Bless-ed— Je - su,   at— Thy word   We— are gath-ered all— to— hear_____ Thee;
Let our— hearts and   soul be stirred   Now to   seek and love and fear——— Thee,

By— Thy teach-ings sweet and ho - ly   Drawn from earth to____ love Thee sole - ly.

[2]
All our knowledge, sense and sight
Lie in deepest darkness shrouded,
Till Thy Spirit breaks our night
With the beams of truth unclouded;

Thou alone to God canst win us,
Thou wilt work all good within us.   (2/3)

## 132. Kyrie, God Our Father Evermore

HYMN†: Anonymous, 1541
MELODY: Anonymous, 1525

KYRIE, GOTT VATER IN EWIGKEIT

TR.: Arthur Tozer Russell, 1851, *alt.*

† Kyrie eleison, Christe eleison (Gk.), "Lord, have mercy, Christ, have mercy."

Ky - ri - e,   God our Fa - ther ev - er
Ky - ri - e,   God our Fa - ther ev - er
Ky - ri - e,   God our Fa - ther ev - er
Ky - ri - e,   God our Fa - ther ev - er

122

## 133. I Believe In But One True God

HYMN: Martin Luther, 1524, (Nicene Creed)
MELODY: Anonymous, 1524

*WIR GLAUBEN ALL AN EINEN GOTT*

TR.: Catherine Winkworth, 1863

love Hath the claim of chil - dren giv - en.

in love Hath the claim of chil - dren giv - en.

love Hath the claim of chil - dren giv - en.

love Hath the claim of chil - dren giv - en.

He in soul and bod - y feeds us, All we

He in soul and bod - y feeds us, All we

He in soul and bod - y feeds us, All we

He in soul and bod - y feeds us, All we want

harm be - tides us; He car - - eth for

_ harm be-tides us; He _ car - - eth for

harm _ be-tides us; He _ car - - eth for us _

harm be - tides _ us; He car - - eth _ for

us, day _ and night, _

us, day _ and _ night, _

day _ and _ night, _

us, day _ and _ night, _

[ 2 ]
I believe in Lord Jesus Christ,
His own Son, our Lord, possessing
An equal Godhead, throne and might,
Whence descends the Father's blessing;

Conceiv'd of the Holy Spirit,
Born of Mary, virgin mother,
That lost man might life inherit;
Made true Man, our Elder Brother,
Was crucifièd for man's sin,
And raised by God to life again.  (2/3)

## 134. Let Who Will Receive Thy Pleasure

*see also:* 87
HYMN: Johann Franck, 1653
MELODY: Johann Crüger, 1649

🎕 *DU, O SCHÖNES WELTGEBÄUDE*

TR.: Catherine Winkworth, 1855, *alt.*

Let who_ will re - ceive thy plea - sure, O_ thou fair and won-drous earth!
Ev - er_ an - guished sor - row's mea - sure Pierc-es through thy seem-ing mirth;

Let thy_ vain de - lights be_ giv - en Un - to them who love not_ heav - en,

My de-sire is__ fixed on__ Thee, Je-sus, dear-est__ far__ to me.

[2]
Some the treacherous waves are daring,
Hidden rock and shifting wind,
Storm and danger they are braving,
Earthly good or wealth to find;

Faith my upward flight is winging,
Starry heights above ascending,
Till I find myself with Thee,
Jesus, dearest Friend to me!   (3/8)

## 135. God the Father, Be Our Stay

HYMN: Martin Luther, 1524
MELODY: Anonymous, 1524

GOTT DER VATER, WOHN UNS BEI

TR.: Anonymous (Selah Song Book, 1936)

1. God the Fa-ther, be__ our stay, When hell's dread pow'rs as-sail_____ us.
Cleanse us from our sins we__ pray, Nor in our__ last hour fail_____ us.

1,2. Keep us__ from the E-.vil One, Firm in__ the__ faith__ a-bid-ing, In__
Let us__ put__ God's ar-mor on: With all__ true Chris-tians run-ning Our__

Christ our Sav-iour hid-ing, And heart-i-ly__ con-fid-ing.
heav'n-ly race, and shun-ning The Dev-il's wiles and cun-ning.

A-men, A-men, this__ be done, So__ sing we__ now Hal-le-lu-jah!

[2]
Jesus Christ, be Thou our stay,
When hell's dread pow'rs assail us.

Holy Ghost, be Thou our stay,
Nor in our last hour fail us.   (2/3)

## 136. Lord Jesus Christ, Be Present Now

HYMN: Wilhelm II of Sachsen-Weimar(?), 1651
MELODY: Anonymous, 1648

❧ HERR JESU CHRIST, DICH ZU UNS WEND

TR.: Catherine Winkworth, 1863

Lord Je-sus Christ, be pres-ent now! And let_ Thy Ho-ly_ Spir-it bow All

hearts in_ love and_ fear_ to-day, To_ hear the_ truth and keep Thy way.

[ 2 ]
Glory to God, the Father, Son,
And Holy Spirit, Three in One!

To Thee, O blessed Trinity,
Be praise throughout eternity.   (4/4)

## 137. Who Puts His Trust in God Most Just

HYMN: Joachim Magdeburg, 1597
MELODY: Joachim Magdeburg, 1571

❧ WER GOTT VERTRAUT, HAT WOHL GEBAUT

TR.: Catherine Winkworth, 1863

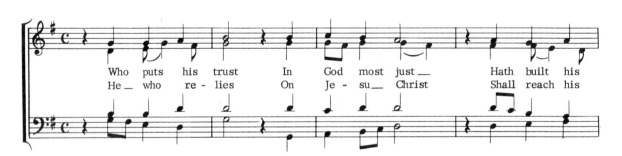

Who puts his trust    In God most just_    Hath built his
He _ who re - lies    On Je - su_ Christ    Shall reach his

house se-cure - ly, Hath built his__ house se-cure - ly;
heav'n most sure - ly, Shall reach his__ heav'n most sure - ly.

Then fix'd on Thee__ My trust shall be,__ For Thy truth can-not al -

ter; While mine Thou__ art,__ Not__ death's worst smart__ Shall

make my cour-age__ fal - ter, Shall make my cour-age fal - ter.

[2]
Though fiercest foes
My course oppose,
A dauntless front I'll show them,
A dauntless front I'll show them.
My champion Thou,
Lord Christ art now,
Who soon shalt overthrow them,
Who soon shalt overthrow them!

And if but Thee I have in me
With Thy good gifts and spirit,
Nor death nor hell,
I know full well,
Shall hurt me, through Thy merit,
Shall hurt me, through Thy merit.  (2/3)

## 138. Jesu, Priceless Treasure

see also: 96, 263, 283, 324, 356
SOURCE: Cantata No. 64, 1723
HYMN: Johann Franck, 1653
MELODY: Johann Crüger, 1653

TR.: Catherine Winkworth, 1869

JESU, MEINE FREUDE

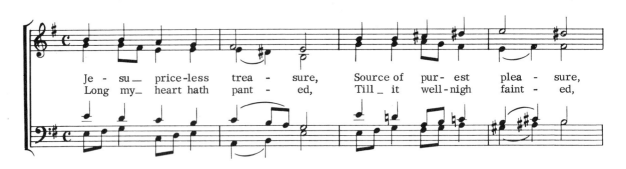

Je - su_ price-less trea - sure, Source of pur - est plea - sure,
Long my_ heart hath pant - ed, Till _ it well-nigh faint - ed,

Tru - est friend to me! Thine I _ am, O spot-less Lamb! I _ will suf-fer
Thirst-ing aft - er Thee!

nought to_ hide____ Thee, Ask_ for nought be - side____ Thee.

[ 2 ]*
Farewell, thou who choosest
Earth, and heav'n refusest,
Thou will tempt in vain;
Farewell, sins, nor blind me,
Get ye far behind me,
Come not forth again;

Past your hour, O pomp and pow'r;
Godless life, thy bonds I sever,
Farewell now forever!   (5/6)

132

# 139. All My Heart This Night Rejoices

*see also:* 357
SOURCE: Christmas Oratorio, 1734
HYMN: Paul Gerhardt, 1653
MELODY: Johann G. Ebeling, 1666

*FRÖHLICH SOLL MEIN HERZE SPRINGEN*
WARUM SOLLT ICH MICH DENN GRÄMEN

TR.: Catherine Winkworth, 1863

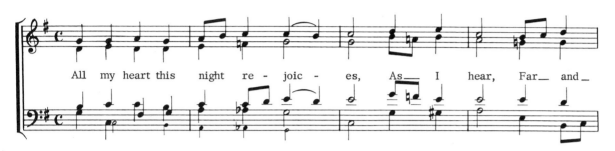

All my heart this night re - joic - es, As_ I hear, Far_ and_

near, Sweet-est_ an - gel_ voic - es; "Christ is_ born! "their choirs are_

sing - ing, Till the air Ev - ery-where Now with joy_ is_ ring - ing.

[ 2 ]*
Thee, dear Lord, with heed I'll cherish,
Live to Thee,
And with Thee
Dying, shall not perish;

But shall dwell with Thee forever,
Far on high
In the joy
That can alter never. (*15/15*)

## 140. Where'er My Task May Take Me

HYMN: Paul Flemming, 1642
MELODY: Anonymous, 1679

TR.: Catherine Winkworth, 1863, *alt.*

*IN ALLEN MEINEN TATEN*

Where-'er my task may take ___ me, May God's true coun-sel guide me, Who ___ rul-eth ___ all ___ things right; Un-less ___ our God ___ doth ___ will ___ it, Our ut-most pains, they fail-eth, And ___ vain must be ___ man's might.

[ 2 ]
My toil is nought availing,
All efforts now are failing
Unless my God is there;
He orders all my being,
His will to me decreeing;
On God I cast my care.   *(2/15)*

## 141. O Eternal Word

HYMN: Adam Drese, 1697
MELODY: Adam Drese(?), 1698

TR.: J. Swertner, 1789

*SEELENBRÄUTIGAM*

O ___ E-ter-nal ___ Word, Je-sus Christ, our Lord, While the hosts of ___

heav'n a - dore Thee, We with awe fall down be - fore Thee, And with rap - ture raise Songs of love and praise.

[ 2 ]
God and man indeed,
Comfort in all need,
Thou becam'st a Man of Sorrows,
To gain life eternal for us,
By Thy precious blood,
Jesus, Man and God.  (3/15)

## 142. Look Up to Thy God Again

SOURCE: Cantata No. 40, 1723
HYMN: Paul Gerhardt, 1653
MELODY: Johann Sebastian Bach(?), 1685–1750

SCHWING DICH AUF ZU DEINEM GOTT

TR.: John Kelly, 1867

Look up to Thy God a - gain, Soul sunk in af - flic - tion!

Shall He be re - proached by me Through thy sore de - jec - tion?

Sa - tan's wiles dost thou _ not see? By se - vere temp - ta - tion,

Glad - ly would he keep from thee Je - su's _ con - so - la - - tion.

[ 2 ]*
Shake thy head in scorn, and "flee,"
Bid the old deceiver:
"Wilt renew thy thrusts at me,
Me to fear deliver?
Serpent, bruis'd thy head I see;
Through His pain hath freed me
From thy grasp, my Lord, and He
To His joy will lead me."   (2/11)

## 143. In Dulci Jubilo

HYMN: Anonymous, fourteenth or fifteenth century
MELODY: Anonymous, 1535

TR.: Catherine Winkworth, 1869, *alt.*

*IN DULCI JUBILO*

In dul - ci ju - bi - lo _____ Sing _ and shout _ be -

Lies in

low! _____ He for whom we're pin - ing Lies _ in _ prae-
Lies in _ prae-

Lies in _ prae-

136

[2]
*O Jesu parvule,*
My heart longs for Thee!
Soothe the sad and ailing,
*O Puer optime,*
With Thy love unfailing!

*O Princeps gloriae,*
*Trahe me post te,*
*Trahe me post te!* (2/3)


## 144. When Man Will Rest in God's Own Sight

*WER IN DEM SCHUTZ DES HÖCHSTEN IST*
HERR, WIE DU WILLST, SO SCHICKS MIT MIR

*see also:* 317, 318(D)
HYMN: Sebald Heyd, 1554, (Psalm 91)
MELODY: Anonymous, 1525

TR.: Robert W. Ottman, 1963

In Thy_ great love Thou sav - est me From Sa - tan's pow'r and_

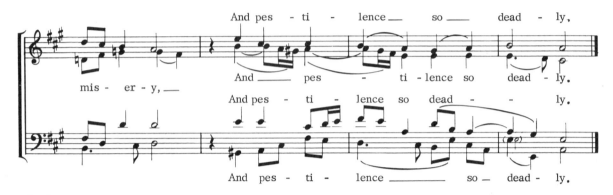

And pes - ti - lence_ so _ dead - ly,

mis - er - y, _ And _ pes - ti - lence so dead - ly.

And pes - ti - lence so dead - ly.

And pes - ti - lence _ so _ dead - ly.

[2]
In peace beneath His wings I lie
In Him to trust completely,
His truth protects from danger nigh,
Affliction cannot reach me.
No evils that abound by night
Nor daily woes can me affright,
His sacred Word defends me.   (2/8)

## 145. Why Art Thou Thus Cast Down, My Heart?

WARUM BETRÜBST DU DICH, MEIN HERZ?

*see also:* 94, 300
HYMN: Hans Sachs(?), 1565
MELODY: Anonymous, 1565

TR.: Catherine Winkworth, 1863

Why art_ thou thus_ cast down, my_ heart? Why_ trou - bled,_ why_ doth_

mourn a - part, O'er nought but_ earth - ly_ wealth? Trust in _ thy_ God, _ be -

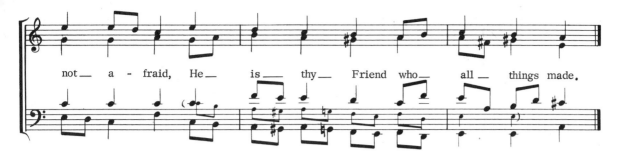

**[ 2 ]**

Dost think thy pray'rs He doth not heed?
He knows full well what thou dost need,
And heav'n and earth are His;

My Father and my God who still
Is with my soul in every ill.  (2/14)

## 146. Who Will but Let Himself Be Guided

*see also:* 62, 104, 112, 204, 339
HYMN: Georg Neumark, 1657
MELODY: Georg Neumark, 1657

✠ *WER NUR DEN LIEBEN GOTT LÄSST WALTEN*

TR.: Anonymous (*Norwegian Evangelical Lutheran Hymn Book*, 1898)

**[ 2 ]**

Wait on the Lord, my heart, in meekness
And cheerful hope; be thou content
To get what-e'er thy Father's kindness
And all discerning love hath sent;
Doubt not that all thy wants are known
To Him who chose thee for His own.  (3/7)

## 147. When Anguished and Perplexed

HYMN: Matthäus Apelles von Löwenstern, 1644, (Psalm 121)
MELODY: Matthäus Apelles von Löwenstern, 1644

TR.: Catherine Winkworth, 1863

When an-guished and _ per-plexed, I lift _ my wea-ry _ eyes Up to _ the _ hills, O _ Lord, And tell _ Thee all _ that grieves me, Thou heark-en'st to my _ sighs, And nev-er _ com-fort-less _ Thy _ in-ner pres-ence leaves _ me.

[ 2 ]
Thou watchest that my foot Should neither slip nor stray,
Thou guidest me Thyself, Though dark the course I travel;
Thou pointest me the way,
The snares of sin and earth for me Thou dost un-ravel. (3/7)

## 148. Lord Jesus Christ, with Us Abide

Duplicate of Chorale 177. Chorale 148 is usually published under the title *Uns ist ein Kindlein heut geborn.*

## 149. O My Soul, Why Dost Thou Grieve

HYMN: Paul Gerhardt, 1647
MELODY: Johann Sebastian Bach, 1736

*NICHT SO TRAURIG, NICHT SO SEHR*

TR.: John Kelly, 1867

O my— soul, why dost thou grieve, Why dost mourn so— bit - ter - ly,
That more free - ly— God doth give Gifts to oth - ers than to thee?

In Thy God— de-light thy— heart, He's the good en - dur - ing part.

[ 2 ]
Know thou art not therefore here
That thou should'st possess the earth;
Look thou up to heav'n so clear,
There's thy gold of priceless worth,
There is honor, there is joy,
Without envy or alloy.   (3/15)

## 150. World, Farewell, I Now Forsake Thee

SOURCE: Cantata No. 27, 1731
HYMN: Johann Georg Albinus, 1649
MELODY AND HARMONIZATION: Johann Rosenmüller,
  1649

*WELT, ADE! ICH BIN DEIN MÜDE*

TR.: Catherine Winkworth, 1863, *alt.*

World, fare - well, I now for -

World, fare - well, _____ I now for -

142

Only peace and love and joy.

no al-loy, On-ly peace and love and joy.

no al-loy, On-ly peace and love and joy.
no al-loy, On-ly peace and love and joy.

no al-loy, On-ly peace and love and joy.

[2]
Here is naught but care and mourning,
Comes a joy, it will not stay;
Fairly shines the sun at dawning,
Night will soon o'ertake the day:

World with thee is war and strife,
Thou with cheating hopes are rife,
But in heaven is no alloy,
Only peace and love and joy.  (5/9)

## 151. Never Will I Part with Christ

HYMN: Anonymous, 1736
MELODY: Anonymous, 1686

🎜 *MEINEN JESUM LASS ICH NICHT, JESUS*

TR.: Anonymous (*Moravian Hymn Book*, 1754)

Nev-er will I part with Christ, Since He died for my sal-va - tion.
Nay, I would be sac-ri-ficed To ob-tain this con-so-la - tion,

That I might en-joy the sight Of His good and gra-cious light.

[2]
Jesus will I never leave
While I breathe and have my senses;
For His merits I receive
Pardon for my past offences;

All the powers of my mind
To my Saviour are resigned.  (2/7)

## 152. Jesus Will I Never Leave

see also: 299, 348
SOURCE: Cantata No. 154, 1724
HYMN: Christian Keimann, 1658
MELODY: Andreas Hammerschmidt(?), 1658

MEINEN JESUM LASS ICH NICHT, WEIL

TR.: Anonymous (*Moravian Hymn Book*, 1908)

Je-sus _ will _ I _ nev - er _ leave, He's _ the _ God _ of _ my _ sal - va - tion; Through His _ mer-its _ I _ re-ceive Par - don, _ life _ and _ con - so - la - tion; All _ the _ pow-ers _ of _ my mind To _ my Sav-iour be _ re-signed.

[ 2 ]*
With my Jesus will I stay
He my soul preserves and feedeth;
He's the Life, the Truth, the Way,
Me to living waters leadeth:
Blessed who can say with me,
Christ, I'll never part with Thee.   (6/6)

144

# 153. Hark! A Voice Saith,"All Are Mortal"

HYMN: Johann Georg Albinus, 1652
MELODY: Jakob Hintze, 1678

*ALLE MENSCHEN MÜSSEN STERBEN*

TR.: Catherine Winkworth, 1863, *alt.*

Hark! A_ voice saith, "All_ are mor-tal, Yea, all_ flesh must fade as_ grass;
On - ly through Death's gloom-y por-tal To a _ bet - ter life ye_ pass;

And this bod - y,_ doom'd to_ lan -guish, Here must stay_ in_ pain and an-guish

Ere it rise_ in glo - rious might, Fit to_ dwell with saints in light."

[ 2 ]
O Jerusalem, how clearly
Dost thou shine, thou city fair!
Lo! I hear the tones more nearly
Ever sweetly sounding there!
There are peace and joy abounding!
Lo, the sun is now arising,
And the breaking day I see
That shall never end for me. (6/8)

145

## 154. O Trinity of Blessed Light

HYMN: Martin Luther, 1544
MELODY: Anonymous, 1545

*DER DU BIST DREI IN EINIGKEIT*

TR.: John Mason Neale, 1852

O Trin-i-ty_ of_ bless-ed light, O U - ni - ty_ of_ prince-ly_ might, The fier-y_ sun now goes his way; Shed Thou with - in_ our hearts Thy ray.

[ 2 ]
To Thee our morning song of praise,
To Thee our evening prayer we raise;
O grant us with Thy saints on high
To praise Thee through eternity.  (2/3)


## 155. Help, O Lord, Behold We Enter

HYMN: Johann Rist, 1642
MELODY: Johann Schop, 1642

*HILF, HERR JESU, LASS GELINGEN†*

TR.: Catherine Winkworth, 1863, *alt*.

† First tune.

Help,_ O Lord,_ be - hold we en - ter On - an - oth - er_ year_ to - day; All _ on Thee our_ hopes now cen - ter,

146

Give us cour-age for the way; Life and strength we

now are ask-ing, Give us hap-pi-ness and bless-ing.

[2]
Every plan and undertaking,
May they all begin with Thee,
Whether sleeping or awaking
Let me know Thou art with me,
When abroad my footsteps guiding,
While at home with me abiding.  (2/16)

## 156. O Lord! How Many Miseries

ACH GOTT, WIE MANCHES HERZELEID

see also: 217, 308(D)

SOURCE: Cantata No. 3, c.1740

HYMN: Martin Moller(?) and Conrad Hojer(?), 1587

MELODY: Anonymous, 1625

TR.: John Christian Jacobi, 1722

O Lord! How man-y mis-er-ies As-sault and dis-com-pose my peace; The

path that leads to Si-on's gate Is full of thorns and ve-ry strait.

[2]*
Preserve my faith from error free,
That I may live and die in Thee.
Lord Jesus Christ, hear my desire,
To hymn Thee in the heav'nly choir.  (18/18)

## 157. If God Withdraweth, All the Cost

WO GOTT ZUM HAUS NICHT GIBT SEIN GUNST

HYMN: Johann Kolross(?), 1525, (Psalm 127)
MELODY: Anonymous, 1535

TR.: Isaac Watts, 1674–1748

If God with-draw-eth, all the cost And pains that build the house are lost; If God the city doth not keep, The watch-ful guards as well may sleep.

[ 2 ]
To Father, Son, and Holy Ghost,
The God whom Heav'n's triumphant host
And suff'ring saints on earth adore,
Be glory now and evermore! (5/5)

## 158. This Glorious Day Is Filled with Joy

DER TAG DER IST SO FREUDENREICH

HYMN: Anonymous, 1529
MELODY: Anonymous, 1531

TR.: Walter E. Buszin, 1952. From *101 Chorales Harmonized by Johann Sebastian Bach*, Copyright 1952 by Hall & McCreary Company. Used by permission of the publishers, Schmitt, Hall & McCreary Company, Minneapolis, Minn.

This glo-rious day is filled with joy, Hearts o'er-flow with rap-ture.
Man-kind loud an-thems doth em-ploy, Glad-ness rich re-cap-ture.

For Je-sus Christ was born this day Of Vir-gin Mar-y, man to save;

Lay there in a man-ger, In a sta-ble, poor and bare; God's own Son man's na-ture shared, As-suaged His Fa-ther's an - ger.

[2]
A wondrous Child was born this day,
Born to be our Savior.
His virgin mother sings to say
Of His Father's favor.
Had this Child not been born to save,
The Foe all men would crush, enslave.

But we have salvation,
Thanks to Jesus, Mary's Son
Who God's grace hath for us won,
Hath caused our jubilation. (2/4)

## 159. That God at Last Might Do

*ALS DER GÜTIGE GOTT*

HYMN: Michael Weisse, 1531
MELODY: Johann Sebastian Bach, 1685–1750     TR.: Henry S. Drinker, 1944

That God at last might do The work that He had planned, His an-gel quick-ly flew To Gal-i-lee's fair land; His name was Ga-bri-el.

[2]
To Nazareth came he,
A virgin there to tell,
To Mary, name adored,
That she one day would be
The mother of our Lord. (2/12)

149

## 160. Praisèd Be Thou, O Jesus Christ

*see also:* 51, 288
SOURCE: Cantata No. 64, 1723
HYMN†: Martin Luther, 1524
MELODY: Anonymous, 1524

⇥ GELOBET SEIST DU, JESU CHRIST

TR.: George Macdonald, 1876

† Kyrieleis or Kyrie eleis from Kyrie eleison (Gk.), "Lord, have mercy."

Prais-èd be Thou, O— Je-sus Christ, That a man— on earth— Thou liest! Born of a maid-en -- it is— true -- In— this— ex-ult the heav'ns al - so.— Ky-rie-leis. Ky-ri-e e - leis. Ky-ri-e e - leis. heav'ns al - so. Ky-ri-e e - leis.

[ 2 ]*
All this for us did Jesus do,
That His great love He might show.

Let Christendom rejoice therefore,
And give Him thanks forever more.
Kyrieleis.   (7/7)

## 161. All Ye Stars and Winds of Heaven

HYMN: Johann Franck, 1655
MELODY: Christoph Peter, 1655

⇥ IHR GESTIRN, IHR HOHEN LÜFTE

TR.: Henry S. Drinker, 1944

All— ye stars— and winds— of Heav - en, Thou— the—
Deep— ra-vines— and loft - y moun-tains, Hills— and—

spa - cious fir - ma - ment,
vales with ech - oes rent,

Shout and sing in
ex - ul - ta - tion, Cleave the clouds with ju - bi - la - tion.

[ 2 ]
In my heart of hearts the chamber
Was a gloomy, dreary place,
All unlike a royal palace;
Thou didst fill it with Thy grace,
Royally its walls adorning,
Like the sunshine in the morning.   (9/9)

## 162. The Old Year Now Hath Passed Away

DAS ALTE JAHR VERGANGEN IST

see also: 314
HYMN: Johann Steurlein(?) and Jakob Tapp(?), 1588          TR.: Catherine Winkworth, 1863
MELODY: Johann Steurlein, 1588

The old year now hath passed a - way,
We thank Thee, O our God, to - day, That

[2]
O help us to forsake all sin,
O help us to forsake all sin,
A new and holier course begin,
Mark not what once was done amiss,
A happier, better year be this,
A happier, better year be this.  (4/6)

## 163. Good Christians All, Rejoice Ye

*FÜR FREUDEN LASST UNS SPRINGEN*

HYMN: Kasperl Peltsch, 1648
MELODY: Anonymous, 1648

TR.: Charles Sanford Terry, 1929. By permission of Oxford University Press, London.

e'er been_ heard on_ earth such_ news ex - cell - ing?

[2]
He who all flesh provideth
With daily fare in plenty
Himself as mortal liveth.
The Son of God Almighty
A virgin's babe now is He born.
How great must be the love for us He beareth!   (2/6)

## 164. To God Let All the Human Race

⁓{ *HERR GOTT, DICH LOBEN ALLE WIR*

*see also:* 334
HYMN: Paul Eber, *c.*1554                                   TR.: John Christian Jacobi, 1722
MELODY: Louis Bourgeois, 1551, (*Old Hundredth*)

To_ God _____ let_ all _____ the_ hu - man   race   Bring
hum - ble wor - ship mixed with ___ grace, Who makes_ His_ love_ and
wis - dom _ known By an - gels that ___ sur - round His   throne.

[2]
Thus God defends us day by day
From many mischiefs in our way,
By angels which do always keep
A watchful eye when we're asleep.   (10/13)

## 165. O Lamb of God, Most Stainless

HYMN: Nikolaus Decius, 1531
MELODY: Anonymous, 1542

*O LAMM GOTTES UNSCHULDIG*

TR.: Catherine Winkworth, 1863

O___ Lamb of ___ God___ most stain-less! Who on___ the___ cross___ didst
So___ pa-tient___ through Thy sor-rows, Though mock'd a-mid___ Thine

lan-___guish; Our sins Thou bear-est for___ us, Else had___ de-spair reign'd
an-___guish; 

o'er___ us:___ Have mer-cy on us,___ O___ Je-su!

[2]
O Lamb of God most stainless!
Who on the cross didst languish,
So patient through Thy sorrows,
Though mock'd amid Thine anguish;
Our sins Thou bearest for us,
Else had despair reign'd o'er us:
Thy peace grant to us, O Jesu! *(3/3)*

## 166. Around God's Throne in Heaven

HYMN: Ludwig Helmbold, 1585
MELODY: Joachim à Burck, 1594

*ES STEHN VOR GOTTES THRONE*

TR.: Robert W. Ottman, 1963

A - round God's throne in ___ heav - en, A - round God's throne in___
Through Christ God's love is ___ giv - en, Through Christ God's love___ is ___

154

heav- en, The guard-ian an- gels stand; Not one on earth re-
giv- en, To men through-out the land;

ject - ing, Nor rich nor poor ne - glect - ing, As

all are born in Him, As all are born in Him.

[2]
Where Christian folk are gathered,
Where Christian folk are gathered,
In dwellings great or small,
From foes we are protected,
From foes we are protected,
God's grace surrounds us all.

Angelic hosts to guard us,
Their vigil ever o'er us,
They hold us in their care,
They hold us in their care.  (3/7)

## 167. Thou Man of Sorrows, Hail

*DU GROSSER SCHMERZENSMANN*

HYMN: Adam Thebesius, 1663
MELODY: Martin Janus(?), 1663

TR.: Arthur Tozer Russell, 1851

Thou Man of Sor- rows, hail! Re- ceive my ad- o- ra- tion: On

Thee the Fa- ther laid Grief for my con- so- la- tion. Thanks

...for Thy an - guish, Lord, -- Bonds, stripes en - dured by Thee: Thanks,

Lord, for_ all _ Thy grief, Thy_ last_ sad_ ag - o - ny.

[ 2 ]
Thy conflict is our crown;
Thy death our life in heaven:
Lord, by Thy bonds to us
Is endless freedom given.

Thy cross our solace is;
Thy wounds salvation give:
Thy blood our ransom price;
By this we sinners live.   (4/7)

### 168. This Day, O Man, Is One of Bitter Pain

*HEUT IST, O MENSCH, EIN GROSSER TRAUERTAG*

HYMN: Matthäus Apelles von Löwenstern, 1644
MELODY: Matthäus Apelles von Löwenstern, 1644

TR.: Henry S. Drinker, 1944

This day, O_ man, is_ one of bit - ter_ pain; This day_ thy Sav - iour

suf - fered and was slain, And ev - en_ down in_ death it - self has lain.

[ 2 ]
This day my God, my God has died for me.
Yes life itself was hanged on Calvary.
Can anyone believe that this could be?   (2/3)

156

# 169. Jesu, Lord of Life and Death

HYMN: Michael Babzien, 1663
MELODY: Anonymous, 1668(?)

*JESU, DER DU SELBSTEN WOHL*

TR.: Charles Sanford Terry, 1929. By permission of Oxford University Press, London.

Je - su, Lord of life and death, Who the grave hast con - quered,

When I draw my lat - est breath Be Thy mer - cy of - fered!

When my thoughts would go a - stray, Deeds of e - vil cher - ish,

Or when Sa - tan blocks my way, Let me, Lord, not per - ish.

[ 2 ]
Jesu, Thou the only Light,
Cast Thy beams upon me,
Shine upon my glazing sight
When death's pains are on me!
Jesu, then be Thou my Shield
'Gainst hell's power accursèd.
Let the might Thy blood doth yield
Draw me to Thee blessèd.  (4/4)

## 170. Come Redeemer of Our Race†

see also: 28
SOURCE: Cantata No. 62, c.1740
HYMN: Martin Luther, 1524
MELODY: Anonymous, 1524

⊰ﬂ *NUN KOMM, DER HEIDEN HEILAND*

TR.: B. M. Craster (stanza 1), by permission of Novello & Co., Ltd., London; Richard Massie, 1800–1887, (stanza 2).

† Sometimes published in the transposed key of A minor.

Come re-deem-er__ of__ our race, Vir-gin__ born by__ Ho-ly__ grace,

Hail'd by__ all__ the__ wond'r-ing__ earth: God__ of__ old__ or-dained His birth.

[ 2 ]*
Praise be to the Father done,
Praise be to the only Son,
Praises to the Spirit be,
Now and to eternity. (8/8)

## 171. Sinners Guilty

HYMN: Matthäus Apelles von Löwenstern, 1644
MELODY: Matthäus Apelles von Löwenstern, 1644

⊰ﬂ *SCHAUT, IHR SÜNDER*

TR.: Charles Sanford Terry, 1929. By permission of Oxford University Press, London.

Sin-ners guilt-y, For you__ I__ suf-fered pain. Ru-ined were ye,

And still in death had__ lain. Through My an-guish Are__ ye__ now

[2]
See, blood floweth
Where cruel men did smite!
It bestoweth
A fountain of delight.
Pour forth, a cleansing flood,
To deliver
Him who hath sin withstood.  (4/7)

## 172. Hear My Pleading, Jesu, Treasure

*SEI GEGRÜSSET, JESU GÜTIG*

HYMN: Christian Keimann, 1663
MELODY: Gottfried Vopelius(?), 1682          TR.: Robert W. Ottman, 1963

[2]
O my Jesu, my salvation,
My heart's joy and consolation,
Lord, Thy wounded body show me
When in doubt I come before Thee.
May I all Thy love inherit
And in death Thy blessing merit.  (2/5)

## 173. O How My Heart Beats Full of Anxious Dreading

♫ O HERZENSANGST, O BANGIGKEIT UND ZAGEN

HYMN: D. Gerh. Müller, 1700
MELODY: Johann Sebastian Bach, 1685–1750

TR.: Jack L. Roberts, 1963

O how my heart beats full of anxious dreading! Whose grave is here, the enemy sore treading? Whose body this, that now they bear before them? I would adore Him.

[2]
Come now, my Lord, come rest on me Thy sadness,
I shall henceforth feel nought but joy and gladness.
See with what joy I'm burning to embrace Thee,—
Do Thou confess me.   (8/9)

## 174. Jesus Christ Who Came to Save Us

♫ JESUS CHRISTUS, UNSER HEILAND, DER DEN TOD

HYMN†: Martin Luther, 1524
MELODY: Anonymous, 1535

TR.: Anonymous

† Kyrie eleison (Gk.), "Lord, have mercy."

Jesus Christ, who came to save us, And

o - ver - came the grave, Is now a - ris - en, And sin hath bound in pris - on. Ky - ri - e e - lei - son.

[ 2 ]
Death and sin and life and mercy,
All in His hands He hath;
Them He'll deliver,
Who trust in Him forever.
Kyrie eleison.  (3/3)

## 175. Jesus Christ, My Sure Defense

*JESUS, MEINE ZUVERSICHT*

see also: 338
HYMN: Luise Henriette, Electress of Brandenburg, 1653     TR.: Catherine Winkworth, 1863
MELODY: Johann Crüger(?), 1653

Je - sus Christ, my sure de - fense And my Sav - iour, ev - er liv - eth;
Know - ing this my con - fi - dence Rests up - on the hope it giv - eth,
Though the night of death be fraught Still with man - y'an anx - ious thought.

[ 2 ]
Nay, too closely am I bound
Unto Him by hope forever;
Faith's strong hand the Rock hath found,
Grasped it, and will leave it never.

Not the ban of death can part
From its Lord this trusting heart.  (3/10)

161

# 176. Our Holy Christ Is Ris'n Today

HYMN: Anonymous, 1544
MELODY: Anonymous, 1555

*ERSTANDEN IST DER HEIL'GE CHRIST*

TR.: Robert W. Ottman, 1963

[ 2 ]
And now let all most joyful be,
Alleluia, Alleluia!
Praise Christ our Saviour lovingly,
Alleluia, Alleluia! (*19/19*)

## 177. Lord Jesus Christ, with Us Abide

*see also:* 148(D)
HYMN: Nikolaus Selnecker, 1611
MELODY: Anonymous, 1589

*ACH, BLEIB BEI UNS, HERR JESU CHRIST*

TR.: Benjamin Hall Kennedy, 1863

Lord Je-sus Christ, with us a-bide, For now, be-hold, 'tis e-ven-tide: And bring, to cheer us through the night, Thy Word, our true and on-ly light.

[2]
O Jesus Christ, Thy Church sustain;
Our hearts are wav'ring, cold, and vain:
Then let Thy Word be strong and clear
To silence doubt and banish fear.   (3/9)

## 178. The Holy Son, the New-born Child

*DAS NEUGEBORNE KINDELEIN*

Duplicate of Chorale 53.

# 179. Wake, Awake, for Night Is Flying

SOURCE: Cantata No. 140, 1731 or 1742
HYMN: Philipp Nicolai, 1599
MELODY: Philipp Nicolai, 1599

WACHET AUF, RUFT UNS DIE STIMME

TR.: Catherine Winkworth, 1863

Wake, a-wake, for night is fly-ing, The
Mid-night hears the wel-come voic-es, And

Wake, a-wake for
Mid-night hears the

watch-men on the heights are cry-ing; A-
at the thrill-ing cry re-joic-es: Come

wake, Je-ru-sa-lem, at last!
forth, ye vir-gins, night is past!

The Bride-groom

comes, a-wake, Your lamps with glad-ness take;

Hal-le-lu-jah! For Him pre-pare a

feast____ most rare, For ____ ye ____ must go ____ to meet Him there.

[ 2 ]*
Now let all the heav'ns adore Thee,
And men and angels sing before Thee,
With harp and cymbal's clearest tone;
Of one pearl each shining portal,
Where we are with the choir immortal
Of angels round Thy dazzling throne;

Nor eye hath seen, nor ear
Hath yet attain'd to hear
What there is ours,
But we rejoice, and sing to Thee
Our hymn of joy eternally.  (3/3)


## 180. The Night Our Saviour Was Betrayed

*ALS JESUS CHRISTUS IN DER NACHT*

HYMN: Johann Heermann, 1636
MELODY: Johann Crüger, 1649

TR.: Henry S. Drinker, 1944

The night our Sav-iour was be-trayed, Be - fore His trib-u-la - tion, A

sol - emn sac - ra - ment He_ made To_ com-pass our_ sal-va - tion.

[ 2 ]
There in His hands He took the bread
And broke it with His fingers,
Gave thanks to God on high, and said,
To His disciple, speaking:  (2/9)

[ 3 ]
"Take this and eat, for this is I,
My body for you broken,
My presence this will testify,
Forever as a token."  (3/9)

## 181. God Gave His Gospel Unto Us

HYMN: Erasmus Alber, 1548
MELODY: Anonymous, 1548

GOTT HAT DAS EVANGELIUM

TR.: Robert W. Ottman, 1963

God gave His Gos - pel un - to us That we might live in

right-eous-ness; The world heeds not this treas - ured Word, The voice of God re -

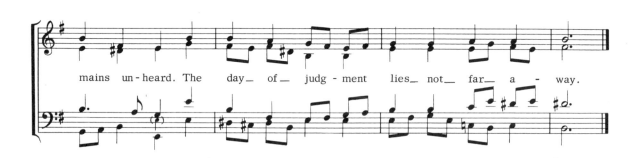

mains un-heard. The day of judg - ment lies not far a - way.

[ 2 ]
Man seeks not words of truth so plain;
For him more profit, greed and gain
Concern him in this earthly sphere;
So sayeth he, "No danger here."
The day of judgment lies not far away.   (2/14)

## 182. Had God Not Come, May Israel Say

WÄR GOTT NICHT MIT UNS DIESE ZEIT

SOURCE: Cantata No. 14, 1735
HYMN: Martin Luther, 1524, (Psalm 124)
MELODY: Johann Walther(?), 1524

TR.: Richard Massie, 1800–1887

Had God not come, may Israel say, Had God not come to aid us, Our enemies on that sad day Would surely have dismayed us; A remnant now, and handful small, Held in contempt and scorn by all Who cruelly oppress us.

[2]*
Thanks be to God, who from the pit
Snatched us, when it was gaping;
Our souls, like birds that break the net,
To the blue skies escaping;

The snare is broken—we are free!
The Lord our helper praisèd be,
The God of earth and heaven. (3/3)

167

## 183. Dear Christians, One and All Rejoice

*NUN FREUT EUCH, LIEBEN CHRISTEN
GMEIN*

HYMN: Martin Luther, 1524
MELODY: Anonymous, 1524

TR.: Anonymous (*Evangelical Lutheran Hymn Book*,
1894)

Dear Chris-tians, one and_ all_ re - joice With ex - ul - ta - tion_
And_ with u - nit - ed_ heart and voice And ho - ly_ rap - ture_

spring - ing,
sing - ing, Tell how_ our_ God_ be - held_ our_ need, And

sing_ His_ sweet and_ won - drous deed; Right dear - ly_ it_ has_ cost_ Him.

[2]
Now to My Father I depart,
From earth to heav'n ascending,
Thence heav'nly wisdom to impart,
The Holy Spirit sending;

He shall in trouble comfort thee,
Teach thee to know and follow Me,
And into truth shall guide thee. (9/10)

## 184. In Death's Strong Grasp the Saviour Lay†

*CHRIST LAG IN TODESBANDE.*

*see also:* 15, 261, 371
SOURCE: Cantata No. 4, c.1740
HYMN: Martin Luther, 1524
MELODY: Adaptation, 1524, of *Christ ist erstanden*

TR.: Catherine Winkworth, 1863, *alt.*

† Sometimes published in the transposed key of D mino

In_ death's strong grasp the Sav - iour lay, For our_ of - fenc - es_ giv - en;
But_ now_ the_ Lord is ris'n to - day, And brings us_ life from heav - en;

Where - fore let us all re-joice And praise God with cheer - ful voice, And sing we loud Hal - le - lu - jahs. Hal - le - lu - jah! Hal - le - lu - jah! Hal - le - lu - jah! Hal - le - lu - jah!

[ 2 ]*
Then let us keep the feast today
That God Himself hath given;
And His pure Word shall do away
The old and evil leaven;

Christ today will meet His own,
Our faith feeds on Him alone,
The living bread come down from heav'n.
Hallelujah! (7/7)

## 185. O Children of Your God, Rejoice

HYMN: Erasmus Alber, c.1549
MELODY: Anonymous, 1546

*NUN FREUT EUCH, GOTTES KINDER ALL*

TR.: Arthur Tozer Russell, 1851, *alt.*

O chil-dren of your God, re - joice: In praise lift to the Lord your voice; With shouts of joy sing to the skies, And un - to Him our praise shall rise.

[ 2 ]
O God the Father, praise to Thee
Throughout our lands forever be;
With all our powers to Thee we raise
Our song of glory, thanks and praise. (3/16)

### 186. O Hear, My God, My Prayer and Sore Complaining

HYMN: Jakob Peter Schechs, 1648
MELODY: Anonymous, 1662

*ACH GOTT, ERHÖR MEIN SEUFZEN UND WEHKLAGEN*

TR.: Walter E. Buszin, 1952. From *101 Chorales Harmonized by Johann Sebastian Bach*, Copyright 1952 by Hall & McCreary Company. Used by permission of the publishers, Schmitt, Hall & McCreary Company, Minneapolis, Minn.

O hear, my God, my pray'r and sore com-plain - ing, Let grief not hide the grace I'm e'er ob - tain - ing. Thou know'st my pain, I need not feign. O help me bear my cross, hear Thou my pray - ing.

[ 2 ]
Without Thy will no evil can befall me;
Thou canst relieve me or in anger fault me.

Thy child I am,
An heir of heav'n;
Heav'n's sunshine send, Thy loving grace recall me.
(2/8)

### 187. Come, Holy Ghost, Our Souls Inspire

HYMN: Martin Luther, 1524
MELODY: Anonymous

*KOMM, GOTT SCHÖPFER, HEILIGER GEIST*

TR.: John Cosin, 1594–1672

Come, Ho - ly Ghost, our souls in - spire, And

light - en with ce - les - tial _ fire; Thou the a - noint - ing _

Spir - it art, Who dost _ Thy sev'n - fold gifts im - part. _

[2]
Thy blessed unction from above
Is comfort, life and fire of love.

Enable with perpetual light
The dullness of our blinded sight.   (3/7)

## 188. I Thank Thee Dearly through Thy Son

*ICH DANK DIR SCHON DURCH DEINEN SOHN*

HYMN: Anonymous, 1586
MELODY: Anonymous, 1595                    TR.: Robert W. Ottman, 1963

I thank Thee dear - ly through Thy Son, My _ God, for _

all _ Thy good - ness, For Thy _ great pow'r _ pro -

tects _ us all _ Through night's long hours _ of dark - ness.

[2]
To God on high, and to His Son
Sing we our praise most joyous;
Praise to the Holy Three in One,
Our God enthroned above us.   (7/7)

### 189. Lord Jesus Christ, True Man and God

HYMN: Paul Eber, 1563
MELODY: Anonymous, 1597

❧ *HERR JESU CHRIST, WAHR MENSCH UND GOTT†*

TR.: Catherine Winkworth, 1855

† First tune.

Lord Je - sus Christ, true Man _ and God, Who bor-est an - guish, scorn the rod, I _
pray Thee through that bit - ter woe Let me, a _ sin - ner, mer - cy _ know.

[ 2 ]
When all my mind is darken'd o'er,
And human help can do no more,
Lead me from this dark vale beneath,
And shorten then the pangs of death.  *(3/8)*

### 190. Lord, Now Let Thy Servant

HYMN: David Behme, *c.*1663
MELODY: Anonymous, 1694

❧ *HERR, NUN LASS IN FRIEDE*

TR.: Catherine Winkworth, 1861, *alt.*

Lord, now _ let _ Thy _ ser - vant Pass in _ peace un - to _____ Thee; _
Life _ on _ earth suf - fic - ing, World, I _ now _ would leave _____ thee:

Let me go if willing, Thy desire fulfilling.

**[2]**

Therefore of His mercy
Will I now be singing,
All my heart most thankful,
Praise to Him be bringing:

Praise Him always, all men,
While the heav'ns cry, Amen! *(9/10)*

## 191. From God Shall Nought Divide Me†

*see also:* 114, 332, 364
SOURCE: Cantata No. 73, *c.*1725
HYMN: Ludwig Helmbold, 1563
MELODY: Anonymous, 1571

❧ *VON GOTT WILL ICH NICHT LASSEN*

TR.: Catherine Winkworth, 1869

† Sometimes published in the transposed key of A minor.

From God shall nought divide me, For He is true alway,
And on my path will guide me, Where else I oft should stray.

His ever bounteous hand At morn and eve is heedful To
give me what is needful,
give me what is needful, Wher-e'er I go or stand.
give me what is needful,

**[ 2 ]\***

For 'tis our Father made us,
And wills our good alone;
The Son hath died to save us
And make God's goodness known;

The Spirit rules our ways,
And dwells through faith within us,
To God and Heaven to win us;
To Him be thanks and praise! *(9/9)*

## 192. My God Makes Ready to Relieve Me

HYMN: Christian Weise, 1682
MELODY: Anonymous, eighteenth century

*GOTTLOB, ES GEHT NUNMEHR ZUM ENDE*

TR.: Paul T. Buszin, 1952. From *101 Chorales Harmonized by Johann Sebastian Bach*, Copyright 1952 by Hall & McCreary Company. Used by permission of the publishers, Schmitt, Hall & McCreary Company, Minneapolis, Minn.

My God makes read-y to re-lieve me Of ev-'ry woe_ and ev-'ry moan;
My Je-sus beck-ons to_ re-ceive me, My Je-sus, who_ calls me_ His own.

And Je-sus is my part-ing word.
I hast-en to_ my home_ pre-ferred, And Je-sus is_ my part-ing_ word.

[ 2 ]
My Jesus by His death defeated
All enemies, Sin, Hell and Death:
Deliverance for me completed
By my dear Jesus' dying breath.
His vict'ry was on me conferred,
So Jesus is my parting word.  (5/7)

## 193. O Why Art Thou Cast Down, My Soul, within Me

*WAS BIST DU DOCH, O SEELE, SO BETRÜBET*

HYMN: Rudolf Friedrich von Schultt, 1704
MELODY: Anonymous, 1704

TR.: Samuel Adler, 1963

O_ why art thou cast down, my_ soul, with-in me? Why down-cast be_ So
That God, the Lord, a cross to_ bear has giv'n thee.

tear-ful-ly  As if,— there-fore, thy_ God_ would nought but_ love____ thee.

[2]
O listen now, and trust the Lord etern'lly,
And let no woe from thy great faith estrange thee.

Mark thou His word:
"Hast thou not heard
My child, I bring you heav'n's eternal glory." (7/8)

## 194. Dearest Immanuel, Lord of the Faithful

*LIEBSTER IMMANUEL, HERZOG DER FROMMEN*

SOURCE: Cantata No. 123, *c*.1740
HYMN: Ahasuerus Fritsch, 1679            TR.: Henry S. Drinker, 1944
MELODY: Anonymous, 1679

Dear-est_ Im-man-u-el, Lord of_ the_ Faith-ful, Come Thou with
Thou art_ my_ heart's de-light, Thou dost_ pos-sess___ it, Glow-ing with

me_ to dwell, Sav-iour_ di-vine! Earth's fu-tile treas-ure
love_ for Thee, yearn-ing_ for Thine.

gives me no pleas-ure, Thou art my heart's de-sire, O_ Sav-iour mine!

[2]*
Get thee gone vanity,
Cease now to cheat me;
Thou Jesus, Thou art mine,
Thine only I;

Gladly I leave the world,
Soon Thou wilt greet me,
Dwell deep within my heart,
There when I die.
Thou art my Being, my life decreeing,
Till in the grave at last one day I lie. (5/5)

### 195. How Bright Appears the Morning Star

*WIE SCHÖN LEUCHTET DER MORGENSTERN*

Duplicate of Chorale 86.

### 196. Now When at Supper They Were Met

*DA DER HERR CHRIST ZU TISCHE SASS*

HYMN: Nikolaus Herman, 1560
MELODY: Anonymous, 1611

TR.: Charles Sanford Terry, 1929. By permission of Oxford University Press, London.

Now when at sup-per_ they were met Their East-er_ Pass-o -ver to_ eat, Did
Their East - er Pass-o-ver to eat.

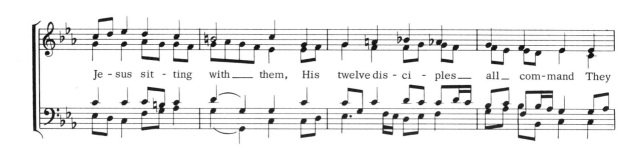

Je -sus sit - ting with ____ them, His twelve dis-ci -ples ____ all_ com-mand They

forth should tell_ in ev - ery land His_ bit - ter_ death and_ suf - f'ring.

[2]
Our praise to Thee, O Christ, we sound,
Who for us hath salvation found,
Thy precious death prevailing.
For we had suffered pain and loss
Hadst Thou not borne the cruel Cross,
Thy Father's anger staying. *(27/28)*

# 197. Christ Is Arisen

HYMN†: Anonymous
MELODY: Anonymous

CHRIST IST ERSTANDEN

TR.: Anonymous (*Lutheran Hymnal*, 1942). Reprinted by permission of Concordia Publishing House from *The Handbook of the Lutheran Hymnal* by W. G. Polack (1942).

† Kyrie eleis from Kyrie eleison (Gk.), "Lord, have mercy."

Christ is a - ris - en __ From the __ grave's dark pris - on. We

now __ re - joice with __ glad - ness; For Christ will end __ all __ sad - ness.

Ky - rie - e - leis!
Ky - rie __ e - leis! All __ our __ hopes were end - ed Had
Ky - rie __ e - leis! __

Je - sus not __ as - cend - ed; Rose from the __ grave tri - umph-ant - ly. For

For

this, Lord __ Christ, we wor - ship Thee,
Ky - rie e - leis!
Ky - rie e - leis!

this, __ Lord Christ, we wor - ship Thee. Ky - rie e - leis! __

Hal - le - lu - jah! Hal - le - lu - jah! Hal - le - lu - jah!_ We_
now_ re - joice with_ glad - ness For_ Christ_ will_ end_ all_
sad - ness. Ky - rie e - leis!
Ky - rie e - leis!
Ky - rie e - leis!

## 198. See the Lord of Life and Light

 CHRISTUS, DER UNS SELIG MACHT

see also: 81, 113, 307(D)
HYMN: Michael Weisse, 1531
MELODY: Anonymous, 1531

TR.: John Troutbeck, 1832–1899, (stanza 1), used by
permission of Novello & Co., Ltd.; John Christian
Jacobi, 1725, (stanza 2).

See_ the_ Lord of_ life_ and_ light,_ Sav - iour_ meek and_
low - ly,_ Tak - en like a_ thief_ at_ night,
Bound by_ hands un - ho - ly. See_ the_ sin - less Son_ of God

[ 2 ]
Grant, O Jesu, blessed Lord,
By Thy cross and passion,
That Thy love may be adored
By Thy whole creation;

Hating sin, the woeful cause
Of Thy death and suff'ring,
Let our hearts obey Thy laws
As our best thanksgiving.  (8/8)

## 199.  O Help Me, Lord, to Praise Thee

see also: 302(D)
HYMN: Heinrich Müller, 1531
MELODY: Anonymous, 1545

✠ HILF, GOTT, DASS MIRS GELINGE

TR.: Charles Sanford Terry, 1929. By permission of Oxford University Press, London.

voice up-raise For Thy blest Word so ho - ly, And guide my fee - ble praise.

[2]
A Comforter He sent us,
The Holy Ghost adored,
In ways of truth to guide us
And teach His holy Word.

And whenso'er we call on Him,
Be sure He'll show Him gracious
And that our prayer is heard. (12/13)

## 200. Christ Our Lord Is Risen

CHRISTUS IST ERSTANDEN

HYMN: Michael Weisse, 1531
MELODY: Anonymous, 1531

TR.: Robert W. Ottman, 1963

Christ our Lord is ris - en From death's dark prison; Christ His grace hath giv - en, Truth doth come from Him.

[ 2 ]
Let all tongues be singing;
Sing Hallelujah!
Praise to Him with singing and Hallelujahs!

Now Thou art arisen,
Lord of Heaven!
Sing His glory, all men,
Sing ye now and ever. Amen.  *(13/13)*

## 201. O Man, Bewail Thy Grievous Fall

*see also:* 306(D)
HYMN: Sebald Heyd, 1525
MELODY: Matthäus Greitter(?), 1525

*O MENSCH, BEWEIN DEIN SÜNDE GROSS*

TR.: Charles Sanford Terry, 1929. By permission of Oxford University Press, London.

The dead He raised again to life, The sick He loosed from pain and strife, Until the time appointed That He for us should shed His blood And take on Him our sin's dark load, Stretched on the cross accursèd.

[2]
Then let us all, with one accord,
Unite to praise our loving Lord
Who took our blame upon Him,
Cast off from us the bonds of sin,
And strive His countenance to win,
His Word and will fulfilling.

And let our hearts toward Him burn
With love, attempting due return
For all He hath endurèd.
O mortals all, the right ensue,
Or surely shall God's wrath pursue
All those who've Him rejected.   *(23/23)*

## 202. Oh, We Wretched Sinners

*⁂ O WIR ARMEN SÜNDER*

HYMN†: Hermann Bonn, 1542
MELODY: Anonymous, 1527

TR.: Thomas S. Harllee, 1963

† Kyrie eleison, Christe eleison (Gk.), "Lord, have mercy
Christ, have mercy."

Oh, we wretch-ed sin - ners! Our most griev - ous deed

In - to which we en - tered And were born there - in,

Has now brought all man - kind To such dam - na - tion dread,
such dam - na - tion dread,
such dam - na - tion dread,

That we have been cast down Ev - er to be dead.

Ky - rie e - lei - son! Chri - ste
Ky - rie e - lei - son! Chri - ste
Ky - rie e - lei - son! Chri - ste
Ky - rie e - lei - son! Chri - ste

e - lei - son! Ky - rie e - lei - son!
e - lei - son! Ky - rie e - lei - son!
e - lei - son! Ky - rie e - lei - son!
e - lei - son! Ky - rie e - lei - son!

[2]

For had Christ not entered
Thus into the world,
On Himself not taken
Our unworthy souls,
Nor for our transgressions
Had died most willingly,

Then for all the ages
We condemned would be.
Kyrie eleison!
Christe eleison!
Kyrie eleison!   (3/6)

## 203. O Man, Christ Jesus Now Behold

*O MENSCH, SCHAU JESUM CHRISTUM AN*

HYMN: Daniel Specht, 1663
MELODY: Anonymous, 1555

TR.: Thomas S. Harllee, 1963

O man, Christ Je - sus now be - hold, Both hu - man
and di - vine, Who cared for us with deeds un -
told By death's most bit - ter sign: What great
pain and suf - f'ring fierce His faith - ful heart did pierce!

[ 2 ]
This balm I have from Jesus' breath
Received within my heart
Upon the moment of His death,
And locked it all apart:

Let, dear Lord, Thy will be done,
My Saviour, God's own Son. (4/5)

## 204. Who Knows How Near Will Be My Ending?

*WER WEISS, WIE NAHE MIR MEIN ENDE!*
WER NUR DEN LIEBEN GOTT LÄSST WALTEN

*see also:* 62, 104, 112, 146, 339
SOURCE: Cantata No. 166 c.1725
HYMN: Emilie Juliane, Countess of Schwarzburg-
Rudolstadt, 1695
MELODY: Georg Neumark, 1657

TR.: Catherine Winkworth, 1863, *alt.*

* Who knows how near will be my end - ing? Time speeds a - way, and death comes on;
How swift - ly, ah, how swift de - scend - ing, May Death be here and Life be gone!

My God, for Je - su's sake I pray Thy peace may bless my dy - ing day.

[2]
The world that smiled when morn was breaking,
May change for me ere close of eve;
For while on earth my home I'm making,
In peril of my death I live;

My God, for Jesu's sake I pray
Thy peace may bless my dying day.  (2/12)

## 205. Our Praise, Lord God, Give We

*HERR GOTT, DICH LOBEN WIR*

HYMN: Martin Luther, 1529
MELODY: Anonymous, 1529(?)

TR.: George Macdonald, 1876, *alt.*

Our praise, Lord God, give we, Lord, we give thanks to Thee.

Thee Fa - ther_ and e - ter - nal God, Earth prai - ses e - ver,_
All an - gels_ and all heav'n's host, And all_ that in_ Thy
The che - ru - bim and se - ra - phim Thee e - ver sing with_

far_ and_ broad.
ser - vice_ boast, Ho - ly_ is_ our_ Lord God!
lof - ty_ hymn:

Ho - ly_ is our Lord_ God,_ the_ God_ of Sa - ba - oth!

Thy god - like might and lord - ship go Wide o - ver heav'n and earth be - low.
The pre - cious mar - tyrs with one voice Praise Thee, O_ Lord, with migh - ty noise.
From all_ Thy wor - thy Chris - ten - dom Thy prai - ses ev' - ry_ day do come.

Thou, King of _ Glo - ry, Christ, a - lone The_ Fa - ther's One e - ter - nal Son,
Thou on - the_ might of death did'st tread, And_ Chris - tians all to_ heaven hast led.
Thou sit - test_ now at God's right hand, With_ hon - or in_ Thy Fa - ther's land.

Let us_ in_ heav - en have_ our place, And_ there the Ho - ly_ One's em - brace. Thy

folk, Lord Je - sus Christ ad-vance, And bless Thine own in - her - i - tance. Them

watch and ward, Lord, ev' - ry day. E - ter - nal - ly them raise, we pray. Dai -

ly, Lord God, we hon - or Thee, And praise Thy name con - tin - ual - ly.

O God of Truth, keep us this day From ev' - ry sin and e - vil way.
Be gra-cious to us, Lord, we plead, Be gra-cious to us in all need.
Show un-to us Thy pi - ty'ng grace, For all our hope in Thee we place.

Dear Lord, our hope is in Thy name; Let us be ne - ver

A - men.

put to shame. A - men.

## 206. O Must Thou Say Good Night Now, Jesus Mine

HYMN: August Pfeiffer, 1688
MELODY: Anonymous, 1694

*SO GIBST DU NUN, MEIN JESU, GUTE NACHT*

TR.: Thomas S. Harllee, 1963

O must Thou say good night now, Je - sus mine? And must Thou die, my dearest One who liv - eth? Yea, Thou art hence, and gone Thy pain di - vine: My God is dead; His spir - it now He giv - eth, My God is dead; His spir - it now He giv - eth.

[2]
Ah, mourn with me! I see the Hero's Strife,
The Father's Word, the Refuge of the Holy,
Man's Blessed Balm, the Lord of Noble Life;
The Prince of Life has come to die most lowly,
The Prince of Life has come to die most lowly.

   (4/24)

## 207. The Holy Ghost's Abundant Grace

HYMN: Johannes Leon(?), c.1570
MELODY: Anonymous, 1627

*DES HEILGEN GEISTES REICHE GNAD*

TR.: Stephen T. Farish, 1963

The Holy Ghost's a - bund - ant grace Our Lord's A - pos - tle's hearts em-brace, And in His Good - ness clasps them all, And makes the Gift of Tongues to fall.

[ 2 ]
Praise to the Worthy Comforter,
The Light of Truth on us confer,

Protection from disgrace afford,
And grant to us Thy great reward.  (6/6)

## 208. Now Forty Days Since Easter Morn

*ALS VIERZIG TAG NACH OSTERN WAR*

HYMN: Nikolaus Herman, 1560
MELODY: Nikolaus Herman, 1560
TR.: Stephen T. Farish, 1963

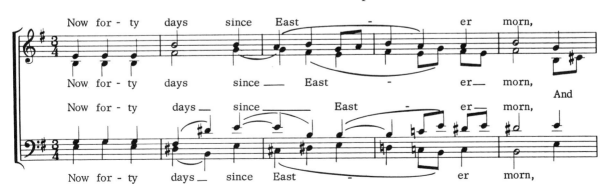

Now for - ty days since East - er morn, And

189

Christ must be to Heaven borne, Called He the
Chosen to the hill, Alleluia! This day the
This day the

prophecy ful-fill. Al - le - lu - ia!
prophecy ful-fill.

[2]
Now go ye forth to all mankind,
That My forgiveness each shall find,

Baptize and teach ye in My Name,
Alleluia!
Until my Kingdom all proclaim.
Alleluia! (5/14)

## 209. Jehovah, Let Me Now Adore Thee

🙣 *DIR, DIR, JEHOVAH, WILL ICH SINGEN*

SOURCE: Notenbuchlein der Anna Magdalena Bach, 1725
HYMN: Barhtholomäus Crasselius, 1697
MELODY: Johann Sebastian Bach, 1725

TR.: Catherine Winkworth, 1863

Je - ho - vah, let me now a - dore Thee, For where is
With song I fain would come be - fore Thee, O let Thy

there a — God — such, Lord, as — Thee?
spir- it — deign to teach me — now To — praise — Thee in His name,

through whom a - lone Our songs — can — please Thee through Thy bless-ed — Son.

[2]
Yes draw me to the Son, O Father,
That so the Son may draw me up to Thee.
Let every pow'r within me gather,
To own Thy sway,·O spirit,—rule in me,

That so the Peace of God may in me dwell,
And I may sing for joy and praise Thee well.   (2/8)

## 210. Lord of Our Life and God of Our Salvation

*CHRISTE, DU BEISTAND DEINER KREUZGEMEINDE*

HYMN: Matthäus Apelles von Löwenstern, 1644
MELODY: Matthäus Apelles von Löwenstern, 1644          TR.: Phillip Pusey, 1799–1855

Lord of — our — life — and God — of — our sal- va -

tion, Star of — our night and hope — of — ev - ery — na - tion, Hear

and re-ceive___ Thy Church-'s sup-pli-ca-___tion, Lord
God Al-might-___y! Lord God___ Al-might-___y!

[2]
Lord, Thou canst help when earthly armor faileth,
Lord, Thou canst save when sin itself assaileth,
Christ, o'er thy rock nor death nor hell prevaileth:

Grant us Thy peace, Lord,
Grant us Thy peace, Lord.  *(2/4)*

## 211. Earth's Frail Pomp and Vanities

HYMN: Michael Weisse, 1531
MELODY: Michael Weisse, 1555

*WELTLICH EHR UND ZEITLICH GUT*

TR.: Charles Sanford Terry, 1929. By permission of Oxford University Press, London.

Earth's frail pomp___ and van-i-___ties,___ De-lights and vain fri-vol-i-___ties, Shall with-er___ as___ the___ grass. All___ its___ might and___ boast-ed pow'r Fall-eth as a fad-ed___ flow'r. This is___

And with care ———— pur-sue Thy course.

[ 2 ]
Live as though the day were near
When thou before God must appear.
When death knocks at the door,
His dread summons must obey,
When He calls thou must not stay.
If thou hast fulfilled God's law
He will welcome thee, be sure.  *(2/10)*

## 212. Lord, at All Times Doth My Soul

*HERR, ICH DENK AN JENE ZEIT*

HYMN: Georg Mylius, 1640
MELODY: Anonymous, 1566

TR.: Charles Sanford Terry, 1929. By permission of Oxford University Press, London.

[ 2 ]
Jesu, save my soul from loss,
In my anguish never leave me!
Save me by the blessed Cross
That did once redeem me!

In Thy pity look on me
Lovingly!
God His son hath called me.  *(6/7)*

193

### 213. Oh, How Blest Are Ye Whose Toils Are Ended

*O WIE SELIG SEID IHR DOCH, IHR FROMMEN†*

HYMN: Simon Dach, 1635
MELODY: Johann Crüger, 1649

TR.: Henry W. Longfellow, 1845

† First tune.

Oh, how blest are ye_ whose toils are end - ed, Who, through death, have un - to_God as-cend - ed! Ye have a - ris - en From the cares which keep us still in_ pris - on.

[ 2 ]
Christ has wiped away your tears forever;
Ye have that for which we still endeavor.

To you are chanted
Songs that ne'er to mortal ears were granted. (4/6)

### 214. In the Midst of Life, We Are

*MITTEN WIR IM LEBEN SIND*

HYMN: Anonymous (stanza 1); Martin Luther, 1524, (stanza 2).
MELODY: Anonymous, 1524

TR.: George Macdonald, 1876

life we are
help us can,

In the midst of_ life,_ we_ are Aye in Death's em-brac - es,
Who is_ there who help_ us_ can, And in fa - vor place_ us?

life_ we_ are
help_ us_ can,

sor -
Thou art He, Lord, Thou on - ly. From ill deeds we sor -
sor -

row - ing turn, That have made Thy an - ger burn. Ho -
row - ing turn,

ly, Ho - ly, Lord God, Ho - ly, might - y Lord God, Ho - ly Sav - iour with the

ten - der heart, Ev - er - last - ing God, Let us not be drown -

O Lord, hear us now!
èd In the pains of bit - ter death. O Lord, hear us now!

[2]
In the midst of pains of Hell
Us our sins are baiting;
Whither shall we flee away
Where a rest is waiting?
To Thee, Lord Christ, Thee only.
Outpourèd is Thy precious blood,
For our sins sufficing good.

Holy, holy, Lord God,
Holy, mighty Lord God,
Holy Saviour with the tender heart,
Everlasting God,
Let us not fall from Thee,
From the comfort of Thy faith.
O Lord, hear us now! *(3/3)*

195

## 215. In These Our Days So Perilous†

see also: 91, 259(D)
SOURCE: Cantata No. 126, c.1740
HYMN: Martin Luther, 1529
MELODY: Anonymous, 1531

VERLEIH UNS FRIEDEN GNÄDIGLICH

TR.: Richard Massie, 1800–1877, alt.

† Sometimes published in the transposed key of G minor.

* In these our days so per-il-ous, Lord, peace in mer-cy send us; No

God but Thee can fight for us, No God but Thee de-fend us: Thou

art our one and on-ly God. Grant to our King and all au-thor-i-

ties Peace and pro-fi-cient rule. That we may live in peace And that,

with our rul-ers, live in qui-et hon-or;
qui-et hon-or; Liv-ing in all
qui-et hon-or;

196

god-li-ness And hon - es - ty. A - men.

## 216. It Is Enough!

SOURCE: Cantata No. 60, 1732
HYMN: Franz Burmeister, 1662
MELODY: Johann Rodolph Ahle, 1662

*ES IST GENUG!*

TR.: J. T. Mueller, 1920. By permission of the Erie Printing Co., Erie, Pennsylvania.

It is e - nough! So take my spir - it, Lord, To Zi - on's gold - en shore; Re - ceive my soul, Which trust - ing in Thy word, Seeks Thee for - ev - er - more; Which day and night in an - guish ly - ing, Is long - ing for Thy pres - ence,

crying: It is__ e - nough! It is e - nough!

[ 2 ]*
It is enough,—
Lord, let it please Thee so,
To take my soul to Thee;—
My Saviour comes
With loving-kindness now,
To heaven leading me.

Farewell, my heart with joy is ringing,
I meet my God with praise and singing:
It is enough!
It is enough!   (5/5)

## 217. O Lord! How Many Miseries

*ACH GOTT, WIE MANCHES HERZELEID*

*see also:* 156, 308(D)
SOURCE: Cantata No. 153, 1727
HYMN: Martin Moller(?) and Conrad Hojer(?), 1587
MELODY: Anonymous, 1625

TR.: John Christian Jacobi, 1722

O Lord! How man - y mis - er - ies As-sault and dis - com-pose my__ peace;.

The path that leads to Zi - on's gate Is full of thorns and ve - ry strait.

[ 2 ]*
So then as long as life shall be,
I'll bear the cross and follow Thee:
O Lord, prepare this heart of mine,
Let it to nothing else incline. (16/18)

[ 3 ]*
Assist me with Thy mighty grace,
With joy to run my Christian race;
Help me to conquer flesh and blood,
And make my Christian warfare good. (17/18)

[ 4 ]*
Preserve my faith from error free,
That I may live and die in Thee.
Lord Jesus Christ, hear my desire,
To hymn Thee in the heav'nly choir. (18/18)

## 218. To Our Trembling Supplication

HYMN: Martin Opitz, 1637, (Psalm 86)
MELODY: Louis Bourgeois, 1547

*LASS, O HERR, DEIN OHR SICH NEIGEN*

TR.: Benjamin Hall Kennedy, 1863

To_ our trem- bling sup- pli- ca- tion,
Lord give ear and ac- cep- ta- tion;
Hear us_ pin- ing_ in_ our
woe, For_ our_ sins_ have brought us_ low. Save the_ souls which Thou did'st
cher - ish, Now up- on_ the point to_ per - ish; Save Thy_
serv- ants who_ have none Help or_ hope_ but_ Thee a - lone.

[ 2 ]
Heav'nly Tutor, of Thy kindness
Teach our dullness, guide our blindness,
That our feet Thy paths may tread,
Which to endless glory led.

Lord of every good the giver,
Kindle in our hearts forever,
When Thy holy name we hear,
Fearful love and loving fear. (2/8)

199

## 219. Oh, How Blest Are Ye Whose Toils Are Ended

*O WIE SELIG SEID IHR DOCH, IHR FROMMEN†*

HYMN: Simon Dach, 1635
MELODY: Anonymous, 1566

TR.: Henry W. Longfellow, 1845

† Second tune.

Oh,— how_ blest_ are— ye whose toils_ are— end - ed,

Who, through death, have un - to God as - cend - ed! Ye have_ a - ris -

en From the cares which keep us_ still_ in_ pris - on.

[ 2 ]
Come, O Christ, and loose the chains that bind us!
Lead us forth, and cast this world behind us!
With Thee th' Anointed,
Finds the soul its joy and rest appointed.   (6/6)

# 220. Shall I Not My God Be Praising?

HYMN: Paul Gerhardt, 1653
MELODY: Johann Schop, 1641

TR.: John Kelly, 1867

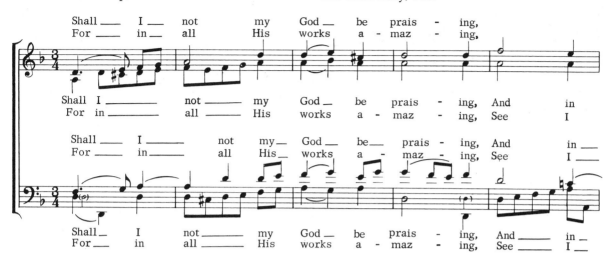

Shall I not my God be praising, And in Him not joyful be?
For in all His works amazing, See I not His care for me?

Him not joyful be?
not His care for me?
Is it not pure

love that filleth, And His faithful heart o'er flows,
When He ever cares for those, Who do

When I sleep, His eye is waking,
When I wake, He strengthens me,
Each new morn fresh courage taking,
I new love and goodness see.

Had my God existed never,
Had His grace not guided me,
From such ills so frequently,
None could have delivered ever.
All things run their course below,
God's love doth forever flow. *(7/12)*

## 221. Lord, in Thy Wrath O Chide Me Not

HYMN: Anonymous, 1610, (Psalm 38)
MELODY: Johann Crüger, 1640

*HERR, STRAF MICH NICHT IN DEINEM ZORN*

TR.: Charles Sanford Terry, 1929. By permission of Oxford University Press, London.

Lord, in Thy wrath O chide me not, Of Thy dear love I pray Thee! Sore full of heaviness am I, By
Could I survive Thine anger hot Or from Thy doom escape me?

**[ 2 ]**

O men of mischief, give ye place!
My God has heard me crying.
My foes He'll bring to swift disgrace,
On Him my soul's relying.

Not ever from me will He turn,
Or let my soul in terror burn,
His love to me denying.  (6/6)

## 222. Now Let Us Singing

*NUN PREISET ALLE GOTTES BARMHERZIGKEIT*

HYMN: Matthäus Apelles von Löwenstern, 1644
MELODY: Matthäus Apelles von Löwenstern, 1644

TR.: Catherine Winkworth, 1863, *alt.*

Now let us sing-ing Praise God the mer-ci-ful; Chris-ten-dom,

proud-ly Tells of His glo-rious rule. Gen-tly He bids___ thee

come be-fore Him; Haste, then, O__ Is-ra-el now a-dore__ Him.

**[ 2 ]**

For the Lord reigneth
Over the universe,
All He sustaineth,
All things His praise rehearse,

The host of angels 'round Him dwelling,
Psalter and harp of His praise are telling.  (2/5)

## 223. I Thank Thee, Lord

HYMN: Johann Freder, 1559
MELODY: Anonymous, 1568

TR.: Robert W. Ottman, 1963

*ICH DANK DIR, GOTT*

[2]
I give to Thee
My spirit free,
Heart, mind, and mood, consigned to Thee,
My life, my all;
That I not fall,

Thine angels fair
For me do care,
And Satan's might
Will not affright,
Nor lead me into sin's delight. *(2/3)*

## 224. O God Almighty, Father, Son

HYMN: Martin Behm, 1608
MELODY: Anonymous, 1713

TR.: Henry James Buckoll, 1842

*DAS WALT GOTT VATER UND GOTT SOHN*

O God Al-might-y, Fa-ther, Son, And Ho-ly Ghost, on heav'n's fair throne, We thank Thee, e'er the sun a-rise, At dawn we stand be-fore Thine eyes.

[ 2 ]
My every path protect today,
Let naught that's ill beset my way;
From sudden death preserve me free;
Where help I need, O help Thou me.   (11/11)

## 225. O God, Who Art the Only Light

HYMN: Johann Rist, 1641
MELODY: Johann Crüger, 1648

TR.: Charles Sanford Terry, 1929. By permission of Oxford University Press, London.

*GOTT, DER DU SELBER BIST DAS LICHT*

O God, who art the On-ly Light, Whose good-ness ev-er shin-eth bright, To Thee be praise un-ceas-ing!
For night's dark hours have passed a-way, And bright-ly dawns an-oth-er day, Thy won-der-work dis-play-ing.

Thou'st held us safe-ly while we_ slept, And from our rest all_ e - vil kept.

[ 2 ]

O God the Father, ever bless!
O Jesus Christ, e'er me confess
And to Thy grace elect me!
O God the Spirit, day and night,
Lift up Thy face on me with might
And with Thy love protect me!
And always, as I go my way,
May God His peace upon me lay!   (15/15)

## 226. Lord Jesus Christ, Thou Hast Prepared

*HERR JESU CHRIST, DU HAST BEREIT*

HYMN: Samuel Kinner, 1638
MELODY: Anonymous, 1742(?)

TR.: Emmanuel Cronenwett, 1880, *alt.* Reprinted by permission of Concordia Publishing House from *The Handbook of the Lutheran Hymnal* by W. G. Polack (1942).

Lord Je-sus Christ, Thou hast pre-pared A feast_ for_ our sal-
It_ is_ Thy bod - y and_ Thy_ blood; And at_ Thy in-vi-

va - tion, As wea-ry_ souls, with_ sin_ op-prest, We
ta - tion

come to___ Thee for need-ed___ rest, For com-fort___and___for par - don.

**[2]**
Lord, I believe what Thou hast said,
Help me when doubts assail me;
Remember that I am but dust
And let my faith not fail me.
Thy Supper in this vale of tears
Refreshes me and stills my fears,
And is my priceless treasure. (4/8)

## 227. Praise God, Thy Father, for His Lovingkindness

*LOBET DEN HERREN, DENN ER IST SEHR FREUNDLICH*

HYMN: Anonymous, 1568, (Psalm 147)
MELODY: Antonio Scandelli, 1568

TR.: Robert W. Ottman, 1963

Praise God,___ thy Fa - ther, Praise God___ thy___ Fa -

ther For His___ lov - ing - kind - ness. For we sin - cere - ly___

sing___ to___ Him___ our___ prais - es, sing to___ Him___ our prais - es;

How love-ly are the sounds we raise to Heav - en To praise our Lord, God. To praise our Lord, God.

[2]
Let all be singing,
Let all be singing,
Singing with thanksgiving;
With harps give praises
For our many blessings,
For our many blessings;

He is our Father,
Powerful and mighty.
O praise our Lord, God.
O praise our Lord, God.   *(2/7)*

## 228. Give Thanks, Sing Praises, for God's Love Is with Us

*DANKET DEM HERREN, DENN ER IST SEHR FREUNDLICH*

HYMN: Johann Horn, 1544
MELODY: Anonymous, 1534

TR.: Robert W. Ottman, 1963

Give thanks, sing prais - es, for God's love is with us, His truth and good - ness, al - ways will they strength - en us.

[2]
He is our God, compassionate and holy;
For us poor creatures He provides most plenteously.
   *(2/6)*

208

## 229. Now Thanks to Thee, Lord God, in Heaven Be Sounded

HYMN: Anonymous, 1612
MELODY: Louis Bourgeois, 1547

ICH DANKE DIR, HERR GOTT, IN DEINEM THRONE

TR.: Charles Sanford Terry, 1929. By permission of Oxford University Press, London.

Now_ thanks to_ Thee, Lord God, in heav'n be_ sound - ed, Through Je - sus_ Christ Thy_ Son, our Lord be - lov - ed, That Thou through-out the night that's past hast guard - ed Our rest_ and all_ that's e - vil_ from us_ ward - ed! And now_ we_ pray, through - out_ the_ hours of_ day - light Thou'lt keep us_ safe_ from sin_ and_ pure in Thy_____ sight.

[ 2 ]

Now take, O Lord, my soul into Thy keeping,
Thy grace from heav'n and sure protection seeking;
Thy holy angel send for my protection,
To guide me ever under his direction!

So shall proud Satan ne'er prevail against me,
Nor all His pow'r avail from Thee to wrest me.
(2/2)

209

### 230. O Christ, Thou Art the Light of Day

HYMN: Erasmus Alber, c.1556
MELODY: Anonymous, 1568

TR.: Robert W. Ottman, 1963

CHRIST, DER DU BIST DER HELLE TA

O Christ, Thou art the light of day, Be - fore whose beams night can - not stay; From God a - bove on us they shine And tell us of His love di - vine, And tell us of His love di - vine.

[ 2 ]
In Thy dear name we all shall sleep
While round us angels watch do keep.

O holy Three in One, may we
Thy praise sing everlastingly,
Thy praise sing everlastingly. (7/7)

### 231. Now God Be with Us

HYMN: Petrus Herbert, 1566
MELODY: Anonymous, 1566

TR.: Catherine Winkworth, 1863, alt.

DIE NACHT IST KOMMEN

Now God be with us, For the night is clos - ing; The light and dark - ness Are of His dis - pos - ing, Be - neath His shad -

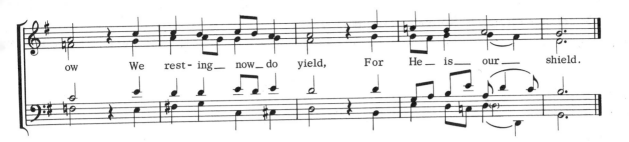

ow We rest-ing now do yield, For He is our shield.

**[ 2 ]**

Let evil spirits
Fly away before us;
Till morning cometh,
O Master watch o'er us;

In soul and body
From heav'n defend thou us,
Thine angels send us.   (2/5)

## 232. The Sun Has Set, All Radiance Has Descended

❀ *DIE SONN HAT SICH MIT IHREM GLANZ GEWENDET*

HYMN: Josua Stegmann(?), 1648
MELODY: Anonymous, 1542

TR.: Samuel Adler, 1963

The sun has set, all ra-diance has de-scend-ed, And in God's plan, an-oth-er day has end-ed. While round a-bout night's man-tle falls with ease, Brings man and beast that e'er de-sir-èd peace.

**[ 2 ]**

I shall sing praise to Thee, O Lord of glory,
That Thou today from pain and want redeemed me.
By Thou strong hand, and ever mighty pow'r
Didst shelter me, and guard me ev'ry hour.   (2/7)

## 233. Jesus, Thou My Soul's Enchantment

≼ *JESU, MEINER SEELEN WONN*
WERDE MUNTER, MEIN GEMÜT

*see also:* 95, 121, 350, 365
SOURCE: Cantata No. 154, 1724
HYMN: Martin Jahn, 1661
MELODY: Johann Schop, 1642
TR.: Henry S. Drinker, 1944, *alt.*

Je - sus, Thou my soul's en - chant - ment, Thou who all my__ cares dis - pel,
Best De - light and Sun of _ Glad - ness, Je - sus whom I __ know so_ well;

With my__ heart and _ soul_ I _ love Thee, Life with - out Thee, O _ so_ lone-ly;

Come Thou, Je - sus, come to me, Stay_ with_ me e - ter - nal - ly.

[ 2 ]*
Jesus, Thou my blest Redeemer,
Jesus, safe retreat from strife,
Jesus, foe of foul blasphemer,
Jesus, beacon of my life!

How my heart will joyous greet Thee,
How my spirit yearns to meet Thee,
Come, O come, I wait for Thee,
Come, my Jesus, dear to me. *(2/19)*

## 234. God Liveth Still

≼ *GOTT LEBET NOC*

HYMN: Johann Friedrich Zihn, 1692
MELODY: Anonymous, 1714
TR.: Frances E. Cox, 1812–1897

God liv - eth still;_____ Trust, my soul,_ and feel no ill:____

God is good, from His compassion Earthly help and comfort flow; Strong is His right hand to fashion All things well for men below: Trial oft the most distressing, In the end has proved a blessing: Wherefore then, my soul, despair? God still lives who heareth prayer.

lives who heareth prayer.

lives who heareth prayer.

lives who heareth prayer.

[2]
God liveth still;
Trust, my soul, and feel no ill:
He who gives the clouds their measure,
Stretching out the heav'ns alone:
He who stores the earth with treasure,
Is not far from every one:

God in hour of need defendeth
Him whose heart in love ascendeth:
Wherefore then, my soul, despair?
God still lives who heareth prayer. (2/8)

## 235. Holy, Holy, Holy

*see also:* 319(D)
HYMN: Sanctus, sanctus, sanctus
MELODY: Anonymous, 1726

HEILIG, HEILIG, HEILIG

TR.: Henry S. Drinker, 1944

Ho - ly,_ ho - ly, ho - ly, Lord_ God_ Thou_ of Sa - ba - oth! All the _ heav - ens Ex - alt _ Thy _ maj - es - ty.

Sing Ho - san - na_ in _ the _ high - est. Ho - san - na, bless - ed _ He who comes _ in _ Thy Name. Sing Ho - san - na_ in _ the _ high - est.

## 236. Lord Jesus Christ, My Life, My Light†

*see also:* 295(D)
HYMN: Martin Behm, 1610
MELODY: Anonymous, 1594

O JESU CHRIST, MEINS LEBENS LICHT

TR.: Catherine Winkworth, 1863

† Sometimes published under the title *O Jesu, du mein Bräutigam.*

Lord Je - sus Christ, my Life,_ my Light, My_ strength by day, my_ trust by_ night, On _

earth I'm but a pass-ing_guest, And_ sore-ly_ with_ my_ sins_ op-press'd.

[2]
And when the last great day is come,
And Thou the Judge shall speak the doom,
Let me with joy behold the light,
And set me then upon Thy right.  (9/14)

## 237. Why Cast Down My Heart within Me

HYMN: Zacharias Hermann, 1690
MELODY: Johann Sebastian Bach, 1685–1750

*WAS BETRÜBST DU DICH, MEIN HERZE*

TR.: Charles Sanford Terry, 1929. By permission of Oxford University Press, London.

Why_ cast down my_ heart with-in me? Where-fore art_ dis- qui-et-ed?

Say then, what doth_ wound and press thee? Why's thy wont-ed cour-age_ fled?

Where-fore comes thy loud com-plain-ing? God's in heav'n, o'er earth is reign-ing.

[2]

Let your will to God be yielded:
Be assured He knoweth best.
Everything shall be fulfillèd
As His word makes manifest:

That all they who trust Him wholly,
And His counsels follow solely,
Never shall be put to shame,
But their dearest hopes obtain. (3/19)

## 238. On That Day That Christ Our Lord Predicted

*ES WIRD SCHIER DER LETZTE TAG HERKOMMEN*

HYMN: Michael Weisse, 1531
MELODY: Anonymous, 1531

TR.: William H. Gardner, 1963

On that day that Christ our Lord predicted,
He will judge the world with sin afflicted.
At the hour that Christ foretold, Judgment shall unfold.

[2]

Grant that we may here on earth be near Thee,
Through our preparation learn to hear Thee,

That we may Thy vision see
For eternity. (19/19)

216

## 239. Father, Lord of Mercy

HYMN: Michael Weisse, 1531
MELODY: Anonymous, 1531

DEN VATER DORT OBEN

TR.: Anonymous (*Moravian Hymn Book*, 1754)

[2]
Lord! accept our graces
With this song of praises,
And forgive what is amiss,
For His sake who gain'd us bliss.

Christ, Thy blest example
Print upon us, that we may
Be God's living temple.  (5/5)

## 240. Now That the Sun Doth Shine No More

HYMN: Johann Friedrich Hertzog, 1692
MELODY: Adam Krieger, 1667

*NUN SICH DER TAG GEENDET HAT*

TR.: Catherine Winkworth, 1863

Now that the sun doth shine no more, And day hath reached its close, They calm-ly sleep who wept be-fore, The wea-ried find re-pose.

[2]
But Thou, my God, no rest doth know
In Thy unslumb'ring might;
Thou hatest darkness as Thy foe,
For Thou Thyself are light.  (2/9)

## 241. How Now, My Soul, Why Makest Sore Complaining

*WAS WILLST DU DICH, O MEINE SEELE, KRÄNKEN*

HYMN: Dietrich von dem Werder, 1653
MELODY: Anonymous, 1682

TR.: Charles Sanford Terry, 1929. By permission of Oxford University Press, London.

How now, my soul, why mak-est sore com-plain-ing? Dost
e'er sup-pose that God thy prayer's dis-dain-ing? Right

God thy prayer's dis-dain-ing?

God thy prayer's dis-dain-ing?

[2]

So, Death and Satan both I do condemn them.
God is my God and I His own possession.
And if a cross I bear, I know 'tis best,
I leave it all to Him and am at rest.
I hold Him closely:
He willeth, so it shall be.

He'll loose the bonds of sin wherein I languish,
And so I calm abide;
For who trusts God, puts else beside,
Shall never know shame's anguish. (9/9)

## 242. O Soul within Me, Why Art Thou So Distressed

*WIE BIST DU, SEELE, IN MIR SO GAR BETRÜBT*

HYMN: Tobias Zeutschner, c.1699
MELODY: Anonymous, 1675

TR.: William H. Gardner, 1963

O soul with-in me, why art thou so dis-tressed? His grace He gives thee, thou whom His love hath blessed. Give of thy-self with gra-cious will-ing And thou wilt find thy sor-rows still-ing.

[2]
If thou dost suffer, then to His voice give ear,
Thou wilt discover He holds thy life so dear.

He whose own life in anguish ended
For thy misdeeds salvation sendeth.  (2/6)

## 243. Jesu, Thou My Dearest Treasure

*JESU, DU MEIN LIEBSTES LEBEN*

HYMN: Johann Rist, 1641
MELODY: Johann Schop, 1642

TR.: Charles Sanford Terry, 1929. By permission of Oxford University Press, London.

Je-su, Thou my dear-est Treas-ure,
All Thou didst for me I meas-ure,
Bride-groom of my
By Thy Pas-sion's
Bride-groom of my lov-
By Thy Pas-sions cru-
Bride-groom of my
By Thy Pas-sion's

lov - ing heart,
cru - el smart.

- ing heart,
- el smart.

Je - su, joy beyond all oth - er, All my
Sav - iour, Lord, and sweet - est treas - ure. Ah, how

lov - ing heart.
cru - el smart.

heart and soul hast won. Thou'rt my Mas - ter, Light, and Sun,
can I worth - i - ly, Je - su, sing my praise to Thee.

[2]
O Thou great and glorious Presence,
Shining from Thy throne divine,
Of eternal good the Essence,
Once on earth to make men Thine!

Well I know that I am mortal,
Worthless, evil in Thy sight,
Dark my soul as blackest night.
Can I dare pass heaven's portal?
Lord, no hope on earth I have
If Thou wilt not stoop to save.  (2/13)

## 244. Jesu, Jesu, Thou Art Mine

*JESU, JESU, DU BIST MEIN*

HYMN: Anonymous, 1687
MELODY: Johann Sebastian Bach, 1736          TR.: Robert W. Ottman, 1963

Je - su, Je - su, Thou art mine, While on earth I must be liv - ing,

I am now and ev - er Thine, All to Thee my fate re - sign - ing.

All_ my life_ to_ Thee be_ grate-ful, E'en in_ death re - main-ing faith-ful;

Bod - y, soul,_ to Thee con - sign, Je - su,_ Je - su, Thou art_ mine.

[ 2 ]
Jesu, Jesu, Thou art mine,
Now in Thee I find my treasure,
In Thy courts of heav'n sublime.
Now to find in fullest measure

All the joys and bliss of heaven;
Angel hosts surround me ever
Where forever I am Thine;
Jesu, Jesu, Thou art mine.  (8/8)

## 245. Christ, Everlasting Source of Light

HYMN: Wolfgang Meusel(?), 1526
MELODY: Anonymous, 1535

*CHRISTE, DER DU BIST TAG UND LICHT*

TR.: John Christian Jacobi, 1725

Christ, ev - er - last-ing_ source of _ light, All things lie_ nak-ed_ in _ Thy sight, Thou

splen-dor_ of _ Thy_ Fa - ther's face, Teach us_ to _ tread the_ path of_ grace.

[ 2 ]
Dispel our sinful drowsiness,
Guard us, when Satan will oppress,

The feeble flesh keep chaste and pure,
That we may rest in Thee secure.  (3/7)

## 246. Sing a New Song to the Lord

HYMN: Matthäus Apelles von Löwenstern, 1644, (Psalm 149)
MELODY: Matthäus Apelles von Löwenstern, 1644

SINGT DEM HERRN EIN NEUES LIED

TR.: Charles Sanford Terry, 1929. By permission of Oxford University Press, London.

Let the con-gre-ga-tion praise Him,
Looking down on earth so lov-ing.

Sing a new song to the Lord, Let the con-gre-ga-tion praise Him,
Who to us doth peace af-ford, Look-ing down on earth so lov-ing.

Let the con-gre-ga-tion praise Him.
Look-ing down on earth so lov-ing.

Is-ra-el there-fore re-joice ye For the good things He hath

done! Help when trib-u-la-tions come, Be as-sured, He'll ne'er de-ny thee.

[2]
Praise, O Zion, praise Thy God,
Let Thy children loudly praise Him,
In high honor Him adore,
To His Name fine anthems raising!

Sound the strings in jubilation,
With the harp make merry sound,
Lauding Him, as ye are bound,
Tell His deeds to every nation. (2/4)

## 247. When in the Hour of Utmost Need

see also: 68
HYMN: Paul Eber, c.1560
MELODY: Louis Bourgeois, 1547

WENN WIR IN HÖCHSTEN NOTEN SEIN

TR.: Catherine Winkworth, 1863

When in the hour of ut-most need We know not where to look for aid, When

days and__ nights of__ anx - ious thought Nor help nor coun-sel__ yet__ have brought.

[2]
Then this our comfort is alone:
That we may meet before Thy throne,
And cry, O faithful God, to Thee,
For rescue from our misery.  (2/7)

### 248.  Oh Praise and Honor God Our King

*SEI LOB UND EHR DEM HÖCHSTEN GUT*
ES IST DAS HEIL UNS KOMMEN HER

TR.: Mevany Roberts, 1936. Copyright 1936 by Breit-kopf & Haertel, Leipzig, reprinted by permission of the original copyright owner and Associated Music Publishers, Inc., New York.

see also: 4, 290, 329, 335, 354(D)
SOURCE: Cantata No. 117, c.1733
HYMN: Johann Jakob Schütz, 1675
MELODY: Anonymous, fifteenth century

Oh__ praise and__ hon - or__ God__ our__ King, The Fa - ther__ of__ all__
The__ God whose won - ders__ all__ men sing, The God__ whose lov - ing__

good - ness,  My__ heart with__ com - fort__ rich__ doth__ fill, The__
kind - ness

God__ who__ pain and__ grief doth__ still. Give God,__ our__ Lord, the__ glo - ry!

[2]*
So come ye now before His Face,
With triumph sing before Him;
Pay now your vows in His High Place,
With joy and praise adore Him:

God in His wisdom and His might
Doth all things well, and all things right!
Give God, our Lord, the glory!  (9/9)

## 249. All Glory Be to God on High

see also: 125, 313, 326, 353(D)
HYMN: Nikolaus Decius, 1525
MELODY: Anonymous, 1539

ALLEIN GOTT IN DER HÖH SEI EHR

TR.: Catherine Winkworth, 1863

All glory be to God on high, Who hath our race befriended!
To us no harm shall now come nigh, The feud at last is
ended;
God showeth His good-will t'ward men, And
peace shall dwell on earth a-gain; Oh thank Him for His good-ness.

[2]
We praise, we worship Thee, we trust
And give Thee thanks forever,
O Father, that thy rule is just
And wise, and changes never:

Thy boundless pow'r o'er all things reigns,
Done is what-e'er Thy will ordains;
Well for us that Thou rulest! (2/4)

## 250. A Safe Stronghold Our God Is Still

see also: 20, 273
HYMN: Martin Luther, 1529
MELODY: Martin Luther, 1529

EIN FESTE BURG IST UNSER GOTT

TR.: Thomas Carlyle, 1795–1881, alt.

A safe strong-hold our God is still, A trust-y shield and weap-on;
He'll help us clear from all the ill That hath us now o'er-tak-en.

The old prince of Hell, His sole pur-pose fell; With craft and with pow'r He wear-eth in this hour; On earth is not his fel - low.

[2]
With force of arms we nothing can,
Full soon we were downridden;
But for us fights the proper man,
Whom God Himself hath bidden.

Ask, Who is this same?
Christ Jesus His name,
Lord Sabaoth's Son;
He, and no other one,
Shall conquer in the battle. (2/4)

## 251. 'Tis Well with Me, for by Thy Might

HYMN: Simon Dach, 1648, (stanza 1); Anonymous
(stanza 2).†
MELODY: Johann Sebastian Bach, 1685–1750

*ICH BIN JA, HERR, IN DEINER MACHT*

TR.: Henry S. Drinker, 1944

† Stanza 2 is found in Schemelli's *Gesang-Buch*, 1736,
where it is associated with stanza 1 of Dach's hymn in a
setting of a melody by Heinrich Albert (1648) with figured
bass line by Bach.

'Tis well with me, for by Thy might, Thou mak-est me to see the light,
Thou count-est well the days and years Still left me in this vale of tears,

'Tis well with me for by Thy might, Thou mak-est me to see the light, To Thee my life it-self is ow - ing,
Thou count-est well the days and years Still left me in this vale of tears, And when from here I must be go - ing.

How, when and where I am to die, Thou know-est, Fa - ther, more than I.

[ 2 ]
Give thou, My child, thyself to Me,
Who one time gave thy life to thee,
And here on earth did well protect it.
'Tis I who give to thee thy breath
And when I shall decree thy death
'Twill come to pass as I direct it.

The time, the place, the very hour
Are in my hands, are in my pow'r.

## 252. Now Join We All to Praise Thee

*JESU, NUN SEI GEPREISET*

see also: 11, 327
HYMN: Johann Hermann(?), 1591
MELODY: Anonymous, 1591

TR.: Henry S. Drinker, 1944

Now join we all to praise Thee, This joy - ous New Year's Day, For
We thank Thee that we meet here At this glad fest - al time, With

all the man - y bless - ings That drive our cares a - way.
gra - cious mer - cy lad - en, And last - ing peace sub - lime;

That free and un - de - feat - ed, The old year we com - plet - ed, To

Thee in deep de-vo-tion, Would we be ev-er near. Pre-

serve us, soul and bod - y, Through-

out the com - ing year, In safe-ty watch and

In safe-ty watch and

In safe-ty watch and

guard us, Through all the com-ing year.

[2]

To Thee alone be glory,
To Thee alone be praise;
In trouble teach us patience,
And govern all our ways,
Until at last in heaven,
From care and trouble free,
In peace and joy and gladness,
We may be one with Thee.

Our needs and ventures measure,
According to Thy pleasure,
And so Thy people, bringing,
To Thee their faith sincere,
With trusting hearts are singing:
Bless Thou this coming year;
With trusting hearts are singing:
Bless Thou this coming year. *(3/3)*

# 253. Ah, God, from Heaven Look Anew†

see also: 3, 262
SOURCE: Cantata No. 77, c.1725
HYMN: Martin Luther, 1524, (stanza 1); David Denicke,
1657, (stanza 2).
MELODY: Anonymous, 1524

ACH GOTT VON HIMMEL SIEH DAREIN

TR.: Henry S. Drinker, 1944

† In the manuscript of Cantata No. 77, no words are
found with this harmonization. Carl Friedrich Zelter (1758–
1832) supplied stanza 8 of David Denicke's hymn, *Wenn
einer alle Ding verstund.*

Ah, God, from heav-en_ look a-new May we_ Thy pi-ty_ wak-
en; How scan-ty_ are_ the_ faith-ful few, Let us_ not_
be_ for-sak-en! Thy Ho-ly Word men_ hold not_ true,
Nor seek, with_ faith, Thy will_ to do; Thy folk are sore-ly_ shak-en.

[2]*
Thou, Jesus, who art far above
All others as love's teacher,
Give me, too, grace and strength to love
My God and fellow creature;

That I may do what-e'er I can,
In friendship true for ev'ry man,
According to Thy pleasure.

## 254. Faithful God, I Lay Before Thee†

see also: 29, 64(D), 67, 76, 256, 282(D), 298
SOURCE: Cantata No. 25, c.1731
HYMN: Johann Heermann, 1630
MELODY: Louis Bourgeois, 1551

*TREUER GOTT, ICH MUSS DIR KLAGEN*
FREU DICH SEHR, O MEINE SEELE

TR.: John Christian Jacobi, 1722

† Sometimes published under the title *Weg, mein Herz, mit dem Gedanken.*

Faith - ful God, I lay__ be - fore Thee All the__ an - guish__ of__ my__ heart:
Though Thou know'st how grief has torn me, Bet - ter__ than I____ can__ im - part:

Lord, my__ weak - ness makes me__ cry In__ temp - ta - tion, when I__ vie

With the fiend that would be - reave me Of__ the faith Thou giv'st to__ save me.

[ 2 ]*
All my life shall be employèd
In Thy praise, with all my might,
That the fiend has been destroyèd
And with shame has lost the fight.
Glorious shall Thy mercy be,
Here and in eternity;
Heav'n and earth, O great Jehovah!
Shall resound with Hallelujahs. *(12/12)*

# 255. What Is the World to Me

see also: 85, 291, 312
SOURCE: Cantata No. 64, 1723
HYMN: Georg Michael Pfefferkorn, 1671
MELODY: Anonymous, 1679

WAS FRAG ICH NACH DER WELT
O GOTT, DU FROMMER GOTT†

TR.: August Crull, 1846–1923, alt. Reprinted by permission of Concordia Publishing House from *The Handbook of the Lutheran Hymnal* by W. G. Polack (1942).

† First tune.

Soprano, Violin I, Trumpet
Alto, Violin II, Trombone I

Tenor, Viola, Trombone II
Bass, Trombone III

Organ, Continuo

* What is the world to me With all its vaunted pleasure, When Thou, and Thou a-lone, Lord Jesus, art my Treasure! Thou on-ly, dearest Lord, My soul's de-light shalt

be; Thou art my Peace, my_ Rest, -- What is_ the_ world to_ me.

[2]
The world is like a cloud
And like a vapor fleeting,
A shadow that declines,
Swift to its end retreating.

My Jesus doth abide,
Though all things fade and flee;
My everlasting Rock,—
What is the world to me!  (2/8)

## 256. Faithful God, I Lay Before Thee†

*see also:* 29, 64(D), 67, 76, 254, 282(D), 298
SOURCE: Cantata No. 194, 1723
HYMN: Johann Heermann, 1630
MELODY: Louis Bourgeois, 1551

❧ *TREUER GOTT, ICH MUSS DIR KLAGEN*
FREU DICH SEHR, O MEINE SEELE

TR.: John Christian Jacobi, 1722

————

† Sometimes published under the title *Jesu, deine tiefen Wunden.*

Oboe I, II

Oboe III

Soprano, Violin I
Alto, Violin II

Faith - ful God, _ I lay _ be - fore_ Thee
Though Thou know'st_ how grief_ has _ torn_ me,

Tenor, Viola
Bass, Continuo

All the_ an - guish of _ my_ heart:
Bet - ter_ than I_ can_ im - part:

Lord, my weak - ness

makes me cry In — temp-ta - tion, when I vie With the — fiend that

would be - reave — me Of — the — faith Thou giv'st to — save — me.

[ 2 ]*
Holy Ghost, of equal honor
With the Father and the Son,
Of all gifts the only donor,
Hear me from Thy Holy throne:
Through Thy mercy I believe,
Let me not myself deceive,
But depend in this my weakness
Of Thy all sufficient greatness. (6/12)

[ 3 ]*
Rescue me from present dullness;
Thy good work in me advance;
And relieve me from the fullness
Of Thy gracious countenance;
Keep the little spark of grace,
That with joy I run my race,
And obtain the prize of Zion
Which I ever keep my eye on. (7/12)

## 257. Awake My Heart Rejoicing

*WACH AUF, MEIN HERZ, UND SINGE*
NUN LASST UNS GOTT DEM HERREN

Duplicate of Chorale 93.

### 258. In God's Most Holy Name, My Eyelids Now I Close

HYMN: Matthäus Apelles von Löwenstern, 1644
MELODY: Matthäus Apelles von Löwenstern, 1644
TR.: Robert W. Ottman, 1963

*MEIN AUGEN SCHLIESS ICH JETZT IN GOTTES NAMEN ZU*

In God's most ho-ly name, my eye-lids now I close, My bod-y wear-i-ly is long-ing for re-pose; Who knows, I may not see to-mor-row's sun a-ris-ing, The time of death for me is of His own ad-vis-ing.

[ 2 ]

I give Thee from my heart my pray'rful thanks and praise,
And still will I give thanks now and throughout my days;

And as my Lord has willed to keep me this day safely,
I fear no evil now, I know no ill can reach me.    (2/6)

### 259. In These Our Days So Perilous

*VERLEIH UNS FRIEDEN GNÄDIGLICH*

Duplicate of Chorale 91.

## 260. 'Tis Sure That Awful Time Will Come

ES IST GEWISSLICH AN DER ZEIT

see also: 362
HYMN: Bartholomäus Ringwaldt, c.1556       TR.: John Christian Jacobi, 1722
MELODY: Anonymous, 1535

'Tis sure that aw-ful_ time will come, When Christ, the_ Lord of glo - ry,
Shall from His throne give men their doom, And change what's trans-i - to - ry.

Who then will ven - ture_ to re - tire When all's_ to_ be con-

sumed by fire, As_ Pe - ter_ has_ de - clar - ed.

[ 2 ]
O Jesu, shorten Thy delay
And hasten Thy salvation,
That we may see that glorious day
Produce a new creation.

O come, O Lord, our Judge and King!
Come! Change our mournful notes to sing
Thy praise forever, Amen.  (7/7)


## 261. Christ in the Bonds of Death Was Laid

CHRIST LAG IN TODESBANDEN

see also: 15, 184, 371
SOURCE: Cantata No. 158, c.1715       TR.: Arthur Tozer Russell, 1851, alt.
HYMN: Martin Luther, 1524
MELODY: Adaptation, 1524, of Christ ist erstanden

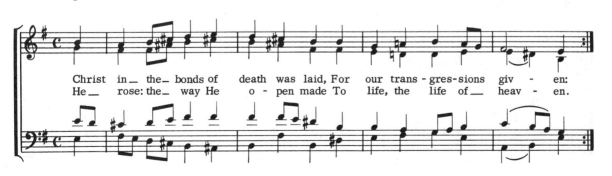

Christ in_ the_ bonds of death was laid, For our trans - gres-sions giv - en:
He_ rose: the_ way He o - pen made To life, the life of_ heav - en.

There-fore we_ will now re-joice, And praise our God with thank-ful_voice, So_

sing we now_ Hal - le - lu - jah.  Hal - le - lu - jah!

Hal - le - lu - jah!

[ 2 ]*
This is the true, the Paschal Lamb,
Assign'd to us from heaven:
His life to love's consuming flame
Upon the cross was given.

If on us His blood appear,
Faith holds by this, though death be near:
Subdued is Satan's awful pow'r.
Hallelujah!  (5/7)

## 262. Look Down, O Lord, from Heaven Behold

*ACH GOTT VOM HIMMEL, SIEH DAREIN*

see also: 3, 253
SOURCE: Cantata No. 2, c.1740
HYMN: Martin Luther, 1524, (Psalm 12)
MELODY: Anonymous, 1524

TR.: Frances E. Cox, 1812–1897

Look down, O Lord, from heav'n be - hold, And let Thy_ pit - y
How few the flock with - in_ Thy fold, Neg - lect - ed_ and for -

wak - en!  Al - most thou'lt seek for_ faith in vain, And those who should Thy
sak - en!

truth_ main-tain Thy Word from_ us_ have_ tak - en.

[ 2 ]*

Thy truth Thou wilt preserve, O Lord,
From this vile generation;
Make us to lean upon Thy word,
With calm anticipation.

The wicked walk on every side
When, 'mid Thy flock, the vile abide
In power and exhaltation.  (6/6)

## 263. Jesu, Priceless Treasure

*ee also:* 96, 138, 283, 324, 356
SOURCE: Motet No. 3, *Jesu meine Freude*
HYMN: Johann Franck, 1653
MELODY: Johann Crüger, 1653

*JESU, MEINE FREUDE*

TR.: Catherine Winkworth, 1869

Je - su, price - less treas - ure, Source of_ pur - est_ pleas - ure,
Long my heart hath pant - ed 'Till_ it_ well - nigh_ faint - ed,

Tru - est_ Friend to me! Thine I am, O spot - less Lamb!
Thirst-ing_ aft - er Thee.

I will suf - fer nought to_ hide_ Thee, Ask for_ nought be - side_ Thee.

[ 2 ]*

Hence all thoughts of sadness!
For the Lord of gladness,
Jesus, enters in.
Those who love the Father,
Though the storms may gather,
Still have peace within;

Yea, what-e'er I here must bear,
Thou art still my purest pleasure,
Jesu, priceless treasure!  (6/6)

237

## 264. Jesus, Thou My Heart's Great Joy

HYMN: Johann Flittner, 1660
MELODY: Johann Rodolph Ahle, 1660

*⸲{ JESU, MEINES HERZENS FREUD*

TR.: William H. Gardner, 1963

Je - sus, Thou my heart's great joy, Bless-ed Je - sus. Would I ___
might Thy love en - joy, Bless-ed ___ Je - sus. To my ___ life Thou
came to bring Joy ful - fill - ing, Je - sus, ___ dear-est Je - sus.

[ 2 ]
Often times I think of Thee, Blessed Jesus.
How I long Thy face to see, Blessed Jesus.

Thou did'st come with love divine,
Saving mankind, Jesus, my Redeemer.    (2/5)

## 265. The Will of God Be Alway Done

*⸲{ WAS MEIN GOTT WILL, DAS G'SCHEH
ALLZEIT*

see also: 41, 115, 120, 349(D)
SOURCE: Cantata No. 144, c.1725
HYMN: Albrecht, Markgraf of Brandenburg-Culmbach,
   c.1554
MELODY: Anonymous, c.1529

TR.: John Troutbeck, 1832–1899, (stanza 1), by permission of G. Schirmer, Inc., New York; Henry S
Drinker, 1944, (stanza 2).

wise -
Him ___

* The will of God be al - way done, His will that ___ wise - ly
His help is nigh to ___ ev - 'ry one Whose faith on ___ Him a -

[2]
Once more, O God, I ask of Thee,
Nor will Thou this deny me:
When base temptations trouble me,
With faith and hope supply me.

O God, our Lord, Thy help afford,
Thy name to render glorious;
And send, I pray, that promised day,
When right will be victorious. *(4/4)*

## 266. Lord Jesus Christ, I Cry to Thee

*HERR JESU CHRIST, ICH SCHREI ZU DIR*
HERR JESU CHRIST, DU HÖCHSTES GUT

*see also:* 73, 92, 294
SOURCE: Cantata No. 48, *c.*1740
HYMN: Anonymous, 1620
MELODY: Anonymous, 1593

TR.: Henry S. Drinker, 1944

Lord Je - sus Christ, I cry_ to_ Thee, In_ woe all_ woe ex - cell - ing.
Let Thou Thy grace de - scend on_ me, And make my_ heart Thy dwell - ing.

The great and griev-ous care and pain Which rends my heart with might and main, Is past all mor-tal tell - ing.

[2]*
My heart, O Lord, is sore distressed
By all the woes that grieve it,
And since to Thee is manifest,
Thou can and will relieve it.
So at Thy side I take my stand,
My heart I place at Thy command;
Do Thou in grace receive it.   (12/12)

### 267.  Remove from Us, O Faithful God

see also: 47, 110, 292
SOURCE: Cantata No. 90, c.1740
HYMN: Martin Moller, 1584
MELODY: Anonymous, 1539

*NIMM VON UNS, HERR, DU TREUER GOTT*
VATER UNSER IM HIMMELREICH

TR.: John Christian Jacobi, 1722

Re - move from us,— O— faith-ful_God, Thy dread-ful and_ a - veng-ing rod, The num-ber_ of our cry-ing crimes Has well de-serv'd a_ thou-sand times, Sad

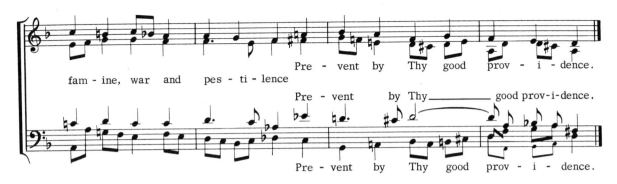

famine, war and pestilence Prevent by Thy good providence.

Prevent by Thy_____ good providence.

Prevent by Thy good providence.

[2]*
O Lord conduct us by Thy Hand,
And bless these realms by sea and land;
Preserve Thy word amongst us pure,
Keep us from Satan's wiles secure;

Grant us to die in peace and love,
And see Thy glorious face above. (7/7)

## 268. My Soul Now Praise Thy Maker

see also: 7, 116, 296

❧ *NUN LOB, MEIN SEEL, DEN HERREN*

HYMN: Johann Graumann, 1540, (Psalm 103)
MELODY: Johann Kugelmann(?), 1540

TR.: Catherine Winkworth, 1863

My soul now praise thy Maker! Let all within me bless His name,
Who maketh thee partaker Of mercies more than thou dar'st claim.

Forget Him not whose meekness Still bears with all thy sin, Who healeth

all thy weakness, Renews thy life within, Whose grace and care are

endless, And sav'd thee through the past; Who leaves no

suf - f'rer friend - less, But rights the wronged at last!

**[2]**
He shows to man His treasure
Of judgment, truth, and righteousness,
His love beyond our measure,
His yearning pity o'er distress;
Nor treats us as we merit,
But lays His anger by;

The humble, contrite spirit
Finds His compassions nigh;
And high as heav'n above us,
As break from close of day,
So far, since He doth love us,
He puts our sins away.   (2/4)

## 269. Jesus, by Thy Cross and Passion

*JESU, DER DU MEINE SEELE*

*see also:* 37, 297, 369
HYMN: Johann Rist, 1641
MELODY: Anonymous, 1642

TR.: Henry S. Drinker, 1944

Je - sus by Thy Cross and Pas - sion, By the
When the E - vil One would hold me, Deep in

bit - ter pain Thou bore, Might - i - ly a - way Thou bore
Hell to suf - fer sore,

me, With a ha - ven safe be - fore me, Through Thy Word, con -

tent - ment sweet, Thou art still my sure re - treat.

**[2]**

Lord, I trust Thee, I adore Thee,
Help my weakness, my despair;
Thou canst strengthen, Thou restore me,
When misdeeds my faith impair.

On Thy loving Grace relying,
God Almighty glorifying,
By Thy side I hope to be
Ever through Eternity. *(12/12)*

## 270. My Heart Is Filled with Longing†

*see also:* 21, 74, 80, 89, 98, 286, 345, 367
SOURCE: Cantata No. 161, 1715
HYMN: Christoph Knoll, 1605
MELODY: Hans Leo Hassler, 1601

→§ *HERZLICH TUT MICH VERLANGEN*

TR.: Catherine Winkworth, 1863, (stanza 1); Henry S.
Drinker, 1944, (stanza 2).

————————

† Sometimes published under the title *Befiehl du deine
Wege.*

Flute I, II

Soprano, Violin I
Alto, Violin II

My heart is filled with long - ing To
For woes are round me throng - ing, And

Tenor, Viola
Bass, Continuo

pass a - way in peace; O fain would I be
tri - als will not cease.

hast - ing From thee, dark __ world of __

gloom, To glad - ness ev - er -

last - ing; O __ Je - sus! __ quick - ly __ come! __

[ 2 ]*
Though worms our flesh devouring,
Deep buried in the earth,
Our souls are soon awaking
Through Christ, assur'd rebirth.

With God in radiant glory,
From care forever free,
In heav'nly joy and rapture,
What fear has death for me?   (4/11)

244

# 271. Have Faith in God, nor E'er Distress Thee

*GIB DICH ZUFRIEDEN UND SEI STILLE*

HYMN: Paul Gerhardt, 1666
MELODY: Johann Sebastian Bach, 1725

TR.: Charles Sanford Terry, 1929. By permission of Oxford University Press, London.

Have faith in God, nor e'er dis - tress thee, Con - stant on His love re - ly - ing;
In Him your joy is found in plen - ty, His love still - eth all thy sigh - ing.
He is our Sun, our Source, Light - giv - er, Who lights us on our path - way ev - er. Faint heart, cease griev - ing, cease griev - ing!

[2]
The dawn's at hand when God shall call us
To His Father's home in glory,
And from the ills that here befall us
Will release our spirit surely.

No more may Death our spirit threaten:
God wipes away all tears in heaven.
Faint heart, cease grieving, cease grieving!   (*14/15*)

245

## 272. We Thank Thee, Lord, for Sending

ICH DANK DIR, LIEBER HERRE

see also: 2, 341
HYMN: Johann Kolross, c.1535
MELODY: Anonymous, 1544

TR.: Henry S. Drinker, 1944

We thank Thee, Lord, for sending A gain the morn ing light,
safe a vert ed The dan gers of the night;

That Thou hast With dark ness deep a round us, We lay in dead ly fear; But foes could not con found us, For Thou, our God wert near.

[ 2 ]
Confer Thou faith upon me
In Jesus Christ Thy Son,
And grant me now the pardon,
That He for me has won.

Thou wilt not now deny me,
That which Thou didst agree;
From sin to purify me,
And lift its load from me.     (4/9)

## 273. A Sure Stronghold Our God Is He

*EIN FESTE BURG IST UNSER GOTT*

*see also:* 20, 250

TR.: Catherine Winkworth, 1863

SOURCE: Cantata No. 80, 1730
HYMN: Martin Luther, 1529
MELODY: Martin Luther, 1529

A — sure strong-hold our God is He, A— trust-y— shield and weap - on;
Our help He'll be— and set us free From ev - ery ill— can hap - pen.

That old ma - li - cious foe Means us— dead-ly woe; Armed with might from—

Hell, And deep-est— craft as— well, On— earth is— not— his— fel - low.

[ 2 ]*
Still shall they leave that word His might,
And yet no thanks shall merit;
Still is He with us in the fight
By His good gifts and spirit.
E'en should they take our life,
Wealth, name, child or wife—
Though all these be gone,
Yet nothing have they won,
God's kingdom our's abideth. (4/4)

247

## 274. Eternity! Tremendous Word

*see also:* 26
HYMN: Johann Rist, 1642
MELODY: Johann Schop, 1642

TR.: John Christian Jacobi, 1722

O EWIGKEIT, DU DONNERWORT

E - ter - ni - ty! Tre - men - dous word. Home - strik - ing_ point, heart-
E - ter - ni - ty! With - out a_ shade, When - ev - er_ fi - ery_

pierc-ing sword, Be - gin - ning with - out end - ing! One_ glimpse of_
bil - lows roar, What is_ Thy sight por - tend - ing?

Thine un - fath - omed deep Would rouse a _ wretch from sin - ful sleep.

[ 2 ]
What pain was ever thought so great
That it must not with time abate
And lose its utmost rigor?
Eternity does never cease,
Admits no manner of release,
But keeps its constant vigor.

Or as our Saviour's words express:
Eternity has no redress.   (2/16)

## 275. O World, Thy Life Doth Languish

*see also:* 50, 63, 103, 117, 289, 355, 363, 366
HYMN: Paul Gerhardt, 1647
MELODY: Anonymous, 1539

O WELT, SIEH HIER DEIN LEBE
O WELT, ICH MUSS DICH LASSI

TR.: Anna Hoppe, 1922. By permission of Erie Printi
Co., Erie, Pennsylvania.

O world, thy life doth lan - guish, Up - on_ the cross in _ an - guish, Thy

dy - ing Sav - iour see! The Prince of Glo - ry of - fers His

life for thee, and suf - fers Scorn, stripes and mal - ice will - ing - ly.

[2]
Draw near in meekness lowly;
Upon His body holy,
The crimson bloodstream see.

Unfathomed woe He knoweth,
His noble heart o'er floweth
With sighs of untold agony.  (2/16)

## 276. Let All Together Praise Our God

❧ *LOBT GOTT, IHR CHRISTEN ALLZUGLEICH*

TR.: Arthur Tozer Russell, 1851

*see also:* 54, 342
HYMN: Nikolaus Herman, 1560
MELODY: Nikolaus Herman, 1554

Let all to - geth - er praise our God Up - on His loft - y

throne; He hath the heav'ns un - clos'd to - day, And

**[2]**
He lays aside His majesty,
And seems as nothing worth,
He takes on Him a servant's form,

Who made both heav'n and earth,
Who made both heav'n and earth.  (3/8)

## 277. Thee, Lord, I Love with Sacred Awe

*HERZLICH LIEB HAB ICH DICH, O HERR*

*see also:* 58, 107
HYMN: Martin Schalling, 1571
MELODY: Anonymous, 1577

TR.: John Christian Jacobi, 1725

and my all, Whose blood re-deem-ed from the fall: Lord Je-sus Christ, Lord

Je-sus Christ, Thy sav-ing name Pre-serve me from e-ter-nal shame!

[2]
'Tis Thy free gift, what's counted mine,
My body, soul and mind is Thine,
With all this life's enjoyment:
Lord grant me such a grateful sense,
To make the praise of providence
My chief and best employment.

Preserve me from delusion free,
Destroy old Satan's tyranny,
In all afflictions bear me up
With Christian courage, faith and hope:
Great Saviour Christ!
Great Saviour Christ, my Sovereign Lord,
In time of death Thy help afford.   (2/3)

## 278. How Lovely Shines the Morning Star

*WIE SCHÖN LEUCHTET DER MORGENSTERN*

TR.: Anonymous, (*Moravian Hymn Book,* 1890)

*see also:* 86, 195(D), 305(D), 323
HYMN: Philipp Nicolai, 1599
MELODY: Philipp Nicolai(?), 1599

How love-ly shines the morn-ing star! The na-tions see and hail a-far The
Thou Da-vid's Son of Ja-cob's race, My bride-groom and my king of grace, For

light in Ju-dah shin-ing; Low-ly, ho-ly, Great and glo-rious, Thou vic-to-rious
Thee my heart is pin-ing!

251

Prince of grac - es, Fill - ing all the heav'n-ly plac - es.
Prince of grac - es,
Prince of grac - es,

[ 2 ]
O joy! To know that Thou, my Friend,
Art Lord, beginning without end,
The First and Last eternal!
And Thou at length, O glorious Grace!
Will take me to that holy place,
The home of joys supernal.
Amen! Amen!
Come and meet me, quickly greet me;
Draw me ever
Nearer to Thyself forever.   (7/7)

## 279. Alas! My God!

ACH GOTT UND HERR

see also: 40

TR.: Catherine Winkworth, 1863

SOURCE: Cantata No. 48, c.1740
HYMN: Johann Major(?) and Martin Rutilius(?), 1613
MELODY: Anonymous, 1625

A - las! My God! My sins are great, My con - science doth up -

braid me; And now I find That at my strait No

man hath pow'r to aid ——————————— me.

aid ———————————————— me.

aid ——————————— me.

[2]*
If pain and woe
Must follow sin,
Then be my path still rougher.
Here spare me not;
If heav'n I win,
On earth I gladly suffer.   (4/6)

## 280. One Thing Needful! Then, Lord Jesus

*EINS IST NOT! ACH HERR, DIES EINE*

HYMN: Johann Heinrich Schröder, 1697
MELODY: Anonymous, 1704

TR.: Frances E. Cox, 1812–1897

One thing need-ful!_ Then, Lord Je-sus, Keep this one thing in_ my_ mind;

All be-side, though first it please us, Soon a griev-ous yoke we_ find:

Be-neath it_ the_ heart is_ still fret-ting and striv-ing,_ No_ true, last-ing

hap - pi - ness___ ev - er de - riv - ing: The___ gain of___ this___ one thing all___

And teach me in all things to find some de - light.

loss can re - quite,

And teach me___ in all things to find some de - light.

And teach me in all things to find some de - light.

And teach me in all things to find some de - light.

[2]
Soul, wilt thou this one thing find thee?
Seek it in no earthly end;
Leave all nature far behind thee,
High above the world ascend:

For where God and man both in one are united,
With God's perfect fullness the heart is delighted;
There, there is the worthiest lot and the best,
My one and my all, and my joy, and my rest.
*(2/10)*

## 281. Ah Whither May I Fly

*WO SOLL ICH FLIEHEN HIN*
AUF MEINEN LIEBEN GOTT

*see also:* 25, 304, 331
SOURCE: Cantata No. 89, *c.*1730
HYMN: Johann Heermann, 1630
MELODY: Anonymous, 1609

TR.: Henry S. Drinker, 1944

Ah whith - er may___ I fly? So sore dis - tressed am I; Where

leav - ing sin___ be - hind___ me, May I de - liv - 'rance find___ me? Though

254

ev - 'ry__ one__ con - dole__ me, The world can - not__ con - sole__ me.

[ 2 ]*
However sore my need,
My Lord will ever heed.
I look for my salvation,
To Jesus' tribulation,

Whereby I triumph glorious,
O'er hell and sin victorious. (7/11)

## 282. Faithful God, I Lay before Thee

TREUER GOTT, ICH MUSS DIR KLAGEN
FREU DICH SEHR, O MEINE SEELE

Duplicate of Chorale 254.

## 283. Jesu, Priceless Treasure†

JESU, MEINE FREUDE

see also: 96, 138, 263, 324, 356
SOURCE: Motet No. 3, *Jesu, meine Freude*, 1723
HYMN: Johann Franck, 1653
MELODY: Johann Crüger, 1653

TR.: Henry S. Drinker, 1944

† Only stanza 4 of the poem *Jesu, meine Freude*, is included here. The contrapuntal harmonization was written specifically for this stanza.

Soprano

*Hence ye earth - ly rich - es,
Hence ye emp - ty splen - dor,

Alto

Hence, hence ye earth - ly rich - es, ye earth-ly
Hence, hence ye emp - ty splen - dor, ye emp-ty

Tenor

Hence, hence a - way ye earth-ly rich - es, ye earth-ly
Hence, hence a - way ye emp-ty splen - dor, ye emp-ty

Bass

Hence, hence, a - way, ye earth - ly rich - es,
Hence, hence, a - way, ye emp - ty splen - dor,

Accompaniment

Nor will an - y tri - al grieve

pain dis - dain, Nor, _____ will tri - al grieve___

pain dis - dain, Nor will tri - al grieve _____

Nor will an - y tri - al grieve _____

me, But that Je - sus leave me.

me, But that my Je - sus leave _____ me.

me, But that my Je - sus leave me, my Je - sus leave __ me.

me, But that my Lord, my Je - sus__ leave _____ me. (4/6)

## 284. Lord Jesus Christ, True Man and God

SOURCE: Cantata No. 127, c.1740
HYMN: Paul Eber, 1563
MELODY: Louis Bourgeois, 1551

*HERR JESU CHRIST, WAHR MENSCH UND GOTT†*

TR.: Catherine Winkworth, 1855

† Second tune.

Lord Jesus Christ, true Man and God, Who bor-est an-guish, scorn, the rod, And died at last up-on the tree, To bring Thy Father's grace to me; I pray Thee through that bit-ter woe Let me, a sin-ner, mer-cy know.

[ 2 ]*
Dear Lord, forgive us all our guilt,
Help us to wait until Thou wilt
That we depart; and let our faith
Be brave and conquer e'en in death,

Firm resting on Thy sacred Word,
Until we sleep in Thee, our Lord. (8/8)

## 285. Had God Not Come, May Israel Say

*WÄR GOTT NICHT MIT UNS DIESE ZEIT*
WO GOTT DER HERR NICHT BEI UNS HÄLT

see also: 31, 301, 336
HYMN: Martin Luther, 1524, (Psalm 124)
MELODY: Anonymous 1535

TR.: Richard Massie, 1800–1887

Had God not come may Is-rael say, Had God not come to aid us,
Our en-e-mies on that sad day Would sure-ly have dis-mayed us;

[2]
Their furious wrath, did God permit,
Would surely have consumed us,
And in the deep and yawning pit
With life and limb entombed us;
Like men o'er whom dark waters roll,
The streams had gone e'en o'er our soul,
And mightily o'erwhelmed us.   (2/3)

## 286. Commit Thou All That Grieves Thee

*BEFIEHL DU DEINE WEGE*
HERZLICH TUT MICH VERLANGEN

*see also:* 21, 74, 80, 89, 98, 270, 345, 367
HYMN: Paul Gerhardt, 1653
MELODY: Hans Leo Hassler, 1601

TR.: Arthur W. Farlander and Winfred Douglas, 1939.
By permission of The Church Pension Fund.

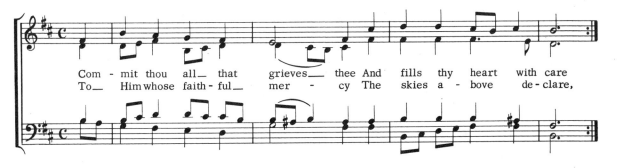

Com - mit thou all__ that grieves__ thee And fills thy heart with care
To__ Him whose faith - ful__ mer - cy The skies a - bove de - clare,

Who gives the winds their cours - es, Who points the clouds their way; 'Tis

He will guide thy foot - steps And be thy staff and stay.

And be thy staff and stay.

**[ 2 ]**

Hope on, then, broken spirit;
Hope on, be not afraid:
Fear not the griefs that plague thee
And keep thy heart dismayed:

Thy God, in His great mercy,
Will save thee, hold thee fast,
And in His own time grant thee
The sun of joy at last.  (6/12)

### 287. Lord, to Thee I Make Confession

*see also:* 33
HYMN: Johann Franck, 1649
MELODY: Johann Crüger, 1649

*HERR, ICH HABE MISSGEHANDELT*

TR.: Catherine Winkworth, 1863

Lord, to Thee I make con - fes - sion, I have sinned and gone a - stray,
I have mul - ti - plied trans - gres - sion, Cho - sen for my - self my way:

Forced at last to see my er - rors, Lord I trem - ble at Thy ter - rors.

**[ 2 ]**

Then on Thee I cast my burden,
Sink it in the depths below!
Let me feel Thy inner pardon,
Wash me, make me white as snow.
Let Thy spirit leave me never,
Make me only Thine forever!  (8/8)

## 288. Due Praises to th' Incarnate Love

GELOBET SEIST DU, JESU CHRIST

see also: 51, 160
HYMN†: Martin Luther, 1524
MELODY: Anonymous, 1524

TR.: John Christian Jacobi, 1722

† Kyrieleis from Kyrie eleison (Gk.), "Lord, have mercy."

Due prais-es to_ th'in - car - nate love Man - i - fest - ed_ from a - bove! All_ men_ and_ an - gels now_ a - dore What we nor_ they have seen _____ be - fore. Ky - rie e - leis!

[2]
The Father's Son, by nature God,
Took amongst us His abode,

And open'd through this world of strife
A way to everlasting life.
Kyrie eleis! (5/7)

## 289. Now All the Woods Are Sleeping

NUN RUHEN ALLE WÄLDER
O WELT, ICH MUSS DICH LASSEN

see also: 50, 63, 103, 117, 275, 355, 363, 366
HYMN: Paul Gerhardt, 1647
MELODY: Anonymous, 1539

TR.: Catherine Winkworth, 1863

Now all the_ woods are sleep - ing, And night and still - ness creep - ing O'er

cit - y,\_ man,\_ and\_ beast; But thou,\_ my\_ heart, a - wake\_ thee, To\_

prayer a - while be - take\_ thee, And praise thy Mak - er \_ e'er thou rest.

[ 2 ]
My heavy eyes are closing;
When I lie deep reposing,
Soul, body, where are ye?
To helpless sleep I yield them,
O let Thy mercy shield them;
Thou sleepless Eye, their guardian be!  (7/9)

## 290. Salvation unto Us Hath Come

*see also:* 4, 248, 329, 335, 354(**D**)
SOURCE: Cantata No. 9, 1731 or later
HYMN: Paul Speratus, 1524
MELODY: Anonymous, fifteenth century

*ES IST DAS HEIL UNS KOMMEN HER*

TR.: Anonymous (*Selah Song Book*, 1936)

Sal - va - tion un - to us\_ has come By\_ God's free grace and fa - vor,
Good works can-not a - vert our doom, They help and save us\_ nev - er.

Faith looks to Je - sus\_ Christ a - lone, Who did\_ for\_ all\_ the\_

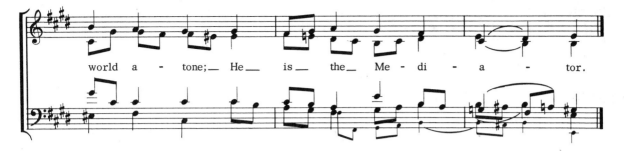

world a - tone;— He — is — the Me - di - a - tor.

[ 2 ]*
Though it may seem He hears thee not,
Count not thyself forsaken;
Thy wants are ne'er by Him forgot,
Let this thy hopes awaken;
His Word is sure, here is thy stay,
Although to this thy heart saith nay,
Let not thy faith be shaken.   *(12/14)*

## 291. What Is the World to Me

see also: 85, 255, 312
SOURCE: Cantata No. 64, 1723, (stanza 2); Cantata No. 94, 1735, (stanza 3).
HYMN: Georg Michael Pfefferkorn, 1671
MELODY: Anonymous, 1679

⋇ *WAS FRAG ICH NACH DER WELT*
O GOTT, DU FROMMER GOTT†

TR.: August Crull, 1846–1923, *alt.* Reprinted by permission of Concordia Publishing House from *The Handbook of the Lutheran Hymnal* by W. G. Polack (1942).

† First tune.

What is the — world to me With all — its — vaunt-ed — pleas - ure, When

Thou, and Thou — a - lone, Lord Je - sus, art my — Treas - ure! Thou

only,— dear-est Lord, My soul's de-light shall be; Thou

art my Peace, my Rest, -- What is the world to me!

[ 2 ]*
The world abideth not;
Lo, like a flash 'twill vanish;
With all its gorgeous pomp
Pale death it cannot banish;
Its riches pass away,
And all its joys must flee;
But Jesus doth abide,—
What is the world to me! (7/8)

[ 3 ]*
What is the world to me!
My Jesus is my Treasure,
My Life, my Health, my Wealth,
My Friend, my Love, my Pleasure,
My Joy, my Crown, my All,
My Bliss eternally.
Once more, then, I declare,—
What is the world to me! (8/8)

## 292. Remove from Us, O Faithful God

NIMM VON UNS, HERR, DU TREUER GOTT
VATER UNSER IM HIMMELREICH

*see also:* 47, 110, 267
SOURCE: Cantata No. 101, *c.*1740
HYMN: Martin Moller, 1584
MELODY: Anonymous, 1539

TR.: John Christian Jacobi, 1722

Oboe I, II, English Horn

Soprano, Flute in 8va, Trumpet, Violin I
Alto, Trombone I, Violin II

Tenor, Trombone II, Viola
Bass, Trombone III, Continuo

Re - move from us, O faith - ful God, Thy

dread - ful ___ and a - veng - ing rod, The num - ber ___ of our ___

cry - ing crimes Has well ___ de - serv'd a thou - sand ___ times, Sad

fa - mine, war and pes - ti - lence Pre - vent ___ by Thy good prov - i - dence.
Thy _____ good prov - i - dence.
Thy good prov - i - dence.

[ 2 ]*
O Lord, conduct us by Thy Hand,
And bless these realms by sea and land;
Preserve Thy word amongst us pure,
Keep us from Satan's wiles secure;
Grant us to die in peace and love,
And see Thy glorious face above. (7/7)

## 293. What-e'er my God Ordains Is Right

see also: 65, 347
SOURCE: Cantata No. 69, 1724
HYMN: Samuel Rodigast, 1676
MELODY: Johann Pachelbel(?), 1690

WAS GOTT TUT, DAS IST WOHLGETAN

TR.: Catherine Winkworth, 1863, *alt.*

What-e'er my God or-dains is right; His Ho-ly_ will a-bid-eth;
I will be still, what-e'er He doth, And fol-low_ where He guid-eth.

He is_ my_ God; Though dark_ my road, From fall-ing_ He_ doth_

hold___ me, Where-fore_ I_ trust_ Him_ sure-ly

[ 2 ]*
What-e'er my God ordains is right;
Here shall my stand be taken;
Though sorrow, need, or death be mine,
Yet am I not forsaken;

My Father's care is round me there;
From falling He doth hold me,
Wherefore I trust Him surely. (6/6)

## 294. Lord Jesus Christ, My Highest Good

see also: 73, 92, 260
SOURCE: Cantata No. 113, c.1740
HYMN: Bartholomäus Ringwaldt, 1588
MELODY: Anonymous, 1593

HERR JESU CHRIST, DU HÖCHSTES GUT

TR.: Catherine Winkworth, 1869, *alt.*

Lord Je-sus Christ, my high-est good, Who show-ers grace up-on___ me,
Be-hold how heav-y_ is my mood, Re-call-ing sins a-gainst_ Thee,

How sore my con-science is be-set With keen-est ar-rows of re-gret That nev-er cease to pierce me.

[ 2 ]*
Thy joyful Spirit give me strength,
Heal by Thy wounds, my Saviour,
When my last hour must come at length
Cleanse Thou my soul forever,

And take me when it seems Thee best,
In Thy true faith to heav'nly rest,
My bonds with Thee ne'er sever.  (8/8)

## 295. Lord Jesus Christ, My Life, My Light

*O JESU CHRIST, MEINS LEBENS LICHT*

Duplicate of Chorale 236.

## 296. My Soul Now Praise Thy Maker

*NUN LOB, MEIN SEEL, DEN HERREN*

see also: 7, 116, 268
HYMN: Johann Graumann, 1540, (Psalm 103)     TR.: Catherine Winkworth, 1863
MELODY: Johann Kugelmann(?), 1540

My soul now praise Thy Mak-er! Let all with-in me bless His name,
Who mak-eth thee par-tak-er Of mer-cies more than thou dar'st claim. For-get Him not whose

meek - ness Still bears with all thy sin, Who heal - eth all thy weak - ness, Re - news thy life with - in, Whose grace and care are end - less, And sav'd thee through the past; Who leaves no suf - f'rer friend - less, But rights the wrong'd at last.

[2]
His grace alone endureth,
And children's children yet shall prove
How God with strength assureth
The hearts of all that seek His love.
In heav'n is fixed His dwelling,
His rule is over all,
Angels in might excelling,
Bright hosts, before Him fall!

Praise Him who ever reigneth,
All ye who hear His word;
Now our poor hymns disdaineth,—
My soul, O praise the Lord! (4/4)

268

## 297. Jesus, by Thy Cross and Passion

see also: 37, 269, 369
SOURCE: Cantata No. 78, c.1740
HYMN: Johann Rist, 1641
MELODY: Anonymous, 1642

JESU, DER DU MEINE SEELE

TR.: Henry S. Drinker, 1944

Je - sus, by Thy Cross and Pas - sion, By the bit - ter pain Thou bore,

When the E - vil One would hold me, Deep in Hell to suf - fer sore,

Might - i - ly a - way Thou bore me, With a ha - ven safe be - fore me,

Through Thy Word, con - tent - ment sweet, Thou art still my sure re - treat.

[ 2 ]*
Lord, I trust Thee, I adore Thee,
Help my weakness, my despair;
Thou canst strengthen, Thou restore me,
When misdeeds my faith impair.
On Thy loving grace relying,
God Almighty glorifying,
By Thy side I hope to be
Ever through Eternity. (12/12)

269

## 298. O My Soul, Be Thou Rejoicing†

see also: 29, 64(D), 67, 76, 254, 256, 282(D)
SOURCE: Cantata No. 19, 1726
HYMN: Anonymous, 1620
MELODY: Louis Bourgeois, 1551

FREU DICH SEHR, O MEINE SEEL

TR.: Henry S. Drinker, 1944, alt.

† Sometimes published under the title *Weg, mein Her* *mit dem Gedanken.*

Trumpet I
Trumpet II, III
Timpani
Soprano, Violin I, Oboe I
Alto, Violin II, Oboe II
Tenor, Viola
Bass, Continuo

O my soul, be thou re - joic - ing, Cast a -
Christ the Lord for you is call - ing, Bids you

side all cares and fears; Out from woe and sore dis - tress,
leave this vale of tears.

Forth to —— joy — and bless - ed - ness, Joy   a - bound - ing, joy — tran-

6    6    6                    4 3 2 3        6          6    6    6  7
          5                                                          5

scend - ing, Ev - er - last - ing, nev - er   end —— ing.

9    8    6
5    -
4    3

[ 2 ]*
Let Thine angels not forsake me,
But to Thee, when life shall cease,
May Elijah's chariot take me
There, like Lazarus, in peace.
Let me rest in Thine embrace,
Fill my heart with joy and grace.
When my days on earth are ended,
May my soul with Thine be blended.   (9/10)

## 299. Jesus I Will Never Leave

see also: 152, 348
HYMN: Christian Keimann, 1658
MELODY: Andreas Hammerschmidt(?), 1658

*MEINEN JESUM LASS ICH NICHT, WE*

TR.: Anonymous (*Selah Song Book*, 1936)

Je - sus I will nev - er leave, Who for me Him - self has giv - en; There-fore un - to Him I'll cleave, Nor from Him be ev - er driv - en; Life from Him doth light re - ceive; My dear Je - sus, I'll not leave.

[ 2 ]
Jesus I will never leave,
While on earth I am abiding;
My full trust He shall receive;
What I have, without dividing,
All to Him I freely give!
My dear Jesus, I'll not leave.  (2/6)

## 300. Why Art Thou Thus Cast Down, My Heart?

see also: 94, 145
HYMN: Hans Sachs(?), 1565
MELODY: Anonymous, 1565

*WARUM BETRÜBST DU DICH, MEIN HERZ*

TR.: Catherine Winkworth, 1863

Why art thou thus cast down, my heart? Why trou - bled, why doth

mourn a-part, O'er nought but earth-ly wealth? Trust in thy God, be
not a-fraid, He is thy Friend who all things made.

[2]
Praise, honor, thanks to Thee be brought,
For all things in and for me wrought
By Thy great mercy, Christ.

This one thing only still I pray,
O cast me ne'er from Thee away.  (13/14)

## 301. Ye Christians Take Your Courage Up

*see also:* 31, 285, 336
SOURCE: Cantata No. 114, *c.*1740
HYMN: Johann Gigas, 1561
MELODY: Anonymous, 1535

*ACH, LIEBEN CHRISTEN, SEID GETROST*
WO GOTT DER HERR NICHT BEI UNS HÄLT

TR.: John Christian Jacobi, 1725

Ye Chris-tians take your cour-age up, Shake off your soul's op-
Will you re-ject the gen-erous cup Of God's own vis-i-

pres-sion! Let us con-fess His judg-ment's just, And
ta-tion?

[2]*
We wake or sleep, we live or die,
We are in God's possession,
Baptised in Christ, we now draw nigh
To God's own habitation:

What we have lost in Adam's fall,
Christ has recovered more than all,
Praised be the Lord of mercy. (6/6)

## 302. O Help Me, Lord, to Praise Thee

*HILF GOTT, DASS MIRS GELINGE*

Duplicate of Chorale 199.

## 303. Lord Christ, by God Engendered

*HERR CHRIST, DER EIN'GE GOTTS SOHN*

*see also:* 101
SOURCE: Cantata No. 96, *c.*1740          TR.: Henry S. Drinker, 1944
HYMN: Elisabethe Cruciger, 1524
MELODY: Anonymous, 1524

[2]*
Transform us by Thy kindness,
Awake us through Thy grace,
That we put on the New Man,
The Old Man's pow'r efface.

While here as mortals living,
With heartiest thanksgiving,
Our trust in Thee we place. (5/5)

# 304. O Whither Shall I Flee

see also: 25, 281, 331
SOURCE: Cantata No. 5, 1735
HYMN: Johann Heermann, 1630
MELODY: Anonymous, 1609

*⊰{ WO SOLL ICH FLIEHEN HIN*
AUF MEINEN LIEBEN GOTT

TR.: Anonymous (*Moravian Hymn Book*, 1789)

O whith-er__ shall I flee, De-pressed with__ mis-er-y? Who is it__ that can ease____ me, And from my__ sins re-lease__ me? Man's help I__ vain have prov-èd, Sin's load re-mains un-mov-èd.

[ 2 ]*
Lord, strengthen Thou my heart;
Such grace to me impart,
That nought which may await me

From Thee may separate me;
Let me with Thee, my Saviour,
United be forever.  (*11/11*)


# 305. How Bright Appears the Morning Star

*⊰{ WIE SCHÖN LEUCHTET DER MORGENSTERN*

Duplicate of Chorale 86.


# 306. O Man, Bewail Thy Grievous Fall

*⊰{ O MENSCH, BEWEIN DEIN SÜNDE GROSS*

Duplicate of Chorale 201.

## 307. See the Lord of Life and Light

Duplicate of Chorale 198.

*CHRISTUS, DER UNS SELIG MACH*

## 308. O Lord! How Many Miseries

Duplicate of Chorale 156.

*ACH GOTT, WIE MANCHES HERZELEID*

## 309. A Lamb Goes Forth: The Sins He Bears

Duplicate of Chorale 5. Chorale 309 is sometimes published in the transposed key of A♭.

*EIN LÄMMLEIN GEHT UND TRÄGT DIE SCHULD*

AN WASSERFLÜSSEN BABYLON

## 310. Thy Bonds, O Son of God Most High

*DURCH DEIN GEFÄNGNIS, GOTTES SOHN*

MACHS MIT MIR, GOTT, NACH DEINER GÜT

see also: 44
SOURCE: St. John Passion, 1723
HYMN: Christian Heinrich Postel, 1658–1705          TR.: John Troutbeck, 1832–1899
MELODY: Johann Hermann Schein, 1629

* Thy bonds, O Son of__ God most high, Have per-fect free-dom brought us.
And free, we to Thy throne come nigh, As Thou by__ grace hast taught__ us.

Hadst Thou dis-dain'd this bond-age sore, We__ had been bound for-ev-er-more.

## 311. While Yet the Morn Is Breaking

HYMN: Johannes Mühlmann, 1618
MELODY: Bartholomäus Gesius(?), 1605

*DANK SEI GOTT IN DER HÖHE*

TR.: Catherine Winkworth, 1863

While yet the morn is breaking I thank my God once more,
Be - neath whose care a - wak - ing I find the night is o'er;
I thank Him that He calls me To life and health a - new, I
know, what - e'er be - falls me, His care will still be true.

[2]
O gently grant Thy blessing
That we may do Thy will,
No more Thy ways transgressing,
Our proper task fulfill;

With Peter's full affiance
Let down our nets again;
If Thou art our reliance
Our toil will not be vain.  (5/7)

## 312. O Lord, We Welcome Thee

*ICH FREUE MICH IN DIR*
O GOTT, DU FROMMER GOTT†

see also: 85, 255, 291
SOURCE: Cantata, "Ehre sei Gott," 1728
HYMN: Caspar Ziegler, 1697
MELODY: Anonymous, 1679

TR.: Composite (*Lutheran Hymnal*, 1942). Reprinted
by permission of Concordia Publishing House from
*The Handbook of the Lutheran Hymnal* by W. G.
Polack (1942).

† First tune.

O Lord, we wel - come Thee, Our hearts for joy are leap - ing. Thou,

Je-sus, dear-est__ Child, Thy pre-cious prom-ise__ keep - ing, Art come from heav'n to __ earth To__ be our__ Broth-er__ dear; Thou gra-cious Son__ of __ God, Wilt__ ban-ish__ all our fear.

[ 2 ]*

To Thee alone we cling,
For Thee all else forsaking;
On Thee alone we build
Though heav'n and earth be quaking.

To Thee alone we live,
In Thee alone we die;
O Jesus, dearest Lord,
With Thee we reign on high.    (4/4)

## 313.  The Lord My Shepherd Is: My Need

*DER HERR IST MEIN GETREUER HIRT, HÄLT*
ALLEIN GOTT IN DER HÖH SEI EHR

*see also:* 125, 249, 326, 353(D)
SOURCE: Cantata No. 112, 1731
HYMN: Wolfgang Meusel, 1531, (Psalm 23)
MELODY: Anonymous, 1539

TR.: Arthur Tozer Russell, 1851, *alt.*

Horn I, II

English Horn I, II

Soprano, Violin I
Alto, Violin II

The__ Lord my Shep-herd__ is:__ my__ need His
He__ doth__ His sheep in__ mer-cy__ lead; On

Tenor, Viola
Bass, Continuo

278

gra - cious hand_ sup - pli - eth: He by His word pro - vid - eth_ peace, By_

Him my_ soul_ re - li - eth. He by His word pro - vid - eth_ peace, By_

hills and streams that ne'er shall cease; My_ wear-ied soul_ He guid - eth.

[2]*

For Thou around my path wilt be
To crown each day with blessing:
Then in Thy house may I with Thee
Abide, Thy name confessing.

All glory be, O God, in one,
The Holy Spirit, Father, Son,
To Thee our praise be given.  (5/5)

## 314. With This New Year We Raise New Songs

‹ DAS ALTE JAHR VERGANGEN IST

see also: 162

HYMN: Johann Steurlein(?) and Jakob Tapp(?), 1588     TR.: John Christian Jacobi, 1722
MELODY: Johann Steurlein, 1588

With this new year we_ raise new songs, With this new_ year we raise new songs, To

praise the Lord with hearts and tongues, For His sup-port in_ trou-bles past, Where-

with our_ life_ was o - ver-cast, Where-with our life_ was_ o - ver-cast.

[ 2 ]
Grant us to lead a Christian life,
Grant us to lead a Christian life;
And when we leave this world of strife,
Then raise us to that joyful day
Where Thou wilt wipe all tears away,
Where Thou wilt wipe all tears away.   (5/6)

### 315. O God, Thou Faithful God

*O GOTT, DU FROMMER GOTT*

*see also:* 337
HYMN: Johann Heermann, 1630
MELODY: Anonymous, 1693

TR.: Catherine Winkworth, 1863

† Second tune.

O_ God, Thou faith-ful_ God, Thou Foun-tain ev - er_ flow - ing,
Who good and per - fect_ gifts In_ mer - cy_ art_ be - stow - ing,

Give me_ a health-y_ frame, And may_ I __ have with - in A_

con - science free_ from blame, A soul_ un - hurt by_ sin.

[ 2 ]

If dangers gather round,
Still keep me calm and fearless;
Help me to bear the cross
When life is dark and cheerless;

To overcome my foe
With words and actions kind.
When counsel I would know,
Good counsel let me find.   (4/8)

## 316. My Life Is Hid in Jesus

*see also:* 6
HYMN: Anonymous, 1609
MELODY: Melchior Vulpius, 1609

*CHRISTUS, DER IST MEIN LEBEN*

TR.: Catherine Winkworth, 1863

My life is hid_ in Je - sus,   Dy -
Dy - ing   ing is_ gain_ to_ me; Then when - so -
e'er_ He pleas - es, I _ meet_ death will - ing - ly.

[ 2 ]

In that last hour, O grant me
Slumber so soft and still,
No doubts to vex or haunt me,
Safe anchored on Thy will.   (6/7)

### 317. Lord, As Thou Wilt, Deal Thou with Me

*see also:* 144, 318(D)
SOURCE: Cantata No. 156, c.1730
HYMN: Caspar Bienemann, 1582
MELODY: Anonymous, 1525

TR.: Emanuel Cronenwett, *alt.*, 1880. Reprinted by permission of Concordia Publishing House from *The Handbook of the Lutheran Hymnal* by W. G. Polack (1942).

*HERR, WIE DU WILLST, SO SCHICKS MIT MIR*

\* Lord, as Thou wilt, deal Thou with me; No oth-er_ wish
In life and_ death I cling to Thee; Oh, do not_ let

— I cher - ish.
— me per - ish! Let not_ Thy grace from me de - part, And

grant an_ ev - er pa - tient heart To bear what Thou _ dost send _ me.

[ 2 ]
Grant honor, truth, and purity,
And love Thy Word to ponder;
From all false doctrine keep me free.
Bestow, both here and yonder,

What serves my everlasting bliss;
Preserve me from unrighteousness
Throughout my earthly journey. (2/3)

### 318. When Man Will Rest in God's Own Sight

*WER IN DEM SCHUTZ DES HÖCHSTEN IST*
HERR, WIE DU WILLST, SO SCHICKS MIT MIR

Duplicate of Chorale 144.

### 319. Holy, Holy, Holy

*HEILIG, HEILIG, HEILIG*

Duplicate of Chorale 235.

## 320. The Lord Bless Thee and Keep Thee

🙙 *GOTT SEI UNS GNÄDIG UND BARMHERZIG*
MEINE SEELE ERHEBT DEN HERREN

*see also:* 130, 358
HYMN: Numbers 6:24–25
MELODY: *Tonus peregrinus*

The Lord bless Thee and keep Thee.

The Lord make His face shine up - on Thee.

## 321. We Christians May Rejoice Today

🙙 *WIR CHRISTENLEUT*

*see also:* 55, 360
SOURCE: Cantata No. 40, 1723
HYMN: Caspar Fuger, 1592
MELODY: Caspar Fuger the younger(?), 1593

TR.: Catherine Winkworth, 1863, *alt.*

We Chris - tians may, We Chris - tians may Re - joice to - day, When

Christ was born to com - fort and to save us; Who thus be - lieves No

long-er grieves, For none are lost who grasp the hope He gave us.

[ 2 ]*
Sin brought us grief,
Sin brought us grief,
But Christ relief,
When down to earth He came for our salvation;
Since God with us
Is dwelling thus,
Who dares to speak the Christian's condemnation.
(3/5)

## 322. When My Last Hour Is Close at Hand

*WENN MEIN STÜNDLEIN VORHANDEN IST*

see also: 52, 351
HYMN: Nikolaus Herman, 1574
MELODY: Nikolaus Herman, 1569
TR.: Catherine Winkworth, 1863

When my last hour is close at hand, And I must hence be-take me, Do Thou, Lord Je-sus, by me stand, Nor let Thine aid for-sake me; To Thy blest hands I now com-mend My soul, at this my

**[2]**
Since I was graft into the Vine,
So will I comfort borrow;
For Thou wilt surely keep me Thine
Through fear, and pain, and sorrow;
Yea, though I die, I die to Thee,
And Thou through death didst win for me
The right to life eternal.  *(3/5)*

## 323. O Morning Star, How Fair and Bright

*WIE SCHÖN LEUCHTET DER MORGENSTERN*

*see also:* 86, 195(D), 278, 305(D)
SOURCE: Cantata No. 172, *c.*1724
HYMN: Philipp Nicolai, 1599
MELODY: Philipp Nicolai(?), 1599

TR.: Catherine Winkworth, 1869

Love - ly art Thou, fair and glo - rious, all\_ vic - to - rious,

rich in\_ bless - ing, Rule and\_ might o'er all\_ pos - sess - ing.

[2]*
But if Thou look on me in love,
There straightway falls from God above
A ray of purest pleasure;
Thy Word and Spirit, flesh and blood,
Refresh my soul with heav'nly food,
Thou art my hidden treasure.
Let Thy grace, Lord, warm and cheer me,
O draw near me; Thou hast taught us
Thee to seek, since Thou hast sought us.   (4/7)

### 324. Jesu, Priceless Treasure

see also: 96, 138, 263, 283, 356
SOURCE: Cantata No. 81, 1724
HYMN: Johann Franck, 1653
MELODY: Johann Crüger, 1653

JESU, MEINE FREUDE

TR.: Catherine Winkworth, 1869

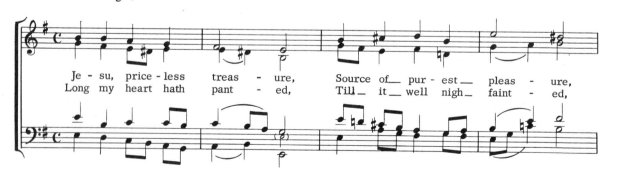

Je - su, price - less treas - ure,    Source of\_ pur - est\_ pleas - ure,
Long my heart hath pant - ed,    Till\_ it\_ well nigh\_ faint - ed,

Tru - est friend to__ me! Thine I__ am, O__ spot - less__ Lamb! I will suf - fer
Thirst-ing aft - er__ Thee!

nought to__ hide____ Thee, Ask__ for__ nought be - side____ Thee.

[2]*
In Thine arm I rest me,
Foes who would molest me
Cannot reach me here;
Though the earth be shaking,
Every heart be quaking,
Jesus calms my fear;

Sin and Hell in conflict fell
With their heaviest storms against me;
Jesus will not fail me.  (2/6)

## 325. In Peace and Joy I Now Depart

*see also:* 49
SOURCE: Cantata No. 83, 1724
HYMN: Martin Luther, 1524
MELODY: Martin Luther(?), 1524

❧ *MIT FRIED UND FREUD ICH FAHR DAHIN*

TR.: George Macdonald, 1876, *alt.*

In peace and joy I__ now__ de - part, As ____ God wills____ me. At

rest and still are mind _____ and heart, He doth save____ me.

[2]*
He is the health and happy Light
Of the heathen,
To feed them and their eyes make bright
Thee to see then.
Of Thy folk Israel is He
The praise, joy, honor, pleasure.  *(4/4)*

## 326. The Lord My Shepherd Is and True

*see also:* 125, 249, 313, 353(D)
SOURCE: Cantata No. 104, *c.*1725
HYMN: Cornelius Becker, 1598, (Psalm 23)
MELODY: Anonymous, 1539

*DER HERR IST MEIN GETREUER HIRT, DEM*
ALLEIN GOTT IN DER HÖH SEI EHR

TR.: Charles Sanford Terry, 1929. By permission of Oxford University Press, London.

doth my soul with glad-ness— fill, Through His— great love and fa - vor.

[2]
He hath a table for me spread,
My foes are vexed to madness;
He doth with oil anoint my head
And fill my soul with gladness.
His goodness never faileth me,
And one day soon at home I'll be
Within His house forever. (3/3)

## 327. Now Join We All to Praise Thee

JESU, NUN SEI GEPREISET

see also: 11, 252
SOURCE: Cantata No. 190, 1725
HYMN: Johann Hermann(?), 1591
MELODY: Anonymous, 1591

TR.: Henry S. Drinker, 1944

Now join we all to praise Thee, This joy-ous New Year's
We thank Thee that we meet here At this glad fes - tal

day,      For all_ the man-y bless-ings That drive our_ cares a-

time,      With gra-cious mer-cy lad - en And last-ing_ peace sub-

way.

lime;      That free and un - de - feat - ed, The

old year we com - plet - ed. To Thee in deep de -
Pre - serve us soul and

vo - tion, Would we be ev - er near.
bod - y, Through - out the com - ing year,

In safe-ty watch and guard us through all the com - ing year.

[2]*

Our New Year greeting bringing,
With grateful hearts we come,
Thy praise and glory singing,
Throughout all Christendom.
Our lives in mercy spare us,
Thy faithful Christian Band,
Let no mishap impair us,
And bless our Fatherland.

Quell war and vain disorders,
Within our country's borders;
Let truth and simple candor
To honor be restored,
Hypocrisy and slander
Be ev'rywhere abhorred.
Hypocrisy and slander
Be ev'rywhere abhorred.  (2/3)

## 328. Blessed Jesu, at Thy Word

⊰ *LIEBSTER JESU, WIR SIND HIER*

Duplicate of Chorale 131.

## 329. Sing Praise to God Who Reigns Above

⊰ *SEI LOB UND EHR DEM HÖCHSTEN GUT*
ES IST DAS HEIL UNS KOMMEN HER

*see also:* 4, 248, 290, 335, 354(D)
SOURCE: Three Wedding Chorales, No. 2
HYMN: Johann Jakob Schütz, 1675
MELODY: Anonymous, fifteenth century

TR.: Frances E. Cox, 1812–1897

Horn I, II

Soprano, Oboe I, Violin I
Alto, English Horn, Violin II

* Sing praise to God_ Who_ reigns a - bove, The_
The God_ of pow'r, the_ God of _ love, The_

Tenor, Viola
Bass, Organ, and Continuo

God of_ all_ cre - a - tion,
God of_ our sal - va - tion;

With heal-ing_ balm my soul He fills, And
ev - ery_ faith-less mur-mur stills; To_ God all praise and glo - ry.

[2]
What God's almighty pow'r hath made
His gracious mercy keepeth;
By morning glow or evening shade
His watchful eye ne'er sleepeth;

Within the kingdom of His might
Lo! All is just, and all is right;
To God all praise and glory.  (3/9)

## 330. Now Thank We All Our God

NUN DANKET ALLE GOTT

see also: 32
SOURCE: Three Wedding Chorales, No. 3
HYMN: Martin Rinkart, 1636
MELODY: Johann Crüger, 1648

TR.: Catherine Winkworth, 1863

Horn I, II

Soprano, Oboe I, Violin I
Alto, English Horn, Violin II

* Now thank we all _ our _ God, With
Who won - drous things hath _ done, In

Tenor, Viola
Bass, Organ, and Continuo

heart, and hands and voi - ces,
whom His world re - joi - ces. Who from our moth - er's

arms Hath blessed us on our way With

count - less gifts of love, And still is ours to - day.

[ 2 ]
All praise and thanks to God,
The Father now be given,
The Son and Him who reigns
With Them in highest heaven,

The One eternal God,
Whom heav'n and earth adore,
For thus it was, is now,
And shall be evermore! (3/3)

# 331. O Whither Shall I Flee

*see also:* 25, 281, 304
SOURCE: Cantata No. 136, c.1725
HYMN: Johann Heermann, 1630
MELODY: Anonymous, 1609

WO SOLL ICH FLIEHEN HIN
AUF MEINEN LIEBEN GOTT

TR.: Anonymous (*Moravian Hymn Book*, 1789)

Violin I

Soprano, Horn, Oboe I, II
Alto, Violin II

Tenor, Viola
Bass, Continuo

O whith - er shall I ___ flee De-

pressed with mis - er - y? Who is it that can ease ___ me ___ And

from my ___ sins re - lease ___ me? Man's help I ___ vain ___ have

prov - èd, Sin's load re - mains un - mov - èd.

[ 2 ]*
Christ, Thine atoning blood,
The sinner's highest food,
Is pow'rful to deliver
And free the soul forever
From all claims of the devil,
And cleanse it all from evil.   *(9/11)*

### 332. From God Shall Nought Divide Me

*VON GOTT WILL ICH NICHT LASSEN*

*see also:* 114, 191, 364
HYMN: Ludwig Helmbold, 1563
MELODY: Anonymous, 1571

TR.: Catherine Winkworth, 1869

From God shall nought di - vide____ me, For He__ is true al - way, And
on my__ path will guide____ me, Where else__ I__ oft__ should stray. His__

[2]
If sorrow comes, He sent it,
In Him I put my trust;
I never shall repent it,
For He is true and just,

And loves to bless us still.
My life and soul, I owe them
To Him who doth bestow them;
Let Him do as He will.  (3/9)

### 333. Would That the Lord Would Grant Us Grace

🎵 *ES WOLLT UNS GOTT GENÄDIG SEIN*

see also: 16, 352
SOURCE: Cantata No. 69, 1730
HYMN: Martin Luther, 1524
MELODY: Anonymous, 1525

TR.: George Macdonald, 1876

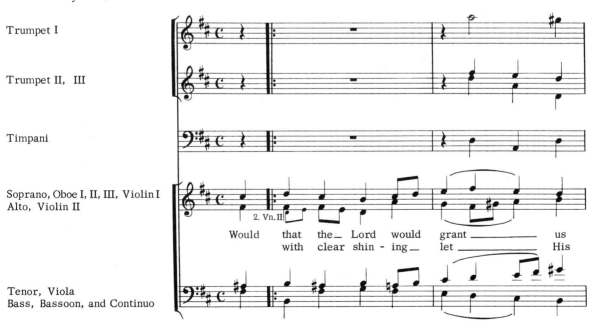

faith do_ place; And Je - sus_ Christ, our health and strength Be_ known to_ all_ the

hea - then race, And un - to_ God con - vert them.

God con - vert them.

God_ con - vert them.

[ 2 ]*
Let them thank God, and Thee adore,
The folk in deeds of grace full.
The land grows fruitful more and more;
Thy word it is successful.

O bless us, God the Father, Son,
O bless us, God the Holy Ghost,
To Whom by all be honor done.
Before Him let men fear the most.
Now heartily say Amen. (3/3)

### 334. Before Thy Throne I Now Appear

*VOR DEINEN THRON TRET ICH HEIMET*
HERR GOTT, DICH LOBEN ALLE WIR

see also: 164
HYMN: Bodo von Hodenberg, 1646
MELODY: Louis Bourgeois, 1551 *(Old Hundredth)*

TR.: John Christian Jacobi, 1722

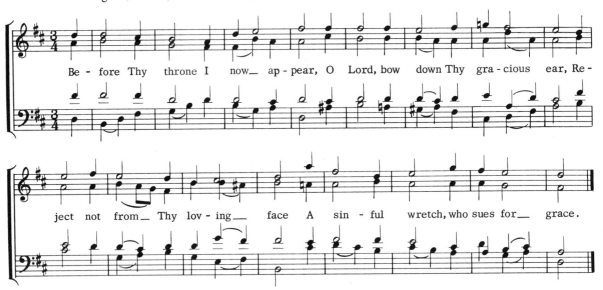

Be - fore Thy throne I now__ ap - pear, O Lord, bow down Thy gra - cious ear, Re -
ject not from__ Thy lov - ing__ face A sin - ful wretch, who sues for__ grace.

[ 2 ]
Thou Father of eternity!
Thine image hath impressed on me:
In Thee I am, and live, and move,
Nor can I breathe without Thy love.   *(2/15)*

### 335. Our Whole Salvation Doth Depend

*ES IST DAS HEIL UNS KOMMEN HER*

see also: 4, 248, 290, 329, 354(D)
SOURCE: Cantata No. 155, 1716
HYMN: Paul Speratus, 1524
MELODY: Anonymous, fifteenth century

TR.: John Christian Jacobi, 1725, *alt.*

Our__ whole sal - va - tion__ doth de - pend On__ God's free__ grace and
All__ our__ good works can__ ne'er pre - tend To__ boast of__ an - y__
spir - it, 'Tis__ faith__ re - ceives its__ right - eous - ness From
mer - it;

Christ and His a - ton - ing Grace, He is our me - di - a - tor.

[2]*
Be not cast down when He delays
To crown thine expectation;
He then is nearest, when thy ways
Seem full of desolation;

On His eternal word rely,
E'en though thy wav'ring heart deny;
And trust in thy Redeemer. *(12/14)*

## 336. If God Were Not upon Our Side

*WO GOTT DER HERR NICHT BEI UNS HÄLT*

*see also:* 31, 285, 301
HYMN: Justus Jonas, 1524, (Psalm 124)
MELODY: Anonymous, 1535

TR.: Catherine Winkworth, 1869, *alt.*

If God were not up - on our side When foes rag'd all a -
Were not Him - self our Help and Guide When war they wag'd a -

round us, Were not He Is - rael's might - y Shield, To
gainst us,

whom their ut - most crafts must yield, We sure - ly should have per - ished.

[2]
But now no human wit or might
Should make us quail for fearing,
God sitteth in the highest height,
Their counsels thus revealing;

When craftiest snares and nets they lay,
God goes to work another way,
And makes a path before us. *(2/8)*

### 337. O God, Thou Faithful God

O GOTT, DU FROMMER GOTT

*see also:* 315
SOURCE: Cantata No. 24, 1723
HYMN: Johann Heermann, 1630
MELODY: Anonymous, 1693

TR.: Catherine Winkworth, 1863

† Second tune.

* O God, Thou faith - ful God,

Thou Foun - tain ev - er

flow - ing,

With - out__ whom__ noth-ing__ is,

All ___ per - fect gifts be - stow ___ ing;

A ___ pure and health - y frame

O give me,⸺ and⸺ with -

in

A⸺ con - science free from⸺

blame,

A soul un-

hurt __ by sin, A soul un - hurt by sin.

sin. ___

sin.

[2]
And let me promise nought
But I can keep it truly,
Abstain from idle words,
And guard my lips still duly;

And grant, when in my place
I must and ought to speak,
My words due pow'r and grace,
Nor let me wound the weak. *(3/8)*

# 338. Up, My Soul, 'Tis God's Great Day

AUF, MEIN HERZ, DES HERREN TAG
JESUS, MEINE ZUVERSICHT

see also: 175
SOURCE: Cantata No. 145, c.1730
HYMN: Caspar Neumann, c.1700
MELODY: Johann Crüger(?), 1563

TR.: Charles Sanford Terry, 1929. By permission of Oxford University Press, London.

\* Up, my soul, 'tis God's great day, Death no long-er can en-thral us!
He who in the dark grave lay Ris'n and glo-rious goes be-fore us.
Ev-er will I trust in Him Who hath bought the world from sin.

[2]
Lord, I lift my song of praise
To my Saviour, loving, faithful.
Thine I am for all my days.
Thou the Prince of Life eternal.
Thanks and glory be to Thee
Now and through eternity! (9/9)

# 339. A Sinner and A Soul Most Wretched

ICH ARMER MENSCH, ICH ARMER SÜNDER
WER NUR DEN LIEBEN GOTT LÄSST WALTEN

see also: 62, 104, 112, 146, 204
SOURCE: Cantata No. 179, 1724
HYMN: Christoph Tietze, 1663
MELODY: Georg Neumark, 1657

TR.: Robert W. Ottman, 1963

A sin-ner and a soul most wretch-ed,
Ah God, may I not be re-ject-ed,

\* A sin-ner and a soul most wretch-ed,
Ah God, may I not be re-ject-ed, Be-fore the
But lead me

A sin-ner and a soul most wretch-ed,
Ah God, may I not be re-ject-ed,

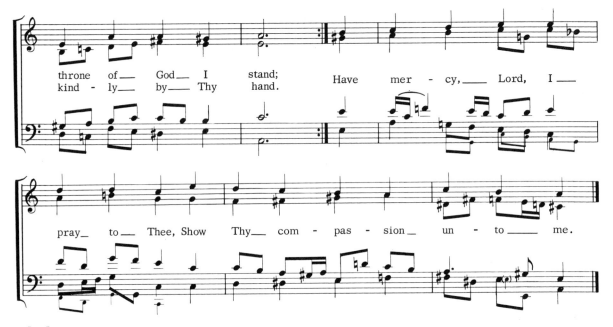

throne of\_\_ God I stand;
kind - ly\_\_ by\_\_ Thy hand. Have mer - cy,\_\_ Lord, I\_\_

pray\_ to\_\_ Thee, Show Thy\_\_ com - pas - sion\_ un - to\_\_\_ me.

[ 2 ]
Anxiety and fear so dreary,
With cares and sins my soul is worn;
Commend Thy grace, O Lord, now help me,
A lonely child and all forlorn.
Have mercy, Lord, I pray to Thee,
Show Thy compassion unto me.  *(2/8)*

## 340. Commit Thou All That Grieves Thee

*BEFIEHL DU DEINE WEGE*

HYMN: Paul Gerhardt, 1653
MELODY: Bartholomäus Gesius(?), 1603

TR.: Arthur W. Farlander and Winfred Douglas, 1939
By permission of the Church Pension Fund.

Com - mit thou all\_\_ that\_\_ grieves thee And fills thy heart with care
To\_\_ him whose faith - ful\_\_ mer - cy The skies a - bove de - clare,

Who gives the\_ winds their cours - es, Who points the clouds their way; 'Tis

He __ will guide thy foot - steps And be __ thy __ Staff and Stay.

[ 2 ]
Hope on, then, broken spirit;
Hope on, be not afraid:
Fear not the griefs that plague thee
And keep thy heart dismayed:
Thy God, in His great mercy,
Will save thee, hold thee fast,
And in His own time grant thee
The sun of joy at last.   (6/12)

## 341. We Thank Thee, Lord, for Sending

*ICH DANK DIR, LIEBER HERRE*

*see also:* 2, 272
SOURCE: Cantata No. 37, 1727                    TR.: Henry S. Drinker, 1944
HYMN: Johann Kolross, c.1535
MELODY: Anonymous, 1544

We __ thank Thee, Lord, for send - ing A - gain the __ morn - ing __ light; That

Thou hast safe a - vert - ed The dan - gers of _____ the night; With

dark-ness_ deep a - round ___ us, We lay in dead-ly fear; But
foes could not con - found _ us,
For Thou, our God ___ wert near.
For Thou ___ our ___ God wert near.
For Thou, our God ___ wert near.

[2]*
Confer Thou faith upon me
In Jesus Christ Thy Son,
And grant me now the pardon,
That He for me has won.

Thou wilt not now deny me,
That which Thou didst agree:
From sin to purify me,
And lift its load from me.    (4/9)

### 342. Let All Together Praise Our God

see also: 54, 276
HYMN: Nikolaus Herman, 1560
MELODY: Nikolaus Herman, 1554

*LOBT GOTT, IHR CHRISTEN ALLZUGLEICH*

TR.: Arthur Tozer Russell, 1851

Let all_ to - geth - er_ praise our_ God Up - on His_ loft - y
throne; He ___ hath _ the _ heav'ns un - closed to - day, And_
And

**[2]**
Behold the wonderful exchange
Our Lord with us doth make!
Lo! He assumes our flesh and blood!
We of His Heav'n partake!
We of His Heav'n partake.   *(6/8)*

## 343. Lord Jesus Christ, Thou Prince of Love†

*see also:* 9, 102, 361(D)
SOURCE: Cantata No. 11, *c*.1735
HYMN: Johann Rist, 1641
MELODY: Johann Schop, 1641

⚜ *DU LEBENSFÜRST, HERR JESU CHRIST*
ERMUNTRE DICH, MEIN SCHWACHER GEIST

TR.: Henry S. Drinker, 1944

† Sometimes published under the title *Nun lieget alles unter dir.*

O - ver_ a_ might - y en - e - my Which Thou hast
Which Thou ___ hast

gained ___ in splen - dor, Our heart - y_ praise we ren - der.

[ 2 ]*

Ruler art Thou of earth and sky,
The Father of creation;
Hither and yon the angels fly
At Thy divine direction.

Princes, obedient to Thy word,
Own Thee their sov'reign overlord;
Earth, air and fire and ocean,
All bow in deep devotion.  (4/14)

## 344. We Sing to Thee, Immanuel

*WIR SINGEN DIR, IMMANUEL*
VOM HIMMEL HOCH DA KOMM ICH HER

*see also:* 46
SOURCE: Christmas Oratorio, 1734
HYMN: Paul Gerhardt, 1653
MELODY: Martin Luther(?), 1539

TR.: Frances E. Cox, 1864

We sing to ___ Thee, Im - man - u - el,

The __ Prince of __ Life, __ Sal - va - tion's __

well,

The __ Flower of __ Heav'n, the __

Star — of — morn, The — Lord — of —

lords, — the — vir - gin - born.

[ 2 ]*
All glory, worship, thanks and praise,
That Thou art come in these our days;
Thou heav'nly guest, expected long,
We hail Thee with a joyful song.    (2/16)

314

## 345. Ah! Lord, How Shall I Meet Thee†

*see also:* 21, 74, 80, 89, 98, 270, 286, 367
SOURCE: Christmas Oratorio, 1734
HYMN: Paul Gerhardt, 1653
MELODY: Hans Leo Hassler, 1601

*WIE SOLL ICH DICH EMPFANGEN*
HERZLICH TUT MICH VERLANGEN

TR.: Catherine Winkworth, 1863

† Sometimes published under the title *O Haupt voll Blut und Wunden.*

* Ah!_ Lord, how shall I _ meet _ Thee, How wel - come Thee _ a - right?
All _ na - tions long to _ greet _ Thee, My hope, my _ sole _ de - light!

Bright - en the _ lamp that burn - eth But dim - ly _ in _ my _ breast, And

teach my soul, that yearn - eth To _ hon - or _ such high quest. _

[ 2 ]
Thy Zion strews before Thee
Her fairest buds and palms,
And I too will adore Thee
With sweetest songs and psalms;

My soul breaks forth in flowers
Rejoicing in Thy fame,
And summons all her powers
To honor Jesu's name. *(2/10)*

## 346. Now at Length the Hour Is Near

*MEINES LEBENS LETZTE ZEIT*

HYMN: Anonymous, 1726
MELODY: Anonymous, 1726

TR.: Charles Sanford Terry, 1929. By permission of Oxford University Press, London.

Now at length the _ hour _ is _ near, On my _ soul _ is _

press-ing close-ly, When death sounds his call so clear, And from earth's mean joys in - vites_ me, Brief's our_ mor-tal_ jour - ney; God hath willed, and_ wise- ly, sure - ly, That our life must, late or_ ear - ly,_ Know an_ end — ing.

[ 2 ]
Jesus only, none but He,
In our last great need availeth
Over fear's proud mastery.
He alone with might prevaileth.

By His blood that flowèd
Hath He to the soul restorèd
Blessed comfort, balm outpourèd,
Joy assurèd.  (4/7)

## 347. What-e'er My God Ordains Is Right

*see also:* 65, 293
SOURCE: Three Wedding Chorales, No. 1
HYMN: Samuel Rodigast, 1676
MELODY: Johann Pachelbel(?), 1690

◁ WAS GOTT TUT, DAS IST WOHLGETAN

TR.: Catherine Winkworth, 1863, *alt.*

Horn I, II

Soprano, Oboe I, Violin I
Alto, English Horn, Violin II

What - e'er my God or - dains_ is_ right; His _
I _ will be still, what - e'er_ He_ doth, And _

Tenor, Viola
Bass, Organ and Continuo

Ho - ly_ Will a - bid - eth; He is_ my God; Though dark my_ road, From
fol - low_ where He _ guid - eth.

fall - ing_ He_ doth hold _ me, Where - fore I trust Him sure - ly.

[ 2 ]
What-e'er my God ordains is right,
Though now this cup in drinking
May bitter seem to my faint heart,
I take it all unshrinking;

Tears pass away
With dawn of day,
My heart with comfort filling,
My pain and grief departing.   (5/6)

## 348. Jesus I Will Never Leave

MEINEN JESUM LASS ICH NICHT, WEIL

see also: 152, 299
SOURCE: Cantata No. 70, 1716
HYMN: Christian Keimann, 1658
MELODY: Andreas Hammerschmidt(?), 1658

TR.: Anonymous (Selah Song Book, 1936)

Violin I, II

Viola

Soprano, Trumpet, Oboe
Alto

Je - sus I _ will nev-er leave, Who for me Him-self has_ giv -

Tenor
Bass, Bassoon and Continuo

en; There-fore un - to_ Him I'll_ cleave, Nor from Him be_ ev - er__ driv - en;

Life from Him doth light re - ceive; My dear Je - sus, I'll not leave.

Life from Him _____ doth light re-ceive; My dear Je - sus, I'll not leave.

Life from Him doth light re - ceive; My dear Je - sus, I'll not leave.

Life from Him doth light re - ceive; My dear Je - sus, I'll not leave.

[ 2 ]
Not for earth's vain joys I crave,
Not for heaven's glorious pleasure;
Jesus who my soul did save
Shall be my desire and treasure;
He redemption did achieve,
My dear Jesus, I'll not leave.  (5/6)

## 349. Father of Mercies! God Most High

*BARMHERZGER VATER, HÖCHSTER GOTT*
WAS MEIN GOTT WILL, DAS G'SCHEH ALLZEIT

Duplicate of Chorale 120. Chorale 349 is sometimes published under the title *Ich hab in Gottes Herz und Sinn.*

## 350. Sink Not Yet, My Soul, to Slumber†

*see also:* 95, 121, 233, 365
HYMN: Johann Rist, 1642
MELODY: Johann Schop, 1642

*⟨ WERDE MUNTER, MEIN GEMÜTE*

TR.: Catherine Winkworth, 1861

† Sometimes published under the title *Jesu, meiner Seelen Wonne.*

Sink not yet, my soul, to slumber, Wake, my heart, go forth and tell
All the mercies without number That this by-gone day befell;

Tell how God hath kept afar All things that against me war,

Hath upheld me and defended, And His grace my soul befriended.

[ 2 ]
Father, merciful and holy,
Thee tonight I praise and bless,
Who to labor true and lowly
Grantest ever meet success;

Many sins and many woes,
Many fierce and subtle foes
Hast Thou checked that once alarmed me,
So that nought today has harmed me. (2/12)

## 351. When My Last Hour Is Close at Hand

*⟨ WENN MEIN STÜNDLEIN VORHANDEN IST*

*see also:* 52, 322
HYMN: Nikolaus Herman, 1574
MELODY: Nikolaus Herman, 1569

TR.: Catherine Winkworth, 1863

When my last hour is close at hand, And I must hence be -

take_____ me, Do Thou, Lord Je-sus,___ by___ me stand, Nor___ let___ Thine aid___ for-

sake_____ me; To Thy blest hands I___ now com-mend My soul, at___ this my

To Thy_____ blest hands I___ now com-mend My soul, at this___ my___

safe-___ ly keep___ it.

earth-ly___ end, And___ Thou wilt safe-___ ly keep_____ it.

earth-ly___ end, And Thou wilt safe-ly keep_____ it.

[ 2 ]

Since Thou from death didst rise again,
In death Thou wilt not leave me;
Thy life declares my fears are vain,
And doubts no more shall grieve me,

For Thou wilt have me where Thou art:
And so with joy I can depart,
And know Thou wilt receive me.  (4/5)

### 352. May God unto Us Gracious Be

*see also:* 16, 333
HYMN: Martin Luther, 1524
MELODY: Anonymous, 1525

🎵 *ES WOLLT UNS GOTT GENÄDIG SEIN*

TR.: Arthur Tozer Russell, 1851

May God un - to us__ gra - cious be,
Lord, show Thy face to__ us_____ through Thee

May God un-to us gra-cious be, And grant to__ us His
Lord, show_____ Thy face_____ to us through Thee E - ter-nal__ life pos-

May God un-to us gra - cious be, __
Lord, show Thy face to us_____ through Thee__

[2]
Thy fold, O God, shall bring to Thee
The praise of holy living;
Thy word shall richly fruitful be,
And earth shall yield thanksgiving.

Bless us, O Father! Bless, O Son!
Grant, Holy Ghost, Thy blessing!
Thee earth shall honor—Thee alone,
Thy fear all souls possessing,
O God, let all say, Amen.  (3/3)

## 353. The Lord My Shepherd Is: My Need

DER HERR IST MEIN GETREUER HIRT, HÄLT
ALLEIN GOTT IN DER HÖH SEI EHR

Duplicate of Chorale 313.

## 354. Oh Praise and Honor God Our King

SEI LOB UND EHR DEM HÖCHSTEN GUT
ES IST DAS HEIL UNS KOMMEN HER

Duplicate of Chorale 248.

## 355. In All That I Am Doing†

see also: 50, 63, 103, 117, 275, 289, 363, 366
SOURCE: Cantata No. 44, c.1725
HYMN: Paul Flemming, 1642
MELODY: Anonymous, 1539

*IN ALLEN MEINEN TATEN*
O WELT, ICH MUSS DICH LASSEN

TR.: Henry S. Drinker, 1944

† Sometimes published under the title *Nun ruhen alle Wälder.*

In all that I am doing, Each en - ter - prise pur - su - ing, I fol - low God's ad - vice; For he who this is heed - ing Is ev - er well suc - ceed - ing, His ven - tures ev - er pay him thrice.

[ 2 ]*
Be His, my soul, forever,
That naught from thee can sever,
Him who created thee.

Whatever ill assail thee,
Thy Father will not fail thee,
Thine ev'ry need will He forsee.    (15/15)

## 356. Jesu, Priceless Treasure

see also: 96, 138, 263, 283, 324
HYMN: Johann Franck, 1653
MELODY: Johann Crüger, 1653

*JESU, MEINE FREUDE*

TR.: Catherine Winkworth, 1869, alt.

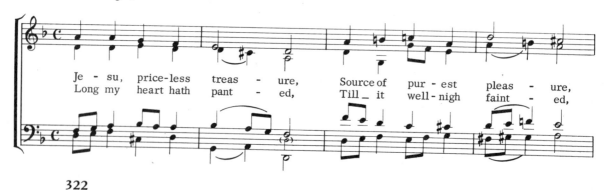

Je - su, price - less treas - ure, Source of pur - est pleas - ure,
Long my heart hath pant - ed, Till it well - nigh faint - ed,

Tru - est_ friend to_ me!
Thirst- ing_ aft - er_ Thee!

Thine I_ am_ O_ spot-less Lamb! I will suf-fer

nought to_ hide_ Thee,
nought to hide _____ Thee,
nought to_ hide Thee,

Ask_ for_ nought be - side _____ Thee.

[ 2 ]
Satan, I defy Thee,
Death, I need not fly thee,
Fear, I bid thee cease!
Rage, O world, thy noises
Cannot drown our voices
Singing still of peace;
For God's pow'r guards every hour,
Earth and all the depths adore Him,
Silent bow before Him.   (3/6)

## 357. Why Should Sorrow Ever Grieve Me

*see also:* 139
HYMN: Paul Gerhardt, 1653
MELODY: Johann G. Ebeling, 1666

WARUM SOLLT ICH MICH DENN GRÄMEN

TR.: John Kelly, 1867

Why should sor - row ev - er_ grieve _____ me? Christ is near, What can

here E'er of Him de - prive \_\_\_\_\_ me? Who can\_ rob me of my\_

heav - en That God's Son, As\_ mine own, To\_ my faith hath giv - en.

[ 2 ]
Shepherd! Lord! Joy's fountain ever,
Thou art mine, I am Thine,
No one can us sever.

I am Thine because Thou gavest
Life and blood
For my good,
By Thy death Thou savest.   *(11/12)*

## 358. Glory Be to God the Father and the Son

*LOB UND PREIS SEI GOTT DEM VATER UND
DEM SOHN*

MEINE SEELE ERHEBT DEN HERREN

*see also:* 130, 320
SOURCE: Cantata No. 10, *c.*1740
HYMN: Doxology
MELODY: *Tonus peregrinus*

TR.: Henry S. Drinker, 1944

\* Glo - ry   be to God the Fa - ther   and\_ the   Son,   And \_\_\_

to the Ho - ly Spir - it.

As   it   was   in   the be -
As   it   was   in
As   it   was\_   in \_\_\_
As   it   was   in   the _____

## 359. Lord Jesus Christ, in Thee Alone

*see also:* 13
HYMN: Johannes Schneesing, *c.*1540
MELODY: Anonymous, 1541(?)

✠ *ALLEIN ZU DIR, HERR JESU CHRIST*

TR.: Catherine Winkworth, 1863, *alt.*

creature here, No angel in the heav'n-ly sphere, Who at thy need can succor me, I cry to Thee, For Thou canst end my misery.

[ 2 ]
My sin is very sore and great,
Beneath its load confining;
O free me from this heavy weight,
My Saviour, through Thy dying;

And with my Father for me plead
That Thou hast suffer'd in my stead;
From me the burden then is roll'd,
And thus lay hold
On Thy dear promises of old.   (2/4)

## 360. Of Fear and Pain, No More Complain

LASST FURCHT UND PEIN
WIR CHRISTENLEUT

see also: 55, 321
SOURCE: Christmas Oratorio, 1734
HYMN: Christoph Runge, 1653
MELODY: Caspar Fuger, the younger(?), 1593

TR.: Robert W. Ottman, 1963

Of fear and pain, Of fear and pain No more complain, For un-to you I bring these joy-ous tid-ings: My words to you, Your

[2]*
Be joyful, sing,
Be joyful, sing
Praise to your King,

Today from heav'n God hath as Man descended.
Though Christ He is,
As Man He lives,
In David's town He lies an infant tended.  (4/8)

## 361. Bestir Thyself, My Feeble Soul

Duplicate of Chorale 9. Sometimes published under the
title *Du Lebensfürst Herr Jesu Christ*.

*ERMUNTRE DICH, MEIN SCHWACHER GEIST*

## 362. Beside Thy Cradle Here I Stand

*ICH STEH AN DEINER KRIPPEN HIER*
ES IST GEWISSLICH AN DER ZEIT

*see also:* 260
SOURCE: Christmas Oratorio, 1734
HYMN: Paul Gerhardt, 1653
MELODY: Anonymous, 1535

TR.: John Troutbeck, 1832–1899, (stanza 1), by permission of G. Schirmer, Inc., New York; John Kelly,
1867, (stanza 2).

soul, my strength, my ev-'ry part, That Thou from me re-quir-est.

[2]
With Thy great love beyond compare,
My soul Thou fillest ever,
Thy glance so sweet, Thine image fair,
My heart forgeteth never.

How otherwise e'er could it be,
How could I ever banish Thee,
From my heart's throne, O Saviour.   (2/15)

## 363. See World, Thy Lord in Anguish

*see also:* 50, 63, 103, 117, 275, 289, 355, 366
HYMN: Paul Gerhardt, 1647
MELODY: Anonymous, 1539

*O WELT, SIEH HIER DEIN LEBEN*
O WELT, ICH MUSS DICH LASSEN

TR.: John Kelly, 1867, *alt.*

See world, thy Lord in an-guish Up-on the cross doth lan-guish, The
Sav-iour sinks in death! The might-y Prince from Heav-en Himself hath free-ly giv-en To shame, and blows, and cru-el wrath.

[2]
I'm bound, my Saviour, ever
By ties most sacred never
Thy service to forsake,

With soul and body ever,
With all my pow'rs endeavor,
In praise and service joy to take.   (9/16)

# 364. From God Shall Nought Divide Me

VON GOTT WILL ICH NICHT LASSEN

*see also:* 114, 191, 332
HYMN: Ludwig Helmbold, 1563    TR.: Catherine Winkworth, 1869
MELODY: Anonymous, 1571

[ 2 ]
What-e'er may be His pleasure
Is surely best for me;
He gave His dearest treasure
That our weak hearts might see
How good His will to us,
And in His Son He gave us
What-e'er could bless and save us:
Praise Him who loveth thus! (4/9)

## 365. Sink Not Yet, My Soul, to Slumber†

see also: 95, 121, 233, 350
HYMN: Johann Rist, 1642
MELODY: Johann Schop, 1642

WERDE MUNTER, MEIN GEMÜTE

TR.: Catherine Winkworth, 1861

† Sometimes published under the title *Jesu, meiner Seelen Wonne.*

Sink not yet, my soul, to slumber, Wake, my heart, go forth and tell
All the mer-cies with-out num-ber That this by-gone day be-fell;

Tell how God hath kept a-far All things that a-gainst me war,

Hath up-held me and de-fend-ed, And His grace my soul be-friend-ed.

[ 2 ]
Yes, our wisdom vainly ponders,
Fathoms not Thy loving thought;
Never tongue can tell the wonders
That each day for us are wrought;

Thou hast guided me today
That no ill hath crossed my way,
There is neither bound nor measure
In Thy love's o'erflowing treasure.   (3/12)

## 366. See World, Thy Lord in Anguish

see also: 50, 63, 103, 117, 275, 289, 355, 363
HYMN: Paul Gerhardt, 1647
MELODY: Anonymous, 1539

O WELT, SIEH HIER DEIN LEBEN
O WELT, ICH MUSS DICH LASSEN

TR.: John Kelly, 1867, *alt.*

See world, thy Lord in an-guish Up-on the cross doth lan-guish, Thy

330

Sav - iour sinks in__ death! The might-y__ Prince from Heav - en Him -

self hath free-ly__ giv - en To__ shame, and__ blows, and__ cru - el__ wrath.

[2]
Thy groaning and Thy sighing,
Thy thousand tears and crying
That once were heard from Thee,
They'll lead me to Thy glory,
Where I shall joy before Thee,
And evermore at rest shall be!  (*16/16*)

### 367. Commit Thou Every Grievance

*BEFIEHL DU DEINE WEGE*
HERZLICH TUT MICH VERLANGEN

*see also:* 21, 74, 80, 89, 98, 270, 286, 345
HYMN: Paul Gerhardt, 1653
MELODY: Hans Leo Hassler, 1601

TR.: Anonymous (*Moravian Hymn Book*, 1890)

Com - mit thou ev - ery griev - ance In - to__ His__ faith - ful__ hands,
To His sure care and guid - ance, Who heav'n and__ earth com - mands;

For He, the cloud's di-rec-tor, Whom winds and seas o-bey, Will

pre-pare thy way.

be thy kind pro-tec-tor, And will pre-pare thy way.

[2]

My soul, then, with assurance  
Hope still, be not dismayed;  
He will from each encumbrance  
Again lift up thy head;

Beyond thy wish extended  
His goodness will appear,  
When He hath fully ended  
What caused thy needless fear. (*3/12*)

## 368. Help, O Lord, Behold We Enter

SOURCE: Christmas Oratorio, 1734  
HYMN: Johann Rist, 1642  
MELODY: Johann Sebastian Bach, 1734

✤{ *HILF, HERR JESU, LASS GELINGEN*†

TR.: Catherine Winkworth, 1863, *alt.*

† Second tune.

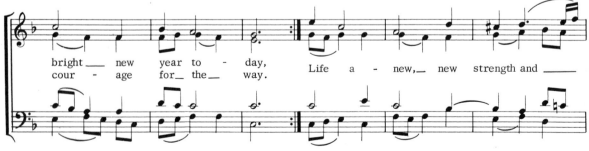

Help, Lord, help, be-hold we en-ter, On this  
All our hopes on Thee now cen-ter, Give us

bright new year to-day,  
cour-age for the way.

Life a-new, new strength and

glad - ness, This__ we ask__ of Thee,__ O bless_____ us.

[ 2 ]*
Jesus, by my side protect me,
Jesus, all my hopes inspire,
Jesus, from my sins protect me,
Jesus, be my heart's desire.
Jesus let me always thank Thee,
Jesus ne'er let me forget Thee.   (15/16)


## 369. Jesu, Who in Sorrow Dying

*see also:* 37, 269, 297
HYMN: Johann Rist, 1641
MELODY: Anonymous, 1642

*JESU, DER DU MEINE SEELE*

TR.: Arthur Tozer Russell, 1851

Je - su,__ who in__ sor - row__ dy - ing, Didst de - liv - 'rance bring to__ me,
Whilst my__ sins for__ ven - geance cry - ing, Nail'd Thee to__ the__ shame - ful tree;

Thou who Sa - tan's pow'r sub - du - est, And the__ sin - ner's hope re - new - est,

Bid - dest all__ so__ gra - cious - ly, That I__ needs must come to__ Thee.

[ 2 ]
Born in sin—my life transgression,
O how have I gone astray!
But I make Thee full confession:
Nought but sin hath marked my way.

Grant me graciously remission,
Who am wounded with contrition.
Be no more my tresspass sought
Which on me Thy wrath hath brought.   (3/12)

## 370. O Father! Send the Spirit Down

see also: 45
SOURCE: Cantata No. 74, 1735
HYMN: Paul Gerhardt, 1653
MELODY: Anonymous, 1530

GOTT VATER, SENDE DEINEN GEIST
KOMMT HER ZU MIR, SPRICHT GOTTES SOHN

TR.: John Kelly, 1867

O Father! Send the spirit down, Whom we are bid-den by Thy Son To seek, from Thy high heav - en: We ask as He taught us to pray, And let us ne'er un - heard a - way From 'fore Thy throne be driv - en.

[ 2 ]*

No mortal man upon the earth
Is of this gift so noble worth,
No merit we've to gain it;

Here only grace availeth aught,
That Jesus Christ for us hath bought,
His tears and death obtain it. (2/12)

# 371. Christ Lay in Death's Dark Prison

CHRIST LAG IN TODESBANDEN

see also: 15, 184, 261
MELODY: Adaptation, 1524, of *Christ ist erstanden*          TR.: Paul England. By permission of Novello & Co., Ltd.

Christ lay in death's dark prison
This day hath He arisen,

Christ lay in death's dark prison
This day hath He arisen, It was our sin that
And sheds new life a-

Christ lay in death's dark prison
This day hath He arisen, And praise our God with

bound Him,
round Him. Therefore let us joyful be, And praise our God with sol-

sol-emn glee, So sing we Hallelujah! Hallelujah!
So sing we Hallelujah! Hallelujah!
-emn glee, So sing we Hallelujah! Hallelujah!
So sing we Hallelujah! Hallelujah!

[ 2 ]
Now Jesus Christ, the Son of God,
For our defense hath risen,
Our grievous guilt He hath removed,
And Death hath bound in prison,

All his might Death must forgo,
For now he's nought but idle show,
His sting is lost forever.
Hallelujah!   *(3/7)*

# APPENDIXES

# Authorization of the Chorales:
## The Bachgesellschaft and Original Sources

This appendix lists the location of the chorales in the Bachgesellschaft. Certain differences in harmonizations between the present edition and the Bachgesellschaft are authenticated in original sources.†
The following abbreviations are used:

AMB, 1725  Notenbuchlein der Anna Magdalena Bach, 1725.

BG  *Johann Sebastian Bach's Werke* herausgegeben von der Bachgesellschaft in Leipzig. Photolithographischen Neudruck der Ausgabe von Breitkopf & Härtel Im Verlag von J. W. Edwards, Ann Arbor, Michigan, U.S.A., 1945.

BH (AMP)  Johann Sebastian Bach 371 Four-part Chorales, Breitkopf & Härtel edition, Associated Music Publishers, Inc., New York.

1765  Johann Sebastian Bachs vierstimmige Choralgesänge gesammlet von Carl

---

† An exhaustive collation of primary sources is available in *The Four-part Chorals of J. S. Bach* edited by Charles Sanford Terry and published by Oxford University Press, 1929.

1769  Philipp Emanuel Bach, Erster Theil. Berlin und Leipzig, gedruckt und zu finden bey Friedrich Wilhelm Birnstiel, Königl. privil. Buchdrucker, 1765.
Johann Sebastian Bachs vierstimmige Choralgesänge. Zweyter Theil. Berlin und Leipzig. Gedruckt und zu finden bey Friedrich Wilhelm Birnstiel, Königl. privil. Buchdrucker, 1769.

1784  Johann Sebastian Bachs vierstimmige Choralgesänge. Erster Theil. Leipzig, bey Johann Gottlob Immanuel Breitkopf, 1784.

1785  Johann Sebastian Bachs vierstimmige Choralgesänge. Zweyter Theil. Leipzig, bey Johann Gottlob Immanuel Breitkopf, 1785.

1786  Johann Sebastian Bachs vierstimmige Choralgesänge. Dritter Theil. Leipzig, bey Johann Gottlob Immanuel Breitkopf, 1786.

1787  Johann Sebastian Bachs vierstimmige Choralgesänge. Vierter Theil. Leipzig, bey Johann Gottlob Immanuel Breitkopf, 1787.

---

1.  BG vol. 39, p. 184
2.  BG vol. 39, p. 224
3.  BG vol. 32, p. 43
4.  BG vol. 20¹, p. 134
5.  BG vol. 39, p. 183
6.  BG vol. 39, p. 191; 1765, No. 8
7.  BG vol. 2, p. 225; 1765, No. 7
8.  BG vol. 7, p. 394
9.  BG vol. 5², p. 59
10. BG vol. 7, p. 300
11. BG vol. 10, p. 58 BG vol. 35, p. 32
12. BG vol. 16, p. 152
13. BG vol. 7, p. 114
14. BG vol. 37, p. 95; 1765, No. 16
15. BG vol. 39, p. 189
16. BG vol. 39, p. 205
17. BG vol. 30, p. 122
18. BG vol. 39, p. 209

19. BG vol. 39, p. 226; 1765, No. 22
20. BG vol. 39, p. 200
21. BG vol. 32, p. 46
22. BG vol. 35, p. 322
23. BG vol. 5¹, p. 272
24. BG vol. 39, p. 263; BH (AMP), No. 24
25. BG vol. 30, p. 260
26. BG vol. 2, p. 317 and p. 327
27. BG vol. 39, p. 204
28. BG vol. 7, p. 258
29. BG vol. 7, p. 80
30. BG vol. 39, p. 234
31. BG vol. 39, p. 178
32. BG vol. 39, p. 248
33. BG vol. 39, p. 216
34. BG vol. 39, p. 202
35. BG vol. 5², p. 208
36. BG vol. 39, p. 247
37. BG vol. 39, p. 227
38. BG vol. 24, p. 132

39. BG vol. 39, p. 179
40. BG vol. 39, p. 178
41. BG vol. 16, p. 166
42. BG vol. 16, p. 246
43. BG vol. 1, p. 241
44. BG vol. 39, p. 242
45. BG vol. 23, p. 230
46. BG vol. 5², p. 47
47. BG vol. 39, p. 263
48. BG vol. 5¹, p. 216; 1784, No. 48
49. BG vol. 39, p. 245
50. BG vol. 4, p. 164
51. BG vol. 22, p. 32
52. BG vol. 39, p. 270
53. BG vol. 26, p. 40
54. BG vol. 32, p. 16
55. BG vol. 23, p. 324
56. BG vol. 26, p. 20
57. BG vol. 39, p. 257
58. BG vol. 35, p. 157
59. BG vol. 12¹, p. 17
60. BG vol. 28, p. 80

61. BG vol. 32, p. 168
62. BG vol. 13¹, p. 144
63. BG vol. 12¹, p. 31;
    1765, No. 65
64. BG vol. 29, p. 124
65. BG vol. 30, p. 87
66. BG vol. 39, p. 190
67. BG vol. 7, p. 348
68. BG vol. 39, p. 272
69. BG vol. 39, p. 57
70. BG vol. 39, p. 211
71. BG vol. 35, p. 234
72. BG vol. 1, p. 176
73. BG vol. 39, p. 218
74. BG vol. 4, p. 214
75. BG vol. 39, p. 195
76. BG vol. 5¹, p. 360
77. BG vol. 5², p. 190
78. BG vol. 4, p. 23
79. BG vol. 39, p. 222
80. BG vol. 4, p. 186
81. BG vol. 12¹, p. 43
82. BG vol. 10, p. 236
83. BG vol. 12¹, p. 39
84. BG vol. 13¹, p. 128
85. BG vol. 10, p. 186
86. BG vol. 7, p. 243
87. BG vol. 12², p. 104
88. BG vol. 5¹, p. 272
89. BG vol. 4, p. 248
90. BG vol. 12², p. 132
91. BG vol. 10, p. 91
92. BG vol. 33, p. 166
93. BG vol. 29, p. 138
94. BG vol. 10, p. 274
95. BG vol. 12², p. 86
96. BG vol. 20¹, p. 152
97. BG vol. 33, p. 192
98. BG vol. 4, p. 53
99. BG vol. 2, p. 198
100. BG vol. 2, p. 252
101. BG vol. 33, p. 88
102. BG vol. 10, p. 126;
     1769, No. 106
103. BG vol. 2, p. 98
104. BG vol. 20¹, p. 178
105. BG vol. 4, p. 192
106. BG vol. 12¹, p. 103;
     1769, No. 110
107. BG vol. 12¹, p. 131
108. BG vol. 12¹, p. 95
109. BG vol. 37, p. 191
110. BG vol. 23, p. 66
111. BG vol. 12¹, p. 52
112. BG vol. 20¹, p. 98
113. BG vol. 12¹, p. 121
114. BG vol. 39, p. 265
115. BG vol. 4, p. 83
116. BG vol. 5¹, p. 316
117. BG vol. 4, p. 42
118. BG vol. 4, p. 151
119. BG vol. 35, p. 198
120. BG vol. 23, p. 94
121. BG vol. 4, p. 173
122. BG vol. 20¹, p. 118

123. BG vol. 37, p. 74
124. BG vol. 39, p. 184;
     1769, No. 128
125. BG vol. 23, p. 116;
     1785, No. 125
126. BG vol. 2, p. 252
127. BG vol. 39, p. 198
128. BG vol. 39, p. 181
129. BG vol. 39, p. 237
130. BG vol. 39, p. 212
131. BG vol. 39, p. 240
132. BG vol. 39, p. 238
133. BG vol. 39, p. 275
134. BG vol. 39, p. 200
135. BG vol. 39, p. 208
136. BG vol. 39, p. 217
137. BG vol. 39, p. 273
138. BG vol. 16, p. 132
139. BG vol. 5², p. 124
140. BG vol. 39, p. 236
141. BG vol. 39, p. 260;
     1769, No. 146
142. BG vol. 7, p. 387
143. BG vol. 39, p. 236
144. BG vol. 39, p. 220
145. BG vol. 39, p. 265
146. BG vol. 39, p. 273
147. BG vol. 39, p. 269
148. BG vol. 39, p. 262
149. BG vol. 39, p. 247
150. BG vol. 5¹, p. 244;
     1769, No. 154
151. BG vol. 39, p. 243
152. BG vol. 32, p. 82;
     1769, No. 156
153. BG vol. 39, p. 181
154. BG vol. 39, p. 196
155. BG vol. 39, p. 223
156. BG vol. 1, p. 94
157. BG vol. 39, p. 276
158. BG vol. 39, p. 197
159. BG vol. 39, p. 182
160. BG vol. 16, p. 118
161. BG vol. 39, p. 236
162. BG vol. 39, p. 194
163. BG vol. 39, p. 206
164. BG vol. 39, p. 213
165. BG vol. 39, p. 255
166. BG vol. 39, p. 204
167. BG vol. 39, p. 199
168. BG vol. 39, p. 221
169. BG vol. 39, p. 229;
     1769, No. 175
170. BG vol. 16, p. 50
171. BG vol. 39, p. 259;
     1769, No. 174
172. BG vol. 39, p. 260
173. BG vol. 39, p. 255
174. BG vol. 39, p. 235
175. BG vol. 39, p. 235
176. BG vol. 39, p. 202;
     BH (AMP), No. 176
177. BG vol. 39, p. 177
178. BG vol. 26, p. 40
179. BG vol. 28, p. 284

180. BG vol. 39, p. 182
181. BG vol. 39, p. 209
182. BG vol. 2, p. 132
183. BG vol. 39, p. 248
184. BG vol. 1, p. 124;
     1785, No. 184
185. BG vol. 39, p. 248
186. BG vol. 39, p. 177;
     1769, No. 152
187. BG vol. 39, p. 238
188. BG vol. 39, p. 225
189. BG vol. 39, p. 219
190. BG vol. 39, p. 219
191. BG vol. 18, p. 104
192. BG vol. 39, p. 210
193. BG vol. 39, p. 267
194. BG vol. 26, p. 60;
     1769, No. 200
195. BG vol. 7, p. 243
196. BG vol. 39, p. 193
197. BG vol. 39, p. 188
198. BG vol. 39, p. 192
199. BG vol. 39, p. 222
200. BG vol. 39, p. 192
201. BG vol. 39, p. 256
202. BG vol. 39, p. 258
203. BG vol. 39, p. 257
204. BG vol. 33, p. 122
205. BG vol. 39, p. 214
206. BG vol. 39, p. 261
207. BG vol. 39, p. 197
208. BG vol. 39, p. 182
209. BG vol. 39, p. 199;
     AMB, 1725
210. BG vol. 39, p. 187
211. BG vol. 39, p. 269
212. BG vol. 39, p. 216
213. BG vol. 39, p. 258
214. BG vol. 39, p. 246
215. BG vol. 26, p. 131
216. BG vol. 12², p. 190
217. BG vol. 32, p. 58
218. BG vol. 39, p. 240
219. BG vol. 39, p. 258
220. BG vol. 39, p. 262
221. BG vol. 39, p. 220;
     1786, No. 221
222. BG vol. 39, p. 250
223. BG vol. 39, p. 224
224. BG vol. 39, p. 195
225. BG vol. 39, p. 208
226. BG vol. 39, p. 218
227. BG vol. 39, p. 241
228. BG vol. 39, p. 193
229. BG vol. 39, p. 226
230. BG vol. 39, p. 186
231. BG vol. 39, p. 198
232. BG vol. 39, p. 198
233. BG vol. 32, p. 65
234. BG vol. 39, p. 210
235. BG vol. 39, p. 212
236. BG vol. 39, p. 218
237. BG vol. 39, p. 267;
     1786, No. 237
238. BG vol. 39, p. 205

| | | | | | |
|---|---|---|---|---|---|
| 239. | BG vol. 39, p. 196 | 284. | BG vol. 26, p. 160 | 328. | BG vol. 39, p. 240; 1787, No. 327 |
| 240. | BG vol. 39, p. 252 | 285. | BG vol. 39, p. 178 | 329. | BG vol. 13$^1$, p. 148 |
| 241. | BG vol. 39, p. 268 | 286. | BG vol. 39, p. 185 | 330. | BG vol. 13$^1$, p. 149 |
| 242. | BG vol. 39, p. 274 | 287. | BG vol. 39, p. 217 | 331. | BG vol. 28, p. 164 |
| 243. | BG vol. 39, p. 230 | 288. | BG vol. 39, p. 207 | 332. | BG vol. 39, p. 264 |
| 244. | BG vol. 39, p. 230 | 289. | BG vol. 39, p. 251 | 333. | BG vol. 16, p. 325 |
| 245. | BG vol. 39, p. 187 | 290. | BG vol. 1, p. 274 | 334. | BG vol. 39, p. 213 |
| 246. | BG vol. 39, p. 260 | 291. | BG vol. 22, p. 127 | 335. | BG vol. 32, p. 96 |
| 247. | BG vol. 39, p. 272 | 292. | BG vol. 23, p. 32 | 336. | BG vol. 39, p. 179 |
| 248. | BG vol. 24, p. 172 | 293. | BG vol. 16, p. 379; BH (AMP), No. 293 | 337. | BG vol. 5$^1$, p. 150 |
| 249. | BG vol. 39, p. 180 | 294. | BG vol. 24, p. 80 | 338. | BG vol. 30, p. 95 |
| 250. | BG vol. 39, p. 201 | 295. | BG vol. 39, p. 218 | 339. | BG vol. 35, p. 292; 1787, No. 338 |
| 251. | BG vol. 39, p. 223 | 296. | BG vol. 39, p. 250 | 340. | BG vol. 39, p. 186 |
| 252. | BG vol. 39, p. 234 | 297. | BG vol. 18, p. 286 | 341. | BG vol. 7, p. 282 |
| 253. | BG vol. 18, p. 254 | 298. | BG vol. 2, p. 288 | 342. | BG vol. 39, p. 242 |
| 254. | BG vol. 5$^1$, p. 188 | 299. | BG vol. 39, p. 244 | 343. | BG vol. 2, p. 32 |
| 255. | BG vol. 16, p. 120 | 300. | BG vol. 39, p. 266 | 344. | BG vol. 5$^2$, p. 90 |
| 256. | BG vol. 29, p. 124 | 301. | BG vol. 24, p. 108 | 345. | BG vol. 5$^2$, p. 36 |
| 257. | BG vol. 29, p. 138 | 302. | BG vol. 39, p. 222 | 346. | BG vol. 39, p. 244 |
| 258. | BG vol. 39, p. 243; 1786, No. 258 | 303. | BG vol. 22, p. 184 | 347. | BG vol. 13$^1$, p. 147 |
| 259. | BG vol. 10, p. 91 | 304. | BG vol. 1, p. 150 | 348. | BG vol. 16, p. 368 |
| 260. | BG vol. 39, p. 203 | 305. | BG vol. 7, p. 243 | 349. | BG vol. 23, p. 94 |
| 261. | BG vol. 32, p. 154 | 306. | BG vol. 39, p. 256 | 350. | BG vol. 39, p. 232 |
| 262. | BG vol. 1, p. 72 | 307. | BG vol. 39, p. 192 | 351. | BG vol. 39, p. 271 |
| 263. | BG vol. 39, p. 61 | 308. | BG vol. 1, p. 94 | 352. | BG vol. 39, p. 206 |
| 264. | BG vol. 39, p. 233 | 309. | BG vol. 39, p. 183 | 353. | BG vol. 24, p. 48 |
| 265. | BG vol. 30, p. 92 | 310. | BG vol. 12$^1$, p. 74 | 354. | BG vol. 24, p. 172 |
| 266. | BG vol. 10, p. 298 | 311. | BG vol. 39, p. 194 | 355. | BG vol. 10, p. 150 |
| 267. | BG vol. 20$^1$, p. 214 | 312. | BG vol. 41, p. 114; 1787, No. 311 | 356. | BG vol. 39, p. 231 |
| 268. | BG vol. 39, p. 249 | 313. | BG vol. 24, p. 48 | 357. | BG vol. 39, p. 266 |
| 269. | BG vol. 39, p. 228 | 314. | BG vol. 39, p. 194 | 358. | BG vol. 1, p. 303 |
| 270. | BG vol. 33, p. 27 | 315. | BG vol. 39, p. 254 | 359. | BG vol. 39, p. 180 |
| 271. | BG vol. 39, p. 207 | 316. | BG vol. 39, p. 191 | 360. | BG vol. 5$^2$, p. 126 |
| 272. | BG vol. 39, p. 225 | 317. | BG vol. 32, p. 114 | 361. | BG vol. 5$^2$, p. 59 |
| 273. | BG vol. 18, p. 378 | 318. | BG vol. 39, p. 220 | 362. | BG vol. 5$^2$, p. 245 |
| 274. | BG vol. 39, p. 253 | 319. | BG vol. 39, p. 212 | 363. | BG vol. 39, p. 252 |
| 275. | BG vol. 39, p. 251; 1786, No. 275 | 320. | BG vol. 39, p. 212 | 364. | BG vol. 39, p. 264 |
| 276. | BG vol. 39, p. 241 | 321. | BG vol. 7, p. 377; 1787, No. 320 | 365. | BG vol. 39, p. 232 |
| 277. | BG vol. 39, p. 221 | 322. | BG vol. 39, p. 270 | 366. | BG vol. 39, p. 252 |
| 278. | BG vol. 39, p. 274 | 323. | BG vol. 35, p. 69 | 367. | BG vol. 39, p. 185 |
| 279. | BG vol. 10, p. 288 | 324. | BG vol. 20$^1$, p. 24 | 368. | BG vol. 5$^2$, p. 166 |
| 280. | BG vol. 39, p. 201 | 325. | BG vol. 20$^1$, p. 76 | 369. | BG vol. 39, p. 228 |
| 281. | BG vol. 20$^1$, p. 194 | 326. | BG vol. 23, p. 116 | 370. | BG vol. 18, p. 146 |
| 282. | BG vol. 5$^1$, p. 188 | 327. | BG vol. 37, p. 257 | 371. | BG vol. 39, p. 190 |
| 283. | BG vol. 39, p. 75 | | | | |

# Location of Chorales in Extant Works of Bach

Cantatas not listed contain either no chorale or chorales not included in *The 371*.

Chorales not listed presumably are from lost cantatas or other choral works.

| Cantata No. | | |
|---|---|---|
| | 2 | 262 |
| | 3 | 156 |
| | 4 | 184 |
| | 5 | 304 |
| | 6 | 72 |
| | 8 | 43 |
| Cantata No. | 9 | 290 |
| | 10 | 358 |
| | 11 | 343 |
| | 13 | 103 |
| | 14 | 182 |
| | 16 | 99 |
| | 17 | 7 |
| | 18 | 100 |
| | 19 | 298 |
| | 20 | 26 |
| | 24 | 337 |

| | | | | | |
|---|---|---|---|---|---|
| Cantata No. | 25 | 254 | Cantata No. | 112 | 313 |
| | 26 | 48 | | 113 | 294 |
| | 27 | 150 | | 114 | 301 |
| | 28 | 23 | | 115 | 38 |
| | 29 | 116 | | 117 | 248 |
| | 30 | 76 | | 121 | 56 |
| | 32 | 29 | | 122 | 53 |
| | 33 | 13 | | 123 | 194 |
| | 36 | 28, 86 | | 126 | 215 |
| | 37 | 341 | | 127 | 284 |
| | 38 | 10 | | 133 | 60 |
| | 39 | 67 | | 136 | 331 |
| | 40 | 8, 142, 321 | | 140 | 179 |
| | 41 | 11 | | 144 | 65, 265 |
| | 42 | 91 | | 145 | 17, 338 |
| | 43 | 102 | | 148 | 25 |
| | 44 | 355 | | 151 | 54 |
| | 45 | 85 | | 153 | 3, 21, 217 |
| | 46 | 82 | | 154 | 152, 233 |
| | 47 | 94 | | 155 | 335 |
| | 48 | 266, 279 | | 156 | 317 |
| | 55 | 95 | | 158 | 261 |
| | 56 | 87 | | 159 | 61 |
| | 57 | 90 | | 161 | 270 |
| | 60 | 216 | | 164 | 101 |
| | 62 | 170 | | 166 | 204 |
| | 64 | 138, 160, 255, 291 | | 168 | 92 |
| | 65 | 12, 41 | | 169 | 97 |
| | 67 | 42 | | 172 | 323 |
| | 69 | 293, 333 | | 174 | 58 |
| | 70 | 348 | | 176 | 119 |
| | 73 | 191 | | 177 | 71 |
| | 74 | 370 | | 179 | 339 |
| | 77 | 253 | | 180 | 22 |
| | 78 | 297 | | 183 | 123 |
| | 80 | 273 | | 187 | 109 |
| | 81 | 324 | | 190 | 327 |
| | 83 | 325 | | 194 | 93, 256 |
| | 84 | 112 | | 197 | 62, 84 |
| | 85 | 122 | Cantata, *Ehre sei Gott* | | 312 |
| | 86 | 4 | Christmas Oratorio | | 9, 35, 46, 77, 139, 344, 345, 360, 362, 368 |
| | 87 | 96 | | | |
| | 88 | 104 | Motet No. 2 | | 69 |
| | 89 | 281 | 3 | | 263, 283 |
| | 90 | 267 | Notenbuchlein der Anna Magdalena Bach | | 209 |
| | 91 | 51 | | | |
| | 94 | 291 | St. John Passion | | 59, 63, 81, 83, 106, 107, 108, 111, 113, 310 |
| | 96 | 303 | | | |
| | 101 | 292 | St. Matthew Passion | | 50, 74, 78, 80, 89, 98, 105, 115, 117, 118, 121 |
| | 102 | 110 | | | |
| | 103 | 120 | Wedding Chorale No. 1 | | 347 |
| | 104 | 326 | 2 | | 329 |
| | 108 | 45 | 3 | | 330 |
| | 110 | 55 | | | |

# Sources of the Translations

Bach, Johann Sebastian, Cantata No. 4, "Christ Lay in Death's Dark Prison," ed. John E. West, English version by Paul England. New York: The H. W. Gray Co., Inc.

———, Cantata No. 8, "Gracious God, When Wilt Thou Call Me," English version by J. Michael Diack. Leipzig: Breitkopf & Härtel, 1931.

———, Cantata No. 61, "Come Redeemer of Our

Race," ed. Ivor Atkins, English version by B. M. Craster. London: Novello and Company, Limited.

———, Cantata No. 117, "Oh Praise and Honor God Our King," English version by Mevanwy Roberts. Leipzig: Breitkopf & Härtel, 1936.

———, The Christmas Oratorio, ed. Max Spicker, English translations by the Rev. Dr. Troutbeck. New York: G. Schirmer, Inc., 1909.

———, The Passion of Our Lord According to St. John, English translation by Rev. J. Troutbeck. London: Novello and Company, Limited.

———, The Passion of Our Lord According to St. John, ed. Ivor Atkins, English translation by Dr. T. A. Lacey. London: Novello and Company, Limited, 1929.

———, The Passion of Our Lord According to St. Matthew, ed. H. W. Nicholl, English translation by Rev. Dr. Troutbeck. New York: G. Schirmer, Inc., 1905.

Bennett, William Sterndale, ed., The Chorale Book for England, the hymns from the "Lyra Germanica" and other sources translated by Catherine Winkworth. London: Longman, Green, Longman, Roberts and Green, 1863.

Bridges, Robert and Woodridge, H. Ellis, ed., The Yattendon Hymnal. London: Oxford University Press, 1920.

Buckoll, Henry James, Hymns Translated from the German. London: Hamilton, Adams and Co., 1842.

Buszin, Walter, ed., 101 Chorales Harmonized by Johann Sebastian Bach. Chicago: Hall & McCreary Company, 1952.

Christian Hymns for Church School and Home. Decorah, Iowa: Lutheran Publishing House, 1898.

A Collection of Hymns for the Use of the Protestant Church of the United Brethren. London, 1789.

A Collection of Hymns of the Children of God in All Ages, from the Beginning till Now. Designed chiefly for the use of the congregations in union with the Brethren's Church. London, 1754.

Cox, Frances E., Hymns from the German. London, Rivington's, 1864.

Drinker, Henry S., ed. The 389 Chorales of Johann Sebastian Bach with English Texts. Association of American Choruses, 1944.

Drinker, Henry S., Texts of the Choral Works of Johann Sebastian Bach in English Translation, 3

volumes. New York: The Association of American Colleges Arts Program, 1942.

Hanser, Adolf T., The Selah Song Book. Erie, Pa.: The Sotarian Publishing Co., 1936.

The Harvard University Hymn Book. Cambridge, Mass.: Harvard University Press, 1926.

The Hymnal of the Protestant Episcopal Church in the United States of America. New York: The Church Pension Fund, 1940.

Hymns of the Evangelical Lutheran Church. St. Louis, Mo.: Concordia Publishing House, 1894.

Jacobi, John Christian, Psalmodia Germanica, Part I. London: J. Young, 1722.

———, Psalmodia Germanica, Part II. London, Joseph Downing, 1725.

Kelly, John, Paul Gerhardt's Spiritual Songs. London: Alexander Strahan, 1867.

Kennedy, Benjamin Hall, Hymnologia Christiana. London: Longman, Roberts and Green, 1863.

Lambert, James F. and Haas, John A. W., Luther's Hymns. Philadelphia, Pa.: General Council Publication House, 1917.

Liturgy and Hymns for the Use of the Protestant Church of the United Brethren or Unitas Fratrum. London: Moravian Publication Office, 1890.

The Liturgy and Hymns of the Unitas Fratrum or the Moravian Church. Bethlehem, Pa.: Moravian Publication Office, 1890.

The Liturgy and Offices of Worship and Hymns of the American Province of the Unitas Fratrum or the Moravian Church. Winston Salem, N.C.: 1908.

Massie, Richard, Martin Luther's Spiritual Songs. London: Hatchard and Son, 1854.

The Poetical Works of Henry Wadsworth Longfellow, volume 6. Boston, Mass.: Houghton Mifflin Co., 1911.

Polack, W. G., The Handbook to the Lutheran Hymnal. St. Louis, Mo.: Concordia Publishing House, 1942.

Russell, Arthur Tozer, Psalms and Tunes. Cambridge, John Deighton, 1851.

Terry, Charles Sanford, J. S. Bach's Four-part Chorals. London: Oxford University Press, 1929.

Winkworth, Catherine, Christian Singers of Germany. New York: Macmillan Company, 1869.

———, Lyra Germanica. London: George Newnes, Limited, 1855.

———, Lyra Germanica, Series II. London: Longman Green, Longman and Roberts, 1861.

# Bach's Scoring of the Chorales

This appendix lists only chorales from extant works of Johann Sebastian Bach. Omitted are the chorales found only in the C. P. E. Bach collections. These contain no obbligatos and are designated simply as four parts.

3. SOPRANO. Violino I col Soprano. ALTO. Violino II coll' Alto. TENORE. Viola col Tenore. BASSO. CONTINUO [figured].

4. [SOPRANO.] [ALTO.] [TENORE.] [BASSO.] [CONTINUO, unfigured.]

7. SOPRANO. Oboe I, II, Violino I col Soprano. ALTO. Violino II coll' Alto. TENORE. Viola col Tenore. BASSO. CONTINUO [unfigured].

8. SOPRANO. Corno I, Oboe I, Violino I col Soprano. ALTO. Oboe II, Violino II coll' Alto. TENORE. Viola col Tenore. BASSO. CONTINUO [unfigured].

9. SOPRANO. Flauto traverso I, II in 8ª, Oboe d'amore

I, II, Violino I col Soprano. ALTO. Oboe da caccia I, Violino II coll' Alto. TENORE. Oboe da caccia II, Viola col Tenore. BASSO. ORGANO e CONTINUO [figured].

10. SOPRANO. Oboe I, II, Violino I, Trombone I col Soprano. ALTO. Violino II, Trombone II coll' Alto. TENORE. Viola, Trombone III col. Tenore. BASSO. Trombone IV col Basso. CONTINUO [figured].

11. TROMBA I. TROMBA II. TROMBA III. TIMPANI. OBOE I. OBOE II. OBOE III. VIOLINO I. VIOLINO II. VIOLA. SOPRANO. ALTO. TENORE. BASSO. ORGANO e CONTINUO [unfigured].

12. FLAUTO I, II. OBOE DA CACCIA I. OBOE DA CACCIA II. SOPRANO. ALTO. TENORE. BASSO. CONTINUO [unfigured].

13. SOPRANO. Oboe I, Violino I col Soprano. ALTO. Oboe II, Violino II coll' Alto. TENORE. Viola col Tenore. BASSO. ORGANO e CONTINUO [figured].

14. SOPRANO. Flauto traverso I, II, Violino I col Soprano. ALTO. Violino II coll' Alto. TENORE. Viola col Tenore. BASSO. CONTINUO [unfigured].

17. SOPRANO. ALTO. TENORE. BASSO. CONTINUO [figured].

21. SOPRANO. Violino I col Soprano. ALTO. Violino II coll' Alto. TENORE. Viola col Tenore. BASSO. CONTINUO [figured].

22. SOPRANO. ALTO. TENORE. BASSO. CONTINUO [unfigured].

23. SOPRANO. Oboe I, Violino I, Cornetto col Soprano. ALTO. Oboe II, Violino II, Trombone I coll' Alto. TENORE. Taille, Viola, Trombone II col Tenore. BASSO. CONTINUO [unfigured] e Trombone III.

25. SOPRANO. ALTO. TENORE. BASSO. CONTINUO [unfigured].

26. SOPRANO. Tromba da tirarsi, Oboe I, II, Violino I col Soprano. ALTO. Oboe III, Violino II coll' Alto. TENORE. Viola col Tenore. BASSO. CONTINUO [figured].

28. SOPRANO. Oboe d'amore I, Violino I col Soprano. ALTO. Oboe d'amore II, Violino II coll' Alto. TENORE. Viola col Tenore. BASSO. ORGANO e CONTINUO [figured].

29. OBOE. VIOLINO I. VIOLINO II. VIOLA. SOPRANO. ALTO. TENORE. BASSO. CONTINUO [unfigured].

35. SOPRANO. Oboe d'amore I, II, Violino I col Soprano. ALTO. Violino II coll' Alto. TENORE. Viola col Tenore. BASSO. ORGANO e CONTINUO [figured].

38. SOPRANO. Corno, Flauto, Oboe d'amore, Violino I col Soprano. ALTO. Violino II coll' Alto. TENORE. Viola col Tenore. BASSO. CONTINUO [figured].

41. SOPRANO. ALTO. TENORE. BASSO. CONTINUO [unfigured].

42. SOPRANO. Corno da tirarsi, Flauto traverso, Oboe d'amore I, Violino I col Soprano. ALTO. Oboe d'amore II, Violino II coll' Alto. TENORE. Viola col Tenore. BASSO. ORGANO e CONTINUO [figured].

43. SOPRANO. Violino I, Flauto traverso in 8ª, Oboe d'amore I, Corno col Soprano. ALTO. Violino II, Oboe d'amore II coll' Alto. TENORE. Viola col Tenore. BASSO. CONTINUO [figured].

45. SOPRANO. Oboe d'amore I, II, Violino I col Soprano. ALTO. Violino II coll' Alto. TENORE. Viola col Tenore. BASSO. CONTINUO [figured].

46. TROMBA I. TROMBA II. TROMBA III. TIMPANI. SOPRANO. Flauto traverso I, II in 8ª, Oboe I, II, Violino I col Soprano. ALTO. Violino II coll' Alto.

TENORE. Viola col Tenore. BASSO. FAGOTTO, ORGANO e CONTINUO [figured].

48. SOPRANO. Corno, Flauto traverso, Oboe I, II, Violino I col Soprano. ALTO. Oboe III, Violino II coll' Alto. TENORE. Viola col Tenore. BASSO. ORGANO e CONTINUO [figured].

50. SOPRANO. Flauto traverso I, II, Oboe I, II, Violino I col Soprano. ALTO. Violino II coll' Alto. TENORE. Viola col Tenore. BASSO. ORGANO e CONTINUO [figured].

51. CORNO I. CORNO II. TIMPANI. SOPRANO. Oboe I, II, III, Violino I col Soprano. ALTO. Violino II coll' Alto. TENORE. Viola col Tenore. BASSO. CONTINUO [figured].

53. SOPRANO. Oboe I, Violino I col Soprano. ALTO. Oboe II, Violino II coll' Alto. TENORE. Taille, Viola col Tenore. BASSO. CONTINUO [unfigured].

54. SOPRANO. Flauto traverso, Oboe d'amore, Violino I col Soprano. ALTO. Violino II coll' Alto. TENORE. Viola col Tenore. BASSO. CONTINUO [unfigured].

55. SOPRANO. Tromba I, Flauto traverso I, II, Oboe I, Violino I col Soprano. ALTO. Oboe II, Violino II coll' Alto. TENORE. Oboe da caccia, Viola col Tenore. BASSO. ORGANO e CONTINUO [unfigured].

56. SOPRANO. Cornetto, Oboe d'amore, Violino I col Soprano. ALTO. Trombone I, Violino II coll' Alto. TENORE. Trombone II, Viola col Tenore. BASSO. CONTINUO [figured]. Trombone III col Continuo.

58. SOPRANO. Oboe I, Violino I, II col Soprano. ALTO. Oboe II, Violino III coll' Alto. TENORE. Taille, Viola I, II, III col Tenore. BASSO. CONTINUO [figured].

59. SOPRANO. Flauto traverso I, II, Oboe I, Violino I col Soprano. ALTO. Oboe II, Violino II coll' Alto. TENORE. Viola col Tenore. BASSO. ORGANO e CONTINUO [figured].

60. SOPRANO. Cornetto, Oboe d'amore I, Violino I col Soprano. ALTO. Oboe d'amore II, Violino II coll' Alto. TENORE. Viola col Tenore. BASSO. CONTINUO [figured].

61. SOPRANO. Oboe, Violino I col Soprano. ALTO. Violino II coll' Alto. TENORE. Viola col Tenore. BASSO. CONTINUO [figured].

62. SOPRANO. ALTO. TENORE. BASSO. CONTINUO [unfigured].

63. SOPRANO. Flauto traverso I, II, Oboe I, II, Violino I col Soprano. ALTO. Violino II coll' Alto. TENORE. Viola col Tenore. BASSO. ORGANO e CONTINUO [figured].

64. Duplicate of 256.

65. SOPRANO. ALTO. TENORE. BASSO. CONTINUO [unfigured].

67. SOPRANO. Flauto I, II in 8ª, Oboe I, II, Violino I col Soprano. ALTO. Violino II coll' Alto. TENORE. Viola col Tenore. BASSO. CONTINUO [unfigured].

69. CORO I.: SOPRANO. ALTO. TENORE. BASSO. CORO II. SOPRANO. ALTO. TENORE. BASSO.

71. SOPRANO. Oboe I, II, Violino I col Soprano. ALTO. Violino II coll' Alto. TENORE. Viola col Tenore. BASSO. CONTINUO [figured]. Fagotto col Continuo.

72. SOPRANO. Violino I, Oboe I, II col Soprano. ALTO. Violino II, Oboe di caccia coll' Alto. TENORE. Viola col Tenore. BASSO. CONTINUO [figured].

74. SOPRANO. Flauto traversi I, II, Oboe I, II, Violino I col Soprano. ALTO. Violino II coll' Alto. TENORE.

Viola col Tenore. BASSO. ORGANO e CONTINUO [figured].

76. SOPRANO. Flauto traverso I, II in 8ᵃ, Oboe I, II, Violino I col Soprano. ALTO. Violino II coll' Alto. TENORE. Viola col Tenore. BASSO. ORGANO e CONTINUO [figured].

77. SOPRANO. Oboe d'amore I, II, Violino I col Soprano. ALTO. Violino II coll' Alto. TENORE. Viola col Tenore. BASSO. ORGANO e CONTINUO [figured].

78. SOPRANO. Violino I, Flauti traversi, Oboi col Soprano. ALTO. Violino II coll' Alto. TENORE. Viola col Tenore. BASSO. ORGANO e CONTINUO [figured].

80. SOPRANO. Flauto traverso I, II, Oboe I, II, Violino I col Soprano. ALTO. Violino II coll' Alto. TENORE. Viola col Tenore. BASSO. ORGANO e CONTINUO [figured].

81. SOPRANO. Flauto traverso I, II, Oboe I, Violino I col Soprano. ALTO. Oboe II, Violino II coll' Alto. TENORE. Viola col Tenore. BASSO. ORGANO e CONTINUO [figured].

82. FLAUTO I a due. FLAUTO II a due. VIOLINO I. VIOLINO II. VIOLA. SOPRANO. Tromba o Corno da tirarsi col Soprano. ALTO. TENORE. BASSO. CONTINUO [unfigured].

83. SOPRANO. Flauto traverso I, II, Oboe I, Violino I col Soprano. ALTO. Oboe II, Violino II coll' Alto. TENORE. Viola col Tenore. BASSO. ORGANO e CONTINUO [figured].

84. SOPRANO. ALTO. TENORE. BASSO.

85. SOPRANO. Flauto traverso I, II, Oboe I, II, Violino I col Soprano. ALTO. Violino II coll' Alto. TENORE. Viola col Tenore. BASSO. CONTINUO [unfigured].

86. SOPRANO. Oboe d'amore I, Violino I col Soprano. ALTO. Oboe d'amore II, Violino II coll' Alto. TENORE. Viola col Tenore. BASSO. ORGANO e CONTINUO [figured].

87. SOPRANO. Oboe I, II, Violino I col Soprano. ALTO. Violino II coll' Alto. TENORE. Taille, Viola col Tenore. BASSO. CONTINUO [unfigured].

88. Duplicate of 23.

89. SOPRANO. Flauto traverso I, II, Oboe I, II, Violino I col Soprano. ALTO. Violino II coll' Alto. TENORE. Viola col Tenore. BASSO. ORGANO e CONTINUO [figured].

90. SOPRANO. Oboe I, Violino I col Soprano. ALTO. Oboe II, Violino II coll' Alto. TENORE. Taille, Viola col Tenore. BASSO. ORGANO e CONTINUO [figured].

91. SOPRANO. Oboe I, II, Violino I col Soprano. ALTO. Violino II coll' Alto. TENORE. Viola col Tenore. BASSO. FAGOTTO, ORGANO e CONTINUO [figured].

92. SOPRANO. Oboe d'amore I, II, Violino I col Soprano. ALTO. Violino II coll' Alto. TENORE. Viola col Tenore. BASSO. CONTINUO [figured].

93. OBOE I. OBOE II. OBOE III. VIOLINO I. VIOLINO II. VIOLA. SOPRANO. ALTO. TENORE. BASSO. CONTINUO [unfigured].

94. SOPRANO. Oboe I, II, Violino I col Soprano. ALTO. Violino II coll' Alto. TENORE. Viola col Tenore. BASSO. CONTINUO [figured].

95. SOPRANO. Flauto traverso, Oboe, Violino I col Soprano. ALTO. Violino II coll' Alto. TENORE. Viola col Tenore. BASSO. CONTINUO [unfigured].

96. SOPRANO. Oboe I, Violino I col Soprano. ALTO. Oboe da caccia I, Violino II coll' Alto. TENORE. Oboe da caccia II, Viola col Tenore. BASSO. CONTINUO [unfigured].

97. SOPRANO. Oboe I, II, Violino I col Soprano. ALTO. Violino II coll' Alto. TENORE. Taille, Viola col Tenore. BASSO. CONTINUO [unfigured].

98. SOPRANO. Oboe I, II, Violino I col Soprano. ALTO. Violino II coll' Alto. TENORE. Viola col Tenore. BASSO. ORGANO e CONTINUO [figured].

99. SOPRANO. Corno di caccia, Oboe I, Violino I col Soprano. ALTO. Oboe II, Violino II coll' Alto. TENORE. BASSO. CONTINUO [unfigured].

100. SOPRANO. Flauto I, II, Viola I. II col Soprano. ALTO. Viola III coll' Alto. TENORE. Viola IV col Tenore. BASSO. Fagotto col Basso. CONTINUO [unfigured].

101. SOPRANO. Oboe I, II, Violino I col Soprano. ALTO. Violino II coll' Alto. TENORE. Viola col Tenore. BASSO. CONTINUO [unfigured].

102. SOPRANO. Tromba I, II, Oboe I, II, Violino I col Soprano. ALTO. Tromba III, Violino II coll' Alto. TENORE. Viola col Tenore. BASSO. CONTINUO [figured].

103. SOPRANO. Flauti, Oboe, Violino I col Soprano. ALTO. Violino II coll' Alto. TENORE. Viola col Tenore. BASSO. CONTINUO [figured].

104. SOPRANO. Oboe d'amore I, II, Violino I col Soprano. ALTO. Taille, Violino II coll' Alto. TENORE. Viola col Tenore. BASSO. CONTINUO [unfigured].

105. SOPRANO. Flauto traverso I, II, Oboe I, II, Violino I col Soprano. ALTO. Violino II coll' Alto. TENORE. Viola col Tenore. BASSO. ORGANO e CONTINUO [figured].

106. SOPRANO. Flauto traverso I, II, Oboe I, II, Violino I col Soprano. ALTO. Violino II coll' Alto. TENORE. Viola col Tenore. BASSO. ORGANO e CONTINUO [figured].

107. SOPRANO. Flauto traverso I, Oboe I, Violino I col Soprano. ALTO. Flauto traverso II, Oboe II, Violino II coll' Alto. TENORE. Viola col Tenore. BASSO. ORGANO e CONTINUO [figured].

108. SOPRANO. Flauto traverso I, II, Oboe I, II, Violino I col Soprano. ALTO. Violino II coll' Alto. TENORE. Viola col Tenore. BASSO. ORGANO e CONTINUO [figured].

109. SOPRANO. Oboe I, II, Violino I col Soprano. ALTO. Violino II coll' Alto. TENORE. Viola col Tenore. BASSO. CONTINUO [figured].

110. SOPRANO. Flauto traverso in 8ᵃ, Oboe I, II, Violino I col Soprano. ALTO. Violino II coll' Alto. TENORE. Viola col Tenore. BASSO. CONTINUO [figured].

111. SOPRANO. Flauto traverso I, II, Oboe I, Violino I col Soprano. ALTO. Oboe II, Violino II coll' Alto. TENORE. Viola col Tenore. BASSO. ORGANO e CONTINUO [figured].

112. SOPRANO. Oboe, Violino I col Soprano. ALTO. Violino II coll' Alto. TENORE. Viola col Tenore. BASSO. CONTINUO [unfigured].

113. SOPRANO. Flauto traverso I, II, Oboe I, II, Violino I col Soprano. ALTO. Violino II coll' Alto. TENORE. Viola col Tenore. BASSO. ORGANO e CONTINUO [figured].

115. SOPRANO. Flauto traverso I, II, Oboe I, II, Violino I col Soprano. ALTO. Violino II coll' Alto. TENORE. Viola col Tenore. BASSO. ORGANO e CONTINUO [figured].

116. TROMBA I. TROMBA II. TROMBA III. TIMPANI. OBOE I, II. VIOLINO I. VIOLINO II. VIOLA. SOPRANO. ALTO. TENORE. BASSO. ORGANO e CONTINUO [figured].

117. SOPRANO. Oboe I, II, Violino I col Soprano. ALTO. Violino II coll' Alto. TENORE. Viola col Tenore. BASSO. ORGANO e CONTINUO [figured].

118. SOPRANO. Flauto traverso I, II, Oboe I, II, Violino I col Soprano. ALTO. Violino II coll' Alto. TENORE. Viola col Tenore. BASSO. ORGANO e CONTINUO [figured].

119. SOPRANO. Oboe I, Violino I col Soprano. ALTO. Oboe II, Violino II coll' Alto. TENORE. Oboe da caccia, Viola col Tenore. BASSO. CONTINUO [figured].

120. SOPRANO. Tromba, Flauto traverso, Oboe d'amore I, II, Violino I col Soprano. ALTO. Violino II coll' Alto. TENORE. Viola col Tenore. BASSO. CONTINUO [unfigured].

121. SOPRANO. Flauto traverso I, II, Oboe I, II, Violino I col Soprano. ALTO. Violino II coll' Alto. TENORE. Viola col Tenore. BASSO. ORGANO e CONTINUO [figured].

122. SOPRANO. Oboe I, II, Violino I col Soprano. ALTO. Violino II coll' Alto. TENORE. Viola col Tenore. BASSO. CONTINUO [unfigured].

123. SOPRANO. Oboe d'amore I, II, Violino I col Soprano. ALTO. Oboe da caccia I, Violino II coll' Alto. TENORE. Oboe da caccia II, Viola col Tenore. BASSO. CONTINUO [unfigured].

125. SOPRANO. Oboe I, Violino I col Soprano. ALTO. Oboe II, Violino II coll' Alto. TENORE. Taille e Viola col Tenore. BASSO. CONTINUO [figured].

126. Duplicate of 100.

138. SOPRANO. Violino I, Cornetto col Soprano. ALTO. Violino II, Trombone I coll' Alto. TENORE. Viola e Trombone II col Tenore. BASSO. Trombone III col Basso. ORGANO e CONTINUO [unfigured].

139. SOPRANO. Flauto traverso I, II in 8ª, Oboe I, II, Violino I col Soprano. ALTO. Violino II coll' Alto. TENORE. Viola col Tenore. BASSO. ORGANO e CONTINUO [figured].

142. SOPRANO. Corno I, Oboe I, Violino I col Soprano. ALTO. Oboe II, Violino II coll' Alto. TENORE. Viola col Tenore. BASSO. CONTINUO [figured].

150. SOPRANO I. Corno, Oboe I, II col Soprano I. SOPRANO II. Violino I col Soprano II. ALTO. Violino II coll' Alto. TENORE. Viola col Tenore. BASSO. Continuo [unfigured] col Basso.

152. SOPRANO. Oboe I, II, Violino I col Soprano. ALTO. Violino II coll' Alto. TENORE. Viola col Tenore. BASSO. CONTINUO [unfigured].

156. SOPRANO. Violino I, Corno, Oboe d'amore I, II col Soprano. ALTO. Violino II coll' Alto. TENORE. Viola col Tenore. BASSO. CONTINUO [unfigured].

160. SOPRANO. Violino I, Cornetto col Soprano. ALTO. Violino II, Trombone I coll' Alto. TENORE. Viola e Trombone II col Tenore. BASSO. ORGANO e CONTINUO [unfigured]. Trombone III.

170. SOPRANO. Corno, Oboe I, II, Violino I col Soprano. ALTO. Violino II coll' Alto. TENORE. Viola col Tenore. BASSO. CONTINUO [figured].

178. Duplicate of 53.

179. SOPRANO. Violino piccolo in 8ª, Corno, Oboe I, Violino I col Soprano. ALTO. Oboe II, Violino II

coll' Alto. TENORE. Taille e Viola col Tenore. BASSO. CONTINUO [figured].

182. SOPRANO. Corno di caccia, Oboe I, II, Violino col Soprano. ALTO. Violino II coll' Alto. TENORE. Viola col Tenore. BASSO. CONTINUO [figured].

184. SOPRANO. Violino I, II, Cornetto col Soprano. ALTO. Viola I, Trombone I coll' Alto. TENORE. Viola II, Trombone II col Tenore. BASSO. Trombone III col Basso. CONTINUO [unfigured].

191. SOPRANO. Corno, Oboe I, Violino I col Soprano. ALTO. Oboe II, Violino II coll' Alto. TENORE. Viola col Tenore. BASSO. CONTINUO [figured].

194. SOPRANO. Flauto traverso I, II in 8ª, Oboe d'amore I, II, Violino I col Soprano. ALTO. Violino II coll' Alto. TENORE. Viola col Tenore. BASSO. CONTINUO [unfigured].

195. Duplicate of 86.

204. SOPRANO. Oboe, Violino I col Soprano. ALTO. Violino II coll' Alto. TENORE. Viola col Tenore. BASSO. CONTINUO [unfigured].

209. [SOPRANO.] [ALTO.] [TENORE.] [BASSO.]

215. SOPRANO. Tromba, Oboe I, II, Violino I col Soprano. ALTO. Violino II coll' Alto. TENORE. Viola col Tenore. BASSO. CONTINUO [figured].

216. SOPRANO. Corno, Oboe d'amore I, Violino I col Soprano. ALTO. Oboe d'amore II, Violino II coll' Alto. TENORE. Viola col Tenore. BASSO. CONTINUO [unfigured].

217. SOPRANO. Violino I col Soprano. ALTO. Violino II coll' Alto. TENORE. Viola col Tenore. BASSO. CONTINUO [figured].

233. SOPRANO. Oboe I, II, Violino I col Soprano. ALTO. Violino II coll' Alto. TENORE. Viola col Tenore. BASSO. CONTINUO [figured].

248. SOPRANO. ALTO. TENORE. BASSO. CONTINUO [unfigured].

253. [SOPRANO.] [ALTO.] [TENORE.] [BASSO.]

254. SOPRANO. Flauto I, II, III, Oboe I, Cornetto, Violino I col Soprano. ALTO. Oboe II, Trombone I, Violino II coll' Alto. TENORE. Trombone II, Viola col Tenore. BASSO. Trombone III col Basso. CONTINUO [unfigured].

255. SOPRANO. Violino I, Cornetto col Soprano. ALTO. Violino II, Trombone I coll' Alto. TENORE. Viola e Trombone II col Tenore. BASSO. Trombone III col Basso. ORGANO e CONTINUO [unfigured].

256. OBOE I. OBOE II. OBOE III. VIOLINO I. VIOLINO II. VIOLA. SOPRANO. ALTO. TENORE. BASSO. CONTINUO [figured].

257. Duplicate of 93.

259. Duplicate of 91.

261. SOPRANO. ALTO. TENORE. BASSO. CONTINUO [unfigured].

262. SOPRANO. Violino I, Oboe I, II, Trombone I col Soprano. ALTO. Violino II, Trombone II coll' Alto. TENORE. Viola, Trombone III col Tenore. BASSO. Trombone IV col Basso. CONTINUO [unfigured].

263. SOPRANO. ALTO. TENORE. BASSO.

265. SOPRANO. ALTO. TENORE. BASSO. CONTINUO [unfigured].

266. SOPRANO. Tromba, Oboe I, II, Violino I col Soprano. ALTO. Violino II coll' Alto. TENORE. Viola col Tenore. BASSO. CONTINUO [figured].

267. [SOPRANO.] [ALTO.] [TENORE.] [BASSO.] [CONTINUO, unfigured.]

270. FLAUTO I. FLAUTO II. VIOLINO I. VIOLINO II. VIOLA. SOPRANO. ALTO. TENORE. BASSO. CONTINUO [figured].

273. [SOPRANO.] [ALTO.] [TENORE.] [BASSO.] [CONTINUO, unfigured.]

279. SOPRANO. Oboe I, II, Violino I col Soprano. ALTO. Violino II coll' Alto. TENORE. Viola col Tenore. BASSO. CONTINUO [unfigured].

281. SOPRANO. Oboe I, II, Corno, Violino I col Soprano. ALTO. Violino II coll' Alto. TENORE. Viola col Tenore. BASSO. CONTINUO [figured].

282. Duplicate of 254.

283. SOPRANO. ALTO. TENORE. BASSO.

284. SOPRANO. Flauto I, II in 8ª, Oboe I, II, Violino I col Soprano. ALTO. Violino II coll' Alto. TENORE. Viola col Tenore. BASSO. CONTINUO [unfigured].

290. SOPRANO. Flauto traverso in 8ª, Oboe d'amore, Violino I col Soprano. ALTO. Violino II coll' Alto. TENORE. Viola col Tenore. BASSO. CONTINUO [figured].

291. SOPRANO. Flauto traverso in 8ª, Oboe I, Violino I col Soprano. ALTO. Oboe II, Violino II coll' Alto. TENORE. Viola col Tenore. BASSO. ORGANO e CONTINUO [figured].

292. SOPRANO. Flauto traverso in 8ª, Oboe I, Cornetto, Violino I col Soprano. ALTO. Oboe II, Trombone I, Violino II coll' Alto. TENORE. Taille, Trombone II, Viola col Tenore. BASSO. Trombone III col Basso. CONTINUO [unfigured].

293. SOPRANO. Tromba I, Oboe I, II, Violino I col Soprano. ALTO. Oboe III, Violino II coll' Alto. TENORE. Viola col Tenore. BASSO. FAGOTTO e CONTINUO [unfigured].

294. SOPRANO. ALTO. TENORE. BASSO.

297. SOPRANO. Flauto traverso in 8ª, Oboe I, Corno, Violino I col Soprano. ALTO. Oboe II, Violino II coll' Alto. TENORE. Viola col Tenore. BASSO. CONTINUO [figured].

298. TROMBA I. TROMBA II. TROMBA III. TIMPANI. VIOLINO I. OBOE I. VIOLINO II. OBOE II. VIOLA e TAILLE. SOPRANO. ALTO. TENORE. BASSO. CONTINUO [figured].

301. SOPRANO. Corno, Oboe I, II, Violino I col Soprano. ALTO. Violino II coll' Alto. TENORE. Viola col Tenore. BASSO. CONTINUO [figured].

303. SOPRANO. Corno, Oboe I, II, Violino I col Soprano. ALTO. Violino II coll' Alto. TENORE. Viola col Tenore. BASSO. CONTINUO [figured].

304. SOPRANO. Violino I, Oboe I, II, Tromba da tirarsi col Soprano. ALTO. Violino II coll' Alto. TENORE. Viola col Tenore. BASSO. CONTINUO [figured].

305. Duplicate of 86.

308. Duplicate of 156.

310. SOPRANO. Flauto traverso I, II, Oboe I, II, Violino I col Soprano. ALTO. Violino II coll' Alto. TENORE. Viola col Tenore. BASSO. ORGANO e CONTINUO [figured].

312. SOPRANO. ALTO. TENORE. BASSO.

313. CORNO I. CORNO II. SOPRANO. Oboe d'amore I, Violino I col Soprano. ALTO. Oboe d'amore II, Violino II coll' Alto. TENORE. Viola col Tenore. BASSO. CONTINUO [figured].

317. SOPRANO. Oboe, Violino I col Soprano. ALTO.

Violino II coll' Alto. TENORE. Viola col Tenore. BASSO. CONTINUO [unfigured].

321. SOPRANO. Corno I, Oboe I, Violino I col Soprano. ALTO. Oboe II, Violino II coll' Alto. TENORE. Viola col Tenore. BASSO. CONTINUO [figured].

323. VIOLINO I. VIOLINO II. VIOLA I. VIOLA II. SOPRANO. ALTO. TENORE. BASSO. CONTINUO [figured]. Fagotto col Continuo.

324. SOPRANO. Oboe d'amore I, II, Violino I col Soprano. ALTO. Violino II coll' Alto. TENORE. Viola col Tenore. BASSO. CONTINUO [figured].

325. SOPRANO. Oboe I, Corno I, Violino I col Soprano. ALTO. Oboe II, Violino II coll' Alto. TENORE. Viola col Tenore. BASSO. CONTINUO [figured].

326. Duplicate of 125.

327. TROMBA I. TROMBA II. TROMBA III. TIMPANI. OBOE I. OBOE II. OBOE III. VIOLINO I. VIOLINO II. VIOLA. SOPRANO. ALTO. TENORE. BASSO. CONTINUO [unfigured].

329. CORNO I. CORNO II. SOPRANO. Oboe I, Violino I col Soprano. ALTO. Oboe d'amore, Violino II coll' Alto. TENORE. Viola col Tenore. BASSO. ORGANO e CONTINUO [figured].

330. CORNO I. CORNO II. SOPRANO. Oboe I, Violino I col Soprano. ALTO. Oboe d'amore, Violino II coll' Alto. TENORE. Viola col Tenore. BASSO. ORGANO e CONTINUO [figured].

331. VIOLINO I. SOPRANO. Corno, Oboe I, II col Soprano. ALTO. Violino II coll' Alto. TENORE. Viola col Tenore. BASSO. CONTINUO [figured].

333. TROMBA I. TROMBA II. TROMBA III. TIMPANI. SOPRANO. Oboe I, II, III, Violino I col Soprano. ALTO. Violino II coll' Alto. TENORE. Viola col Tenore. BASSO. FAGOTTO e CONTINUO [unfigured].

335. SOPRANO. Violino I col Soprano. ALTO. Violino II coll' Alto. TENORE. Viola col Tenore. BASSO. CONTINUO [unfigured].

337. CLARINO. OBOE I, II. VIOLINO I. VIOLINO II. VIOLA. SOPRANO. ALTO. TENORE. BASSO. CONTINUO [figured].

338. SOPRANO. ALTO. TENORE. BASSO.

339. SOPRANO. Oboe I, II (Violino I) col Soprano. ALTO. (Violino II coll' Alto.) TENORE. (Viola col Tenore.) BASSO. CONTINUO [unfigured].

341. SOPRANO. Oboe d'amore I, Violino I col Soprano. ALTO. Oboe d'amore II, Violino II coll' Alto. TENORE. Viola col Tenore. BASSO. CONTINUO [figured].

343. SOPRANO. Flauto traverso I, II in 8ª, Oboe I, Violino I col Soprano. ALTO. Oboe II, Violino II coll' Alto. TENORE. Viola col Tenore. BASSO. CONTINUO [unfigured].

344. FLAUTO TRAVERSO I. FLAUTO TRAVERSO II. OBOE D'AMORE I. OBOE D'AMORE II. OBOE DA CACCIA I. OBOE DA CACCIA II. VIOLINO I. VIOLINO II. VIOLA. SOPRANO. ALTO. TENORE. BASSO. ORGANO e CONTINUO [figured].

345. SOPRANO. Flauto traverso in 8ª, Oboe I, II, Violino I col Soprano. ALTO. Violino II coll' Alto. TENORE. Viola col Tenore. BASSO. Violoncello col Basso. FAGOTTO, ORGANO e CONTINUO [figured].

347. CORNO I. CORNO II. SOPRANO. Oboe I, Violino I col Soprano. ALTO. Oboe d'amore, Violino II coll' Alto. TENORE. Viola col Tenore. BASSO. ORGANO e CONTINUO [figured].

348. TROMBA. OBOE. VIOLINO I. VIOLINO II. VIOLA. SO-
PRANO. ALTO. TENORE. BASSO. FAGOTTO e CON-
TINUO [unfigured].
349. Duplicate of 120.
353. Duplicate of 313.
354. Duplicate of 248.
355. SOPRANO. Oboe I, Violino I col Soprano. ALTO.
Oboe II, Violino II coll' Alto. TENORE. Viola col
Tenore. BASSO. FAGOTTO e CONTINUO [unfigured].
358. SOPRANO. Violino I, Oboe I, II, Tromba col Soprano. ALTO. Violino II coll' Alto. TENORE. Viola
col Tenore. BASSO. CONTINUO [figured].
360. SOPRANO. Flauto traverso I, II in 8ª, Oboe I, II,
Violino I col Soprano. ALTO. Violino II coll' Alto.

TENORE. Viola col Tenore. BASSO. ORGANO e CON-
TINUO [figured].
361. Duplicate of 9.
362. SOPRANO. Oboe I, II, Violino I col Soprano. ALTO.
Violino II coll' Alto. TENORE. Viola col Tenore.
BASSO. ORGANO e CONTINUO [figured].
368. CORNO I. CORNO II. OBOE I. OBOE II. VIOLINO I.
VIOLINO II. VIOLA. SOPRANO. ALTO. TENORE. BASSO.
ORGANO e CONTINUO [figured].
370. SOPRANO. Tromba I, Oboe I, Violino I col So-
prano. ALTO. Oboe II, Violino II coll' Alto.
TENORE. Oboe da caccia, Viola col Tenore. BASSO.
CONTINUO [figured].

# INDEXES

# Index of English Titles

Numbers in parentheses are cross references to the Hymn-Tune Index, which gives the name of the hymn-tune (melody) and the name of the German hymn (poem), as well as the names of other German hymns associated with the melody and the translations. (D) indicates a duplicate chorale, in which no music is found under the chorale number; (I) indicates that the chorale contains an instrumental obbligato.

A child is born in Bethlehem (51)    *12*

A Lamb goes forth: the sin He bears (15)    *5, 309(D)*

A mighty fortress is our God (50)    *20*

A safe stronghold our God is still (50)    *250*

A sinner and a soul most wretched (200)    *339*

A sure stronghold our God is He (50)    *273*

Ah, God, from heaven look anew (4)    *253*

Ah, holy Jesus, how hast Thou offended (96)    *111*

Ah! Lord, how shall I meet Thee (95)    *345*

Ah whither may I fly (17)    *281*

Ah wounded heart that bearest (95)    *98*

Alas, dear Lord, what law then hast Thou broken (96)    *59, 78, 105*

Alas! My God! (3)    *40, 279*

All glory be to God on high (9)    *249*

All mankind fell in Adam's fall (49)    *100, 126(D)*

All my heart this night rejoices (188)    *139*

All praise to Jesus' hallowed name (68)    *51(I)*

All things wait on our possessing (11)    *128*

All ye stars and winds of heaven (72), (110)    *35, 161*

Around God's throne in heaven (62)    *166*

As sure I live, my Master saith (181)    *110*

As willed the Three (37)    *75*

Awake my heart (16)    *124*

Awake, my heart, rejoicing (151)    *93(I), 257(D)*

Awake ye souls, this is the day (112)    *77*

Before Thy throne I now appear (82)    *334*

Beside Thy cradle here I stand (60)    *362(I)*

Bestir thyself, my feeble soul (55)    *9, 361(D)*

Blessed is the Spirit (120)    *96*

Blessed Jesu, at Thy word (134)    *131, 328(D)*

Christ, everlasting source of light (25)    *245*

Christ in the bonds of death was laid (23)    *15, 261*

Christ is arisen (22)    *197*

Christ lay in death's dark prison (23)    *371*

Christ our Lord is risen (30)    *200*

Christ, who freed our souls from danger (124)    *30*

Come and hear our blessed Saviour (65)    *67*

Come, Holy Ghost, our souls inspire (127)    *187*

Come, Holy Spirit, God and Lord (128)    *69*

Come Redeemer of our race (150)    *28, 170*

Comfort, comfort ye My people (65)    *76*

Commit thou all that grieves thee (20), (95)    *286, 340*

Commit thou every grievance (95)    *80, 367*

Deal with me, God, in mercy now (137)    *44*

Dear Christians, one and all rejoice (149)    *183*

Dearest Immanuel, Lord of the faithful (133)    *194*

Deck thyself, my soul, with gladness (171)    *22*

Due praises to th' incarnate love (68)    *288*

Earth's frail pomp and vanities (195)    *211*

Entrust thy ways unto Him (95)    *21*

Eternity! Tremendous word (155)    *26, 274*

Faithful God, I lay before Thee (65)    *64(D), 254, 256(I), 282(D)*

Farewell I gladly bid thee (180)    *24, 108*

Father, Lord of Mercy! (38)    *239*

Father of Mercies! God most high (192)    *120, 349(D)*

For me to live is Jesus (28)    *6*

From God shall nought divide me (184)    *114, 191, 332, 364*

From heav'n above to earth I come (183)    *46(I)*

Give thanks, sing praises, for God's love is with us (33)    *228*

Glory be to God the Father and the Son (139)    *358*

God gave His Gospel unto us (73)    *181*

God liveth still (74)    *234*

God the Father, be our stay (71)    *135*

Good Christians all, rejoice ye (67)    *163*

Gracious God, when wilt Thou call me (132)    *43*

Had God not come, may Israel say (186), (206)    *182, 285*

Hark! A voice saith, "All are mortal" (8)    *153*

Have faith in God, nor e'er distress thee (69)    *271*

Hear my pleading, Jesu, treasure (174)    *172*

Help, O Lord, behold we enter (100), (101)    *155, 368*

Hence my heart, and cease such thinking (65)    *29*

His own God ne'er neglecteth (126)    *129*

Holy, holy, holy (79)    *235, 319(D)*

How bright appears the morning star (203)    *86, 195(D), 305(D)*

How lovely shines the morning star (203)    *278*

How many they, how many rail (4)    *3*

How now, my soul, why makest sore complaining (193)    *241*

I believe in but one true God (205)    *133*

I cry to Thee, my dearest Lord (109)    *71*

I into God's own heart and mind (192)    *41*

I thank Thee dearly through Thy Son (105)    *188*

I thank Thee, Lord (103)    *223*

If God were not upon our side (206)    *336*

If God withdraweth, all the cost (207)    *157*

If thou but suffer God to guide thee (200)    *62, 104*

In all that I am doing (166)    *103, 355*

In death's strong grasp the Saviour lay (23)    *184*

352

# Index of German Titles

This index includes names of the German hymn-tunes (melodies), first lines of German hymns (poems) and alternate German titles mentioned in footnotes to the chorales.

Numbers in parentheses are cross references to the Hymn-Tune Index where a detailed listing of the association of hymns and hymn-tunes may be found. (D) indicates a duplicate chorale, in which no music is found under the chorale number; (F) indicates that the title is located in a footnote; (I) indicates that the chorale contains an instrumental obbligato.

# Hymn-Tune Index

This index lists by its German name each hymn-tune (melody) used in *The 371*. When more than one hymn (poem) is associated with the hymn-tune, the first line of each hymn is listed, together with its English translation(s). When only one German title appears, the names of the hymn-tune and the hymn are identical.

The numbers following the English titles are those of the stanzas in the original hymn. A number in parentheses after a German title is a cross reference to another hymn-tune where the same hymn may be located.

The symbol (D) indicates a duplicate chorale, with no music presented under its number. The symbol (I) indicates that the chorale contains an instrumental obbligato.

1. Ach bleib bei uns, Herr Jesu Christ   *148*(D), *177*
   Lord Jesus Christ, with us abide: 1, 3
2. Ach Gott, erhör mein Seufzen und Wehklagen   *186*
   O hear, my God, my prayer and sore complaining: 1, 2
3. Ach Gott und Herr   *40, 279*
   Alas! My God!: 1, 2   *40*
   1, 4   *279*
4. Ach Gott vom Himmel, sieh darein   *3, 253, 262*
   Ach Gott vom Himmel, sieh darein
   Ah, God, from heaven look anew: 1, 8†   *253*
   Look down, O Lord, from heaven behold: 1, 6   *262*
   Schau, lieber Gott, wie meine Feind
   How many they, how many rail: 1, 7   *3*
5. Ach Gott, wie manches Herzeleid   *156, 217, 308*(D)

O Lord! How many miseries:
   1, 16, 17, 18   *217*
   1, 18   *156*
6. Ach! was soll ich Sünder machen   *39*
   What shall I, a sinner, do, Lord: 1, 2
7. Ach wie flüchtig, ach wie nichtig   *48*
   O how cheating, O how fleeting: 1, 13
8. Alle Menschen müssen sterben   *153*
   Hark! A voice saith, "All are mortal": 1, 6
9. Allein Gott in der Höh sei Ehr   *125, 249, 313*(I), *326, 353*(D)
   Allein Gott in der Höh sei Ehr
   All glory be to God on high: 1, 2   *249*
   Der Herr ist mein getreuer Hirt, dem
   The Lord my Shepherd is and true: 1, 2   *125*
   1, 3   *326*
   Der Herr ist mein getreuer Hirt, hält
   The Lord my Shepherd is: my need: 1, 5   *313*(I)
10. Allein zu dir, Herr Jesu Christ   *13, 359*
    Lord Jesus Christ, in Thee alone: 1, 2   *359*
    1, 4   *13*
11. Alles ist an Gottes Segen   *128*
    All things wait on our possessing: 1, 6
12. Als der gütige Gott   *159*
    That God at last might do: 1, 2
13. Als Jesus Christus in der Nacht   *180*
    The night our Saviour was betrayed: 1, 2, 3

† See footnote to Chorale 253.

**358**

† See footnote to Chorale 251.

361

# Index of Composers

# Index of Authors

# Index of Translators